WHEN CATS REIGNED LIKE KINGS

OTHER BOOKS BY GEORGIE ANNE GEYER

*The New Latins: Fateful Change in
South and Central America*

The New 100 Years' War

The Young Russians

*Buying the Night Flight: The Autobiography
of a Woman Correspondent*

Guerrilla Prince: The Untold Story of Fidel Castro

*Waiting for Winter to End: an Extraordinary Journey
Through Soviet Central Asia*

Americans No More: The Death of Citizenship

When Force Fails: Flawed Intervention

Tunisia: A Journey Through a Country That Works

WHEN CATS REIGNED LIKE KINGS

On the Trail of the Sacred Cats

GEORGIE ANNE GEYER

Andrews McMeel Publishing

Kansas City

05 06 07 08 RR2 10 9 8 7 6 5 4

Library of Congress Cataloging-in-Publication Data
Geyer, Georgie Anne, 1935–
   When cats reigned like kings : on the trail of the sacred cats / Georgie Anne Geyer.
     p. cm.
   ISBN-13: 978-0-7407-4697-0
   ISBN-10: 0-7407-4697-9
   1. Cats—History. 2. Cats—Religious aspects—History. 3. Geyer, Georgie Anne, 1935– I.
Title.

   SF442.6.G49 2004
   636.8'009—dc21

                                                2004049694

Book design by Holly Camerlinck

Attention: Schools and Businesses
Andrews McMeel books are available at quantity discounts with bulk purchase for educational, business, or sales promotional use. For information, please write to: Special Sales Department, Andrews McMeel Publishing, 4520 Main Street, Kansas City, Missouri 64111.

To my dear friends
Harriet Wilson Ellis, Pasha's secret love,
Carol Krametbauer Petersen, Nikko's best girl,
and Winifred Reidy, beloved of all cats everywhere

contents

PART ONE

ON THE TRAIL OF THE ROYAL
AND SACRED CATS ... 1

PART TWO
THE FAMILY OF CAT ... 163

PREFACE

Many people will doubtless wonder, given my background in the world of international affairs, why I became so fascinated with the history of the royal and sacred cats. After all, my beat for many years has been foreign cultures, various national histories, and other political and social systems. I view myself and all foreign correspondents as unique "in-between" people who rove between different and often mutually hostile societies carrying messages from people to people and trying to make some sense of things. How, then, did I become so enthralled with cats?

Well, frankly, after covering Vietnam, Lebanon, El Salvador, Iraq, Angola, and other hot spots around the world, cats looked pretty good to me compared to humans!

What's more, as I've traveled around the world for the last forty years, always immersed in my first love of history, I began to find an intriguing, fascinating, and largely unknown story unfolding before my eyes. Across our known human history and in very differing cultures, human beings had made cats into royal and sacred creatures. Alone of all the animals of the world, cats were sacred in many cultures. Egypt, of course, came first, but then there were ancient Siam, Burma, Japan, Turkey, and probably to some extent China, and even Persia.

If we explore the world of the big cats—pumas, jaguars, and tigers—we find still other cultures, from the Inca to the Maya to the great tribes of Africa—all of whom used them to represent their search for the spiritual. I have not attempted to deal with the big cats here, but only with our beloved little household "gods," the cats that we think we know so well.

Thus, inspired by my first beloved cat, Pasha, the "Egyptian god cat," and then by my second dear cat, Nikko, the Japanese "Buddhist good fortune cat," I traveled around the world to find out the true history, legends, and sagas of the cats who served the human need for symbols of the spirit and of sacredness and royalty.

My voyages took me to the ruins of the great cat temple at Bubastis in Egypt, to the wild northeast of Burma to a magnificent Buddhist monastery where cats leap endlessly and devotedly through hoops, to the royal family in Siam or today's Thailand, to Buddhist temples in Japan, and to veterinary schools in Turkey.

In the Library of Congress in Washington, I found a rare copy of a charming book by the founder of cat shows, Harrison Weir, titled *Our Cats and All About Them,* published in 1889. It has loving sketches of the varied breeds by the author himself. The book was so delicate that in order to read it, I had to place it on a little stand designed to protect the pages from being pulled down too far. I was enchanted as I read the words of this fine Victorian gentleman who had done so much to bring cats to the attention of the world, and thus to protect and love them:

> Among animals possibly the most perfect, and certainly the most domestic, is the cat. I did not think so always, having a bias against it, and I was some time coming to the belief, but such is the fact. The cat is more critical in noticing things than the dog. I never knew but one dog that would open a door by moving the fastening without being shown or taught how to do it. The cat seems to take note of time as well as place.

Then, just when I thought that I knew a lot about the "time of the cat" in history and as I was finishing the book, a veritable bombshell was dropped about the history of cats. It had long been assumed, and proven, that cats were first domesticated by about 2000 B.C. in Egypt. But in the spring of 2004, scientists discovered feline remains alongside a human burial site in the village of Shillourokambos on the island of Cyprus. This exploration suggested that people and cats were living together as early as 9,500 years ago or at approximately

7500 B.C. The fossils indicated that the animal was larger than today's domestic cats, but it was found so close to the human skeleton that researchers believe that the cat had been tamed and even had some "spiritual significance."

Jean-Denis Vigne of Paris's Museum of Natural History reported that wild cats were never native to Cyprus, and thus were surely brought there by humans. "Possibly tamed cats were devoted to special activities or special human individuals in the village," he wrote, adding that the burial "emphasizes the animal as an individual." Zooarchaeologist Melinda Zeder of the Smithsonian National Museum of Natural History in Washington further confirmed that the burial provided good evidence that the animal, the same furry *Felis silvestris* as the Egyptian cats, had been tamed by then.

Today, cats are "royal" and "sacred" in other ways. Many are beloved of their human families, and the breeds take part in competitions designed to raise their status among all humans. Cats are America's favorite pet, having bypassed dogs in household numbers some years ago. One thinks of Shakespeare's Hamlet who says, "'The cat will mew, the dog will have his day.'" The cat is still mewing, and meowing, and RRRAGHHRING, but the cat's day is clearly now.

acknowledgments

I want to thank a number of people for helping me bring through to fruition an admittedly unusual book.

My biggest thanks go to Universal Press Syndicate and its sister company Andrews McMeel Publishing in Kansas City. Its legendary founder, John McMeel, with his eye for the workable unusual, gave me most welcome encouragement. Publisher Tom Thornton could not have been more enthusiastic and helpful. Very special thanks go to Chris Schillig, my editor, who painstakingly saw the book through to fruition and offered too many excellent suggestions even to mention.

Original research was done for me as early as the 1990s by my former assistant, Ariane de Vogue, who scoured the Los Angeles libraries for marvelous old books on the historic Family of Cat. Her work laid the basis for the book and was invaluable. My trusted and treasured assistant of fourteen years, Rita Tiwari, saw me through the book at every stage with her charm, her intelligence, and her indefatigable organizational sense. In earlier years, my goddaughter Rebecca Coder also worked on the book with her wonderful capacity for originality, efficiency, and grace.

My literary agent, Fredrica Friedman, constantly offered invaluable advice. Her patience, her enthusiasm, and her excellent suggestions buoyed me when I dared to consider that maybe cats were *not* royal or sacred, after all. Bill Fitz-Patrick, the legendary White House photographer, was kind enough to take picture after picture of Nikko and me, despite Nikko's obvious reticence to be in the spotlight that day.

I could never have gotten the marvelous pictures for the Family of Cat without the help of my respected former editor, Elizabeth Andersen, and a fine Kansas City photographer, Gloria Berkel. With extraordinary patience, they scoured the Internet, going from cattery to cattery to find the best pictures of the different breeds, always hitting upon just the most beautiful and the most evocative photographs.

I want to especially thank the breeders of the catteries for their spontaneous generosity in providing us with such unforgettable pictures.

Two superb professional photographers, Helmi Flick and Linda Beatie contributed immeasurably to the photo exhibitions.

To all, I thank you for allowing my mind to wander—and for going with me.

WHEN CATS REIGNED LIKE KINGS

PART ONE

ON THE TRAIL OF THE ROYAL AND SACRED CATS

CHAPTER ONE

an egyptian god cat, lost on the streets of chicago

If the traveler can find
A virtuous and wise companion
Let him go with him joyfully
And overcome the dangers of the way.
BUDDHIST PROVERB FROM THE DHAMMAPADA,
THE SAYINGS OF THE BUDDHA

CHICAGO:

There was no reason to go out that hot, sticky July morning in 1975. There was no possible excuse for me to leave my mother's apartment on Barry Avenue in Chicago at exactly 10:28 A.M. and walk to the corner to mail one letter. It was not even an important letter and could easily have waited until later. I was home with my mother between trips. As a foreign correspondent, I struggled to study, understand, and somehow encapsulate the complex human cultures of the world, and I was usually writing at that time.

There are many who will rightly insist that nothing was foreordained about such a fated meeting on a Chicago street corner. There are those who will also argue that it was crazy to dream of finding a royal cat, albeit one of recent and suspicious lineage and travels, masquerading as a Chicago street cat. They are right on one point: five or ten minutes either way, and I wouldn't have seen the charming creature at all!

Indeed, when I came upon that lean, scrawny, Wizard of Oz scarecrow of a kitty lost on the streets of Chicago, with his long legs and his pinched little face and an odd black spot on the very end of his nose, I had never heard the names Bastet or Mau, much less Freyja or Maneki Neko. Oh, I had heard loosely of the sleek Siamese cat and her fluffy, pug-nosed Persian half sister, but I had never heard of all the other great breeds of the Family of Cat, such as the confounding Burmese, the mysterious Birman, the curious Chinchilla, the avidly swimming Turkish Van, or the slightly scary, black-as-night Bombay. I could never have guessed how impoverished I really was.

Before I found the kitty that summer's day of 1975, displaced on the streets of Chicago by some still-unknown destiny, I had barely known that the cat was considered a god in ancient Egypt. I had no knowledge of those ancient biblical tales that contend that, during the long weeks when Noah's Ark floated over the invading waters, rats and mice increased so alarmingly that Noah passed his hand three times over the head of the lioness, before she then sneezed forth the cat. Because of its success in eliminating vermin, it was also the cat that led the procession out of the ark when the rains finally stopped.

I was not aware that the Prophet Muhammad was so devoted to his pet cat Muezza that he once cut off the sleeve of his garment rather than disturb the little fellow who had fallen asleep there. Or that centuries later, in his African hospital, Albert Schweitzer began to write his prescriptions with his left hand because his beloved cat, Sizi, would fall asleep on the right arm of his shirt. I surely had never heard of Lao-Tsun Temple, although eventually there would come a time when I was sorry that I had heard of it!

I had yet to discover that the furry Birman cat had earned its pristine white paws centuries ago when it touched the bier of its king or that the Peruvian city of Cuzco is laid out in the form of the sacred puma. I still did not know that the charming, poetry-creating bushmen of southern Africa, who were so respectful of the supernatural qualities of lions that the very word for the beast—*n!l,* spoken with a clicking sound made by the tongue—was like the name of God and could not be uttered in daylight. Yet although I did not exactly know these things, I was hardly surprised to learn that writers (Petrarch, Charles Baudelaire, John Keats, Percy Bysshe Shelley, William Wordsworth, T. S. Eliot, to name only a few) loved cats, while most dictators (Hitler, Napoleon, and Stalin, among others) not surprisingly hated them: cats were simply too free and self-determining ever to prove agreeable to such human tyrants.

I did not know then, although I sensed it on different and mysterious levels, that after this fated meeting I would enter a new world, a world that is still with me and will be forever. It is a world in which I would be driven to explore, examine, and immensely enjoy history's lessons in order to understand the relationship of cat to man.

It was most unusual to see a friendly young animal like this in our area of high-rises and busy streets. Thus, on that auspicious July day, I stopped in my tracks when I saw him—he was pacing efficiently in little measured steps, back and forth, along a brick ledge that edged the sidewalk—and we stared at each other for a long and searching moment. He had a most forthright gaze, charmingly clear, and as our eyes met I had the strangest feeling that I had known him for many, many years—even centuries.

Still, I only patted him on the head, and as I did so, the small creature purred like a veritable industrial machine at the height of production hour. Then he suddenly elongated his whole body in what I would come to call his "Halloween Cat" stretch, arching his back and thrusting his tail out in a daring, saucy greeting. His flexible little shoulders hunched up as if to attack, but he only purred some more. Then he meandered with the studied and casual nonchalance of a feline Fred Astaire over to some nearby bushes, and proceeded to sip some milk from a plastic container placed there, probably by the wanton person who had left him out all alone.

Before I could escape this encounter, with a flick of his tail he was back, staring at me fixedly, the yellow eyes as deep and impenetrable as amber pools. This kitty's fur was revealing. He had a rich but flat white coat with black spots scattered artistically down his back, long white legs, and a dramatic black spot of fur right on the top of his head, which looked like a hairpiece parted exactly in the middle of his head. All I really knew was that he was assuredly one adorable young kitten, probably between four and six months old, with a black-as-midnight tail that flicked like lightning, twitched creatively, and managed to cover astonishingly large expanses in every direction. As I greeted him, he acknowledged my every word with a quirky swish of his luxuriant tail.

I had always loved animals, but in our modest bungalow on the South Side of Chicago, our family had only small "black-and-tan" dogs that came from a farm in Ohio. Cats were not exactly favored or pampered pets in those days. They were left outside to roam and range, and so they were almost always mangy, furtive, and unfriendly. My favorite books as I was growing up were Albert Payson Terhune's volumes about his beautiful collies in New Jersey, all extraordinarily valiant creatures whose noble deeds would leave me recurrently and inconsolably in tears throughout my childhood.

"I hope that kitten is gone when I get back," I said to myself halfheartedly that day as I crossed the street to the mailbox. After all, I was about to move to Washington, D.C., and at this point in my life a pet would only be a burden. My mother already had a cat—a scourge against humanity named Mookie—and hardly needed another such "pet," given her wretched experience. Yet when I returned moments later, there he was, staring at me with such an ineffable calm that now I unhesitatingly scooped him up and swept him into the apartment, where he settled into my arms like some sweet child who had been lost and now was found.

In our first hours together, he adjusted to the apartment just as easily and comfortably as if he were thoroughly inured to the ways of the city. After introducing him to my big brother, Glen, and to our close friends, I began to wonder about an appropriate name—but that could wait until tomorrow. It had already been a full day.

The next morning, I found the kitten—*my* kitty now—sleeping next to me. It evoked in me the strangest feelings to see that he was curled up on his side in the same position in which I had been sleeping, his lanky cat limbs surreally askew exactly the way mine were. Already I sensed in our relationship a parallelness and a strange and even magical togetherness that would soon enough come to haunt me. When I got up, he barely stirred, but when he did, he stretched briefly, with a consciously restrained movement that seemed strange in such a small, young, lost animal. Then he examined me again with that penetrating gaze, his eyes staring fixedly into mine. At that moment he seemed to be an ancient and wise creature.

He also immediately began to invent and then display his games for me. For instance, that first morning the summer sun was gleaming and glittering in a kaleidoscope of light reflecting off Lake Michigan and playing all over the walls. How the kitten loved these flittering, flickering pools of light that were playing such wondrous tricks on him! First, a beam would appear, and he would naturally try to climb the offending wall. What else could any self-respecting cat be expected to do? Then several beams would sweep the ceiling, and the little puss would leap up and down, trying not to let a single beam escape. He reminded me at times of a philosopher searching in every dark corner for the light of truth. How he scampered around the apartment that morning, trying with all the charming abandon of youth to catch and capture the light!

I knew the intention: I had tried to do the same many times. He never quite did catch it, but then, how many of us do?

—

I had already been to Egypt several times in the late 1960s and 1970s in my work as a correspondent for the *Chicago Daily News,* and I had seen the Egyptian cats etched on the walls of tombs and on every sort of statue in the Egyptian Museum in Cairo. For just a fleeting moment that first morning with my kitten, I thought those Egyptian cats reminded me a lot of this cat, with his long, lean, almost languorous body, his pinched and knowing face, and his regal, upright bearing. Could he perhaps be a feline from somewhere far, far away? Being quite enough of a romantic, I did not dismiss the possibility, but how could he have arrived at Barry Avenue on the North Side of Chicago?

I decided it might well be appropriate for him to have a Middle Eastern royal name. I tried Emir—no, the syllables were too harsh. I toyed with Sultan—again, not enough of those imprecisely warm sounds that cats like so much. Then I hit upon Pasha. The pashas were men of high military and civil rank in both Egypt and Turkey. More important, the *shhhh* sound absolutely engrossed the cat!

"Pasha," I said aloud to him that first afternoon. "PASH-a!" His ears twitched with excitement as he came to attention, and his regal plume of a tail plop-plopped uncontrollably with all the unpretentious, natural spirit of a plebian cat who had suddenly come across a field of sparrows. "PASSHHA . . ." I repeated. At this, he rolled over onto his side, tipping his head toward me, his ears on the alert and his eyes gleaming. I had to admit that some of the historical, spiritual, or even cultural implications of the name were lost in his spontaneous response.

But they were not lost on me. The name had the correct political connotations. The Egyptians had abolished the office and even the term "pasha" in 1952, when they entered their modern nationalist and revolutionary period. Thus, I could not be accused of elitism but only of historical romanticism. Pasha it was—ever after.

Of course, being a responsible person, I did have some lingering concern that he might actually belong (if that word can be applied to any cat) to someone else. So I scoured the papers for a few days, and if I had found an ad in the "Lost" column saying, "Royal Egyptian cat from the Third Dynasty lost at Barry Avenue and Sheridan Road at 10:28 A.M. on July 28. Answers to the name 'Pasha.'" I would surely have returned him.

So it was that a game centered around Pasha's origins soon became a most serious search. All my life as a journalist and as a writer, I had been searching for truths about different cultures and how they related to one another. I had often remarked to people, "I became a journalist and explored the world in order to explain it to myself." Now I had with me a mysterious, devoted creature whom I could not explain at all; much less describe our special relationship.

I began to wonder, "Who am *I*, and where did *I* come from?" and "Who is *he* and where did *he* come from?" Those questions would soon take me across the entire globe.

———————

First, of course, I tried to "place" Pasha by his breed—if indeed he had one— through the nice veterinarians at our local McKillip Animal Hospital, where I took young Pasha for his shots and exams. He needed extra care, for he obviously was a cat with a "shady" past. Pasha would sit quietly in his carrier until he saw the vet. Then, some spirit of ancient shaman, some streak of banshee, some strain of hyena, perhaps, would suddenly overcome him, and he would begin to howl! I do not mean cry. The noise, which was truly terrible, would pause only at those moments when he needed to catch his breath, and then move on, sotto voce. All his life, this otherwise serene, composed creature hated vets with an unquenchable rage.

In between the bloodcurdling screams, I would always find time to implore the vet for information on my friend's unknown past: "Do you think he might be Siamese? Oriental? After all, he doesn't meow, he gurgles."

The vet invariably looked at me pityingly and pronounced with a tight, unequivocal smile: "American Shorthair!"

At first this response hurt me to the quick. Then it came to me: I had before me a Chicago example of what happened all the time in Asia and other parts of the Third World. In many of those lands, they protected babies from kidnapping, from mortal danger, and from the resentment and jealousy of the gods by pretending that a beautiful newborn baby was hideously ugly. They would say of the child: "He's an ugly little mud pie, isn't he?" Or, "Too bad, she'll never get a husband."

After that, the vet's words never hurt me again. Indeed, sometimes I would tickle Pasha on the head and ears and say fondly, "Hello, my little shorthair." It was all in the true spirit of Catherine the Great, who, upon choosing a handsome colonel for her bed, would cajole him endearingly with, "Hello, my sweet serf."

Another reason I knew that Pasha was unusual was that he was a mischievous and endlessly creative prankster. He designed tricks and then displayed them to me, sometimes with notable impatience if I did not take part immediately. He would jump over a box in the apartment, then come over to me and put his head in my lap, then jump over the box again, until he felt I was paying him sufficiently fond attention. Then he would tire, of course, and like all good cats, would need a little snooze for, say, sixteen or eighteen hours.

Indeed, Pasha was a classic rogue operator, an engaging trickster ever full of artful maneuvers. One day he suddenly came racing out of the bedroom toward an innocent visitor, terrifying her so much that she put her hands up to protect her face before he turned on a dime and streaked away, not to reappear for hours (and then without the slightest hint of shame). Another day, I brought some cans of peanuts for the staff members who had been working on one of my books, and I warned them not to leave the nuts out in the open, for most cats love peanuts. One staffer paid no heed and placed the peanuts atop a tall chest. I suddenly glanced up from my work to witness Pasha ambling across the room with a deceptiveness that outdid the Borgias, looking the very soul of innocence with a mien that would have shamed many prophets. In fact, he then leapt with Machiavellian purposefulness up onto a chair from which he reached the top of the chest and, with a flick of his quick paw, whiffed the peanuts to the floor. There, he quickly gobbled them all up before we could get to him. Of course, he immediately got quite sick and threw up all over the rug, leaving it majestically for his supposed "owner" to clean up.

Pasha loved food of almost any kind. The first time I gave a party after finding him, I discovered the miscreant in the act of licking his way across the hors d'oeuvres. It was a purposeful feat that was accomplished in the veritable flick of an eyelid while I was putting on lipstick, for he could cover an immense amount of territory with that scratchy little tongue. (Sometimes good cats do bad things.) I never felt it quite necessary to tell the guests who, of course, immediately arrived, that someone else had "touched" their delicious hors d'oeuvres before they had. So far as I know, no one perished from the experience.

It is said in cat veterinary circles that some cats hesitate before eating and make faces at their food dishes. This is duly explained by experts who say that the strange, almost sneering expression is called the "Flehman response," and occurs when the scent is transferred to the Jacobson's organ in the roof of the cat's mouth. I can assure you that Pasha did not waste any of his time on such ridiculous beliefs.

As students of animal rites point out, cat games have their own rules and rituals, and these are neither random nor accidental. In fact, cats seldom break a rule in their play. Some would attribute that fact to lack of intelligence, but it is really simply part of their cleverly patterned little minds. Studies have shown that cats can recall problem-solving mechanisms for as long as sixteen hours, but Pasha's own particular gamesmanship only alerted me still more to the mystery of the origins of my little pet.

I began to wonder: Do god cats behave so? Then I remembered the gods in ancient Greece who were always cavorting about, drinking excessively, and surely mating without any noticeable exclusivity. I concluded that such behavior was actually *proof* of Pasha's royal lineage.

After all, a rogue cat could not be an alley cat, for alley cats expend all their energies in foraging for food, fighting with their fellows, and engaging in the most morally distressing sexual encounters by moonlight. Only aristo*cats* or cosmopolo*cats* could afford to be rogue cats or devilish mephisto*cats*, with all that means in playfulness, and a satiric view of life. Question answered!

In the months after finding Pasha and bringing him into my life, I began a secret little scrapbook for him. It is a small and deliberately unassuming brown book called a *Pet Passport*. Where it asks for type of pet and breed, I wrote, "Egyptian temple cat from Second Dynasty." Where it asked hair length, I wrote "Sassoon cut." Where it asked for ID or license, I put in "Clearly unlicensable." Where it asked for pedigree or registration, I wrote, "Ramses II, Cairo, Egypt, summer home, Luxor." At the end, I wrote, "Beware of his powers. When he looks in the flames and then fastens his all-knowing eyes on you, he penetrates your soul."

Throughout history royalty and sacredness are inevitably confronted by vulgarity and evil. By that token, in that same magical summer there was . . . MOOKIE! Repeat the name to yourself only in silence and in secret: Mookie. For it is a name that should not be spoken in the light or day or within the hearing of man. Pasha's encounter with that bad customer would eventually serve to assure me even further of his noble character, but not, unfortunately, before a most unpleasant confrontation.

How does one describe such a thoroughly bad cat as Mookie? My elderly mother loved pets, and so my brother, Glen, brought her a little gray kitten, whom she immediately named after a white angora kitten she had when she was first married. This Mookie could have had the best life in the world. She could have been the most loved and appreciated cat ever, but Mookie, incapable of love, dedicated herself only to mayhem.

Almost from the very beginning, Mookie, her fluffy physical beauty not at all reflected in her personality and character, ran wild in the apartment, apparently incapable of any modicum of decent cohabitation, much less any *civilized* domestication. For a small kitty, she spent abnormal amounts of time growling and hissing and running around the apartment, all the while uttering terrifying war cries reminiscent of the onslaught of the Mongol hordes as they raged across Central Asia and into Europe in the twelfth century. (It has also been suggested to me by shadowy observers that there is a Mookie file at the CIA, and perhaps the FBI and the attorney general's office as well; but I was never able actually to confirm such rumors.)

Mother would not hear of getting rid of Mookie, so there we were, locked in the apartment with this mad cat. It was August by then, and my mother had been at our Wisconsin home with Mookie all summer, and I wanted to introduce mother to Pasha before he and I left for Washington.

As I relate this story, it is important to remember that Pasha was a very, very tiny kitten, weighing only three or four pounds. He was surely not more than four months old, although we could not know his birthdate for sure. His coat was so sleek that he looked even smaller than he actually was. Mookie, on the other hand, was a huge and threatening creature, with bushy gray hair and wild eyes that made her look like some great Tatar warrior ready to sweep across the central plains of ancient Russia. Glen and I and our friends were a little concerned about putting them together, so I carried Pasha through the door into the little house. We called to Mookie, who was out on the porch straining for possible prey among any of the local robins, raccoons, chipmunks, skunks, squirrels, bunnies, and lake cats that might randomly or foolishly stumble by, not to speak of human ankles, wrists, cheeks, ears, or fingers that might happen to present lively opportunity. The fact that she could not get at them, but could only growl and scream and wildly paw at the porch screens only drove her on to greater displays of unnatural temper.

I put tiny little Pasha down on the dining-room floor, and he immediately looked about in some confusion. After all, this was his second home in as many weeks, after all his voyaging around and across the world. He very carefully picked his steps, moving slowly and nonthreateningly out to the porch to greet Mookie. He actually made it close-up to try and rub noses with her. In fact, I watched the entire ballet with fascination; he was so careful, so deliberate, and so measured in edging up to greet her with his wet nose that I thought at once, "Pasha, the great Egyptian peacemaker." (An Anwar Sadat of cats, perhaps?)

As she perused the front yard, Mookie seemed to spot the movement of foreign fur out of her left eye. At this first sight of Pasha, Mookie's entire body stiffened until she was like a corpse, only standing up. Her eyes seemed to bulge from their sockets, and her ears went flat back on her head until they were almost even with her shoulders. She began to snarl and cough and hiss, but not, frankly, for very long. Almost immediately, she actually jumped out of the porch through the screen, tearing a huge hole in it, and leaving all of us in a total panic as she raced crazily across the yard before climbing our huge oak tree and staying there for many hours. Frankly, the thought did occur to us to just leave her there.

Instead, it took Glen all those hours to get a high ladder, climb most of the way up to her, and reason with her to come down. He finally grabbed her, stuffed her into a pillowcase, and lowered her, hissing and screaming inside, to the ground. Once again captive in the house, she stayed under the bed for three full days, a relief to everyone.

Now I had seen Pasha, the diplomat, the peacemaker, the cat destined for great things, in full action—so confident and noble, trying to reason with that evil, treacherous Mookie—and somehow I sensed already that he would become a very famous and beloved cat indeed. I also had a brave companion to drive with me for two days to the nation's capital, where all the laws and decisions of the land are so masterfully made and so flawlessly executed. To tell the truth, I was more frightened than excited, for I was just starting my own syndicated column, and such an undertaking was an equivocal thing, depending totally upon the unsureness of how many papers would buy the column, whether I could keep up the strain of telling the entire world how to live, three times a week in exactly 750 words, and whether people would actually like having me tell them how to live those three times a week.

Then, just at the moment when all my plans seemed to be coming together, a new problem raised its pesky head. I had bought a condominium in D.C., but since it would not be ready until December, I planned to stay at the old Fairfax Hotel on Massachusetts Avenue. It had once been elegant—and it would be again in years to come, when it became the Westin Embassy Row—but at this time, it was a seedy, worn old lady, still genteel to be sure, but way down on her luck and growing a little careless with her appearance. Al Gore had been raised there because his family owned it, and as a child he liked to go up on the roof and dangle rubber ducks outside the windows to scare residents. The hotel also had the prestigious Jockey Club Restaurant in one corner, where senators and leading journalists presided in a suitably dark and sulky atmosphere. Most important, it was the only place where I had found a small two-room apartment at the right price for a short period of time. Now I realized that they did not permit pets! What to do?

I decided to write to the general manager of the Fairfax, saying that I had my heart set upon staying there my first months in Washington. I would flatter him about how wonderful his run-down apartments were. I would tell him that I dreamed about going down to Sunday breakfast in the Jockey Club where I could absorb the atmosphere of all the great political decisions that had been made there the night before. But there was one little problem: I had this wonderful pet. I decided to change Pasha's delineation once again—to parody him, just as cats had sometimes been so richly parodied in Egyptian temples and indeed in other ancient cultures. "Pasha has just got his press card to cover the White House with me," I wrote, "and he would be absolutely inconsolable if he could not stay at the famous Fairfax Hotel."

In the return mail, I received this kind letter from George C. Donnelly, assistant to the general manager, dated August 12, 1975:

Dear Ms. Geyer:

I am sure that we can accommodate you and Pasha for as long as you wish. I will block a one-bedroom apartment beginning September 15, 1975, for a period of two months. If you should wish to extend your stay, I am sure that we will be happy to do so.

Looking forward to your arrival, I remain,

Sincerely, George C. Donnelly,
Ass't. to Gen. Mgr.

Our first voyage together had begun.

———

When Pasha and I arrived at the Fairfax Hotel that hot September evening after a long drive through the stifling late-summer heat of Pennsylvania and Maryland, I exhaustedly began to take the bags out of my little Fiat Spider sports car, but the doormen would not let me proceed. They whispered among themselves, bustling mysteriously about, like men who knew something that we did not know. Finally, they motioned for me to wait just a moment while they directed furtive little glances at the small carrier sitting right exactly in the middle of the lobby—Pasha, all big eyes and long legs, stuffed inside.

Suddenly, the general manager strode purposefully out from his office. A big, stalwart man, he had a broad smile on his face, as he fixed his gaze, not upon me but upon the carrier. "Hello, Pasha," he said in a booming voice. "Welcome to the Fairfax!" And everyone in the lobby smiled, laughed, and poked each other in the ribs, pointing at the first cat ever in the history of the Fairfax Hotel. If Eloise was the literary sweetheart of The Plaza in New York, then Pasha soon was the darling of the Fairfax in our nation's capital.

As we settled into our odd, dark, and grimy apartment at the end of a long hallway, the young kitten charmed everyone. If I was away overnight, I would just call one of the young clerks on the desk, and he would seem overjoyed to go up and feed and pet the little fellow. If I had any problems at all, I just went straight to the general manager; he had now become my ally and co-conspirator against all those foolish "rules."

I had read about President Franklin D. Roosevelt's White House cat, Slippers, who often attended glittering White House dinners. So on Sunday mornings in the Jockey Club, Pasha would come down to breakfast and sit next to me. The dimly lit room, with its seasoned dark woods and its mood of having seen everything and everybody (if, not yet, every*cat*) was in sharp contrast to the sunlight just outside on Massachusetts Avenue. I would carry Pasha down in my arms into this darkness and, though he was rough-and-tumble upstairs, he would invariably sit quietly and serenely by my side while I had my scrambled eggs and sausage. It was strange how at ease he was there, but then, he always had a natural way with power, almost as if, I kept thinking, he had been born to it.

A Pawnote: This is not, I would soon learn, unusual in cats of accomplishment and status. In the journals of early courtiers of the Siamese kings, royal Siamese cats were brought into the full court ceremonies, whose meaning they symbolized. One observer noted, "By their nature, animals are restless. Yet when the ceremonies started, the cat was quite still, and not at all restless. The ceremony must have been very sacred."

One Sunday morning, Pasha was curled up next to me on the couch in the Jockey Club when a couple came in and, apparently not realizing that it was Sunday morning, took up directly from the night before and began drinking Bloody Marys with a certain noticeable gusto. Pasha had been resting quietly and properly, but suddenly his little head popped up, and he laid his paw on my leg as though in request or warning. He seemed to be sniffing for something. Then his ears trembled, and his whiskers began to move ever so slightly. Finally he looked directly, with amazing steadiness, at the noisy couple. After a few moments, to my utter amazement—and then even more to theirs—he got up, stretched appropriately for effect, and ambled over to their table.

Before I could stop him, he jumped up onto it, upsetting not a single thing, and started sipping the woman's Bloody Mary, his rough little tongue lapping it up as fast as he could. I lunged for him, and he gave no resistance. He was clearly happy because he already had the Bloody Mary all over his whiskers, his cheeks, and his paws. He snuggled up in my arms and used his long tongue to clean up his face.

To make it worse, the couple howled with laughter. The waiters stood in a line and clapped their hands. Three other people at breakfast paused, first in wonderment and then in pleased acknowledgment of what was surely a singular feline achievement. From that moment on, Pasha always loved Bloody Marys. Once we had the new apartment, if someone was having one, he would always try to sneak a sip. There are those who say the liver problems that came later stemmed from this unlikely love, but personally, I never believed that.

It was at the Fairfax that Pasha also illustrated the comical and uncommon qualities that further convinced me that he was an extraordinary cat. There were many moments when he momentarily lost his obviously inherited sophistication and appeared to be just a kitten. Sometimes, for instance, when I was taking a shower in the little tub with the bath curtain closed about me, he would run full-speed into the bathtub, leaping right through the shower curtain until he was right there with me under the flowing water! Then he would race out again, shaking himself all over the apartment as though the devil himself were in him or after him.

You must understand that in those days the Fairfax was not exactly a temple of cleanliness and order. Old furniture and newspapers sat out in the halls for weeks, and the maid, when she deigned to clean at all, would sit in my apartment and discuss Washington politics until her time was up, and she would then duly say, "Well, time to go home."

Like many children, Pasha kept his good behavior for when he was "out" at places like the Jockey Club. When he was home, he always exhibited his true and exuberant self. So if I inadvertently left the door open, he loved to "escape" and run down the long hall to . . . well, who really knows where he thought he was going, or why? The problem was that there were so many layers of wax on the floor that his sharp claws stuck into it. In fact, he would invariably get no more than six feet before he was brought to a humiliating stop. In truth, I found it quite amusing to see him there, literally stuck in the eternal wax of the Fairfax's dirty floors, trying his best to free his sticky little paws.

Finally he would slink back into the apartment in humiliation, his head hung low, his long black tail wagging back and forth, back and forth, *plunk-plunk-PLUNK,* with rage and embarrassment. At that moment I could not think of him any more as a special cat; he merely seemed to be a very funny, charming, normal young cat whom I loved more and more.

Pasha's epic confrontation with the Fairfax's slack housekeeping occurred one day when we heard a terrible roaring noise just outside our apartment. Hesitantly peeking out, I found a man with a floor polisher actually cleaning the hall! This was truly amazing because that floor had probably not been cleaned throughout the entire twentieth century. On this day, after the busy man had been *RRRRhhing* and *RRRRawrrring* with his machine up and down the long hall for some time, Pasha decided once again to make a run for it. Inadvertently,

I had left the door ajar just a whit; he pushed it open with his nose and took off. I watched, first irked by my carelessness and finally amazed at what I saw. For Pasha was used to taking off down the hall and being slowed to defeat by many layers of wax. Now that those were disappearing before our eyes, his journey was speeded up by the unaccustomed polish on the floor. He tried to stop himself with his front paws, but they only acted like wheels, speeding him to the end of the hall at an ever faster momentum.

I watched with amazement as my little cat went sliding down the hall as if on a toboggan, rivaling the best cartoons of cats tumbling all over themselves. Not wanting to hurt his feelings or offend his self-image, I never mentioned it to him again.

Many weeks after our splendid entrance at the Fairfax, we bade farewell to the new friends we had grown to know and love there and moved into our very own apartment near the Watergate complex. Now I had both a cat and a home of my own. The night we moved in, I slept on the floor in a sleeping bag, and every time I awoke, Pasha was pacing the floor, looking, gazing, and wondering. It was a magical night. I remembered the words of the twentieth-century French writer, actor, and librettist Jean Cocteau: "I love cats because I love my home, and little by little by little they become its visible soul." So it surely was with me.

For the next sixteen years our lives were intricately linked and Pasha did indeed live like royalty in our apartment. He certainly behaved like a king! Always comically regal, he would go up to every guest like a young prince or dauphin, sometimes with a slight bow of his head, making no sound. He would put his paw on the person's knee or thigh or sometimes arm and wait until the person responded appropriately. Then he would stare at the person in a deep and penetrating way for some seconds before moving on. It was his way of shaking paws. He would usually sit on the piano during the most active part of a party—clearly enjoying the music—and then curl up in the most beautiful woman's lap to rest from all the excitement. Once a beautiful blonde Uruguayan friend named Susana came by, and the minute she came into the apartment, Pasha's ears began to twitch uncontrollably back and forth. Every time Susana moved, Pasha moved with her. When she went into the kitchen, he posed on the edge of a chair, looking around the corner so he could see her the minute she emerged. When she reappeared, he had an unmistakably lascivious look on his "innocent" little face. Then he lay on *her* lap all evening.

Jealous? *Moi?*

Meanwhile, my suspicions about his royal lineage began to grow. They were confirmed by his shamanistic bent, probably something he brought with him from the Middle East, and they were illuminated by the fact that he would sit for hours lowering his paws slowly right down close to the very top of candle flames. At moments like these, I thought he must be a feline magician. Sounds also fascinated him, and his little ears would tremble with joy. Since cats have thirty muscles in each ear, which allow them to twist, turn, and flex their ears in many directions as they pick up passing sounds, all of him was very busy. He also copied me: when I lay on the floor doing exercises, he would lie down beside me and do much the same things. The French writer Colette famously wrote, "There are no ordinary cats." But Pasha gave new meaning to her words.

He was agile like a prince, yet gracious and generous when faced with conflict. When he was young, he would stand by the floor-to-ceiling windows in the living room and leap clear to the ceiling if a bird even showed its face on the balcony. Like all truly regal creatures, he became notably nonviolent in his mellow later years. Then he would lie on his back letting out a small warning cackle, really for appearances' sake, when bothersome birds dared to roost on *his* balcony.

Pasha was also a clotheshorse. While most cats hate anything on their "person," even the collar that protects them, Pasha just loved . . . hats. He had a Jungle Jim hat, white and fit for the jungle, and an assortment of others. His very favorite was a small cap like those that men in Europe wore at the turn of the century, with a little brim that made him look rather like a Pomeranian railroad man. The hat had an elastic band that fit under his chin, so he could—and would—sit for hours with it on, while people laughed and tittered. Frankly, much like his mistress, he just loved attention—any attention.

I should mention that for a time, he also had his red-and-white-striped tent with a pom-pom on the top. It was just big enough for him, and he didn't mind retiring into it. In fact, he was rather proud of it. One day when a badly behaving five-year-old child stopped by with his parents and brattishly insisted on climbing into the tent, Pasha looked at this display with disbelief, then sauntered over and gave the kid's backside a couple of swats with his right paw.

———————

Soon Pasha became a famous cat. Not Madonna-famous, or Henry Kissinger–famous, or Elvis-famous, but still famous. When I wrote columns about him and his charming ways, the *Chicago Sun-Times,* which was by then publishing my column, ran a headshot of him instead of me. There he would be, his pinched white head with the black toupée parted in the center and his pert little ears, next to the likes of Robert Novak, George Will, and Mike Royko. When I wrote about traveling with him by car, Joel Rochon, the cartoonist with what was then the *Tucson Daily Citizen,* designed a charming cartoon of the two of us riding in a car, Pasha's profile most definitely dominating the scene.

I once interviewed King Hussein of Jordan in his golden stone palace in Amman, and he told me with great relish—doubtless ever so relieved to get off the endless subject of the Israel-Palestine war—that all his life he had lovely little cats that his American wife, Queen Noor, obtained for him in London. "Every night," he told me, "they wait at the bottom of the stairs for me, and then we go up together." His were another kind of royal cats!

I also found myself employing, with substantial success, the analogy of the cat that Pasha's regal presence suggested to me. When I gave speeches around the country, I would explain complex strategic subjects through homey references to Pasha, whom I always identified as "the Egyptian god cat." With their essential good nature, Americans always want to believe that people can "change." They want to think that even the worst tyrants and the most mischievous rascals and miscreants can somehow be reformed—if *we* do the right thing. After I published my biography of Fidel Castro, someone in the audience would often ask me: "But, Miss Geyer, surely Fidel would change if only we recognized him. . . . If only we lifted the embargo. . . . If only we had not supported the Batista dictatorship!"

Well, you can't undo history, but you can be reasonable about what is happening today, and about the human personality and its relationship to power,

greed, and aggression. I knew that such men as Castro, Saddam Hussein, Aya-
tollah Khomeini, Muammar Qaddafi, or Juan Perón—only a few of the
unpleasant charismatic leaders whom I had the "pleasure" of interviewing—
would not ever have changed their personalities or intentions. In fact, it was
self-absorbed on our part to think they would or could. I began to use Pasha to
explain the conundrum to my audiences. "I have the smartest cat in the world,"
I would say. "He is really very intelligent and very sensitive." At this, I would
see their eyes begin to rove. Then I would add, "But no matter how hard Pasha
tries, he cannot bark!"

Then the audience understood the implacability of culture and psychology.

The analogy became known across the country as the "My-Cat-Can't-
Bark" doctrine of understanding foreign leaders. Okay, so it wasn't Manifest
Destiny, it wasn't "Cold War Deterrence and Containment." Nor was it Met-
ternich, Brzezinski, Sun-tzu, Machiavelli, or Von Clausewitz: still, it worked.
Pasha, once lost on the streets of Chicago, had come to represent a certain type
of strategic thinking; he had come to personify how the realistic person judges
the personality and character of leaders. Ramses II or Queen Hatshepsut would
have understood.

———

Just when our lives were going along well and everything seemed within reach,
tragedy nearly struck. It was this event that led us both to our meeting with
Pasha's royal and sacred past.

Ever since I found him that fortuitous day, Pasha had had medical problems, especially with his liver. It didn't really have to do with the sips of Bloody
Marys, I am convinced of that. I did occasionally catch him giving a sidewise
look to a bottle of German "Zeller Schwarze Katz" wine, and at least once, to
a bottle of Victorian-era British gin called Old Tom, but no, his liver was often
clogged up so it simply could not digest his food.

You must remember that Pasha had traveled a long way to come to me, and
such travel—across rivers and valleys, up mountain ranges, over deserts, and
through swampy mires, and especially crossing time zones and probably centuries—is exhausting for any cat. One picks up many diseases and maladies along

———

the way, and who knew how many centuries it actually took him to get to Chicago from Luxor and Alexandria? You must remember, too, that he was a god cat in hiding, without a passport, birth certificate, driver's license, voter's registration, Social Security number, or Visa card. After World War II, we would have called him a "displaced kitten." Today, we could have called him an "illegal cat-alien," or an "undocumented feline worker." What is clearly true is that he had brilliantly eluded everyone on his long journey, this innocent but stalwart creature, for I never got one single call or visit from the INS, the FBI, or even the CIA.

Thus, in addition to the liver problem, one core psychological issue revealed itself to me: *Pasha did not really know who he was!* We humans, despite all of our problems, live with webs of remembrance all tangled up inside ourselves, with systems of memory that are constantly jolting us to new levels of under-standing, and with early experience of socialized responses that we do not even recall, much less consult, as we live and age. Most of us have roots, most of us know where we came from, and therefore, where we might go. But Pasha, lack-ing this, had none of those webs, systems, or experiences.

Then one night we were watching on television a film on Egypt, its antiq-uities, the Nile, the great days of magnificent cities along the river in ancient times. Chants rose above the great temples, haunting Egyptian music filled the air, and a picture of a cat sailing down the Nile like a queen suddenly flashed across the screen. Pasha jumped up into my lap, but instead of cuddling, he sat up very straight, transfixed by the sounds and the sights. He was breathing heavily and even shaking a bit. Then he leapt off my lap—he never did this—and jumped up onto the television set. He lay along the top, pawing at the Egyptian scenes on the screen for a full fifteen minutes, until I grew a bit fright-ened by his odd movements and turned off the set.

Only a matter of days later, once again he could not eat. He was obviously in pain, and I rushed him to Dr. Wesley Bayles on M Street in Georgetown. The good veterinarian looked at me soberly. "I am going to have to operate on his liver," he said. I knew it was serious. I hugged the little creature, who despite his pain and fright was howling like a hyena at the doctor, and I went home in considerable pain myself. Every day after the surgery, it was touch and go. One day he was better; next day he was worse. By this time we had been together for six years, and the idea that I might lose him was simply too much to bear. We still had so much to discover and experience together.

One night, I was sure he was gone—I could hear it in Dr. Bayles's voice—but Pasha survived. Little by little, he began to get better. By the time I brought him home two weeks later, he had gone from a splendid full-grown male cat with beautiful fur and a swishing tail to a pitiful, scrawny creature, his coat all matted and thin, his eyes lifeless and his tail nearly immobile. He would lie beside me at night, as always, but now he sniffed and breathed heavily. I nursed him and cared for him, and slowly he got stronger.

Even at the worst, he still dreamed; he would shake and cry out, more like a dog. I always wondered: What is he dreaming about? Then one night I woke up and Pasha was sitting by the window looking at the moon. The light of the heavenly body was reflected in his eyes. Indeed, they glowed as if from within with a magical and almost catatonic intensity, so much so that I almost shuddered. At that moment, I knew something else: his body was healing, but his spirit was still somewhere else. I needed to bring that "somewhere else" to him, to make him whole again.

So it was that I began to study the history of the cat. I went to the library, bought books, looked through magazines. I quickly realized there was much to be learned.

For instance, cats had been on earth for about 40 million years, on every continent except Antarctica and Australia, and they had (as hard as this is to accept) the same origins as dogs, raccoons, bears, and pigs. Ancient Egypt always cropped up. For it was there, several thousand years before Christ, that the cat strolled insouciantly out of the deserts of North Africa, at first apparently welcomed in order to kill a burgeoning rat population and soon deified by the grateful, awed Egyptians.

I discovered that at the temple of Bubastis in the northeastern Nile Delta, the cat goddess Bastet was worshiped by hundreds of thousands as a god. We are certain that by the second millennium B.C., Egypt alone of all the empires and courts of the world had fully domesticated the cat, and worshiped it as well. We also know that in the tomb of Ti from 2563 B.C., the honored cat in that tomb is wearing not a hat but *a collar!* (Just try that on Mookie, I thought.)

Soon cats were being mummified. While alive, cats in Egypt were groomed and bathed and anointed with fragrant oils; once dead, the animal would be wrapped in fine linen perfumed with cedar oil. I discovered that Bastet is most often seen in Egyptian paintings and hieroglyphs as a slim, beautiful woman wearing a long evening dress and, always, earrings. I pored over books to discover that, once the cats became little gods, it was forbidden for anyone to kill them. Indeed, the great Greek historian Diodorus Siculus visited Egypt in 60 to 57 B.C. and wrote in *Bibliotheca Historica*, his history of the world, "Whoever kills a cat in Egypt is condemned to death, whether he committed this crime deliberately or not." It seems that some unfortunate Roman contemptuously killed a cat in Egypt, and "the multitude rushed in a crowd to his house," while "neither the officials sent by the king to beg the man off nor the fear of Rome . . . were enough to save the man from punishment."

Another strange habit of the Egyptians of these times was remarked upon by none other than Herodotus, the great Greek historian and traveler of the fifth century B.C. "On every occasion of a fire in Egypt, the strangest prodigy occurs with the cats," he wrote in his *History*, book 2: "The inhabitants allow the fire to rage as it pleases, while they stand about at intervals and watch these animals which, slipping by the men or else leaping over them, rush headlong into the flames. When this happens, the Egyptians are in deep affliction."

Cats were also at the battle of Pelusium in 525 B.C., when the evil Persian monarch Cambyses, son of Cyrus I and father of Cyrus II, the Great, ordered his soldiers to carry cats instead of shields into battle. When the Egyptians saw this desecration, they surrendered to the Persians. We know further, from the sacred Book of the Dead of the pharaohs, parts of which date from 3500 B.C., that the cat eventually came to be equated with the greatest Egyptian god of all, the sun god Ra, who could take the form of a cat at will. The two were interchangeable in the minds and souls of the people.

As I read further every night, Pasha always slept by my side, obviously dreaming, because he would awake, startled, every once in a while. I wondered whether my reading was influencing him: Was he dreaming of ancient days, when he strode the streets and roamed the wharfs of Luxor and the streets of Philae? Was he directing sea battles off Alexandria? Luxuriating on the Nile during one of the many X-rated festivals at Bubastis, when the cat goddess reigned at the site of the cat temple on the Nile?

Pasha never really told me, the rogue, but our lives had become so interconnected that I sensed he somehow understood the lore, and it excited him. At the same time, incongruously, his dreams became calmer. He would lie there and take a deep breath, as cats do when they seem pleased with themselves. His little concave chest would heave for just a second, and then he would drift off. It was as if his dreams were becoming ordered and he was putting something together.

As for myself, I began to realize that I would have to go back to Egypt. This time, I would dig deeply into the pharaonic cat culture and try to understand it. I knew which questions I would begin with: What were the qualities in the cat that so enchanted the ancient Egyptians? Did they ascribe certain qualities to the cat, or did the cat cause them to be aware of certain virtues they wished to emulate? Why did the Egyptians make the cat, alone of all animal creatures, into a god across the entire width and breadth of their empire?

That part was just for Pasha, and it would become only a small piece of my search. I was also searching on behalf of all those humans who love cats: what is the very nature of mankind's long fascination—its love affair and complex relationship—with cats? What is this unique relationship between man and animal? What should it mean to us, in an age of fancy breeds, when we "worship" animals in a different way, but do not truly seek to analyze them and their qualities? If I could not uncover those mysteries in ancient cultures that had such deep and profound relationships with their felines, how could I expect to discover them anywhere?

I said good-bye to Pasha some weeks later when I left for Egypt. I told him, "Don't worry, little friend, you will be amazed at what I will find for you." I tried to tell him, too, that this was no normal trip. I was going to explore—for both of us—wondrous things: gods and devils, the sacred and the royal, the enlightening, the frightening, and the shameful. This voyage was not about the evidence of everyday life, but of eternity—the strange dark trips to the underworld and of preparations for them. This was not about simple prayers and recitations but about transcendence over life's mendacities and even a "transmigration of souls," or the exchange of souls between humans and animals. It would not be told from the viewpoint of the human family, but from that of the great and little-known Family of Cat. I could see Pasha's ears twitching as I whispered all of this to him, and he took a very deep sigh and then stretched himself out.

Pasha looked strangely peaceful the morning I left. He lay curled in a ball, his long midnight tail wound around him like a black feather boa, and he was fast asleep before I was even out the door. He had begun his part of the journey as well.

CHAPTER TWO

BACK HOME IN EGYPT—
REIGNING CATS

They made them gods because they were so beautiful.
DR. MOHAMED HASSAN SALEH, DIRECTOR
OF THE EGYPTIAN MUSEUM, TO THE AUTHOR

CAIRO

Flying into Cairo in the late afternoon, I could see beneath me the looming sentinels of time, the pyramids, out on the edge of the vast desert that pushes ever southward into Africa. Sitting regally before them was the Sphinx, that great reclining beast with the body of a lion and the face of a human, stretching out his paws with a kind of lofty disdain toward the cacophonous city. I already knew from my studies that such fabulous catlike beasts—like the legendary Greek griffin and the Chimera, brothers and sisters of the Sphinx—could be found across history in many cultures and climes. And as I studied this new world below me, I remembered that such mythological creatures and their humans could be compared to the Mayan shamans of Central America, who draped themselves in jaguar skins so that they might be filled with the spirit of the most powerful animal in the jungle.

But I was here to see and understand the small, domestic cat gods: I knew it would deeply hurt Pasha's self-esteem if I began comparing him to these behemoths. So I deliberately put the Sphinx aside for the infinitely more personal purpose of my searchings.

I arrived in Cairo in the early evening, when the streets were jammed with the crush of cars and people, the cries of hawkers vying with the call to prayer of the muezzin—and I had an odd sense of wonder. For a cat, after all, finally going to Egypt was like a Roman Catholic making a pilgrimage to the Vatican, a Jew traveling to the Wailing Wall, a Muslim journeying to Mecca, or a Hindu finding his way once a year to the sacred Ganges. I was the cat's emissary, not unlike the plenipotentiary who goes ahead to prepare the tableau for the prime minister. Or, I occasionally wondered, was I perhaps a mere cat's paw, being used by these clever felines to accomplish *their* missions, not mine?

I knew that later Egyptian history was filled with sagas about cats. In her book, *The Cats of Cairo: Egypt's Enduring Legacy,* Annemarie Schimmel wrote, "When the British Orientalist E. W. Lane lived in Cairo in the 1830s, he was quite amazed to see, every afternoon, a great number of cats gathering in the garden of the High Court, where people would bring baskets full of food for them. In this way, he was told, the *qadi* (judge) fulfilled obligations dating from the thirteenth-century rule of the Mamluk Sultan al-Zahir Baybars. This cat-loving monarch had endowed a 'cats' garden,' a pious foundation where the cats of Cairo would find everything they needed and liked."

The Prophet Muhammad was also a cat lover. He once said, according to the holy writings, that "Cats are not impure; they keep watch around us." He used water from which a cat had drunk for his purifications, and his beloved first wife, Ayisha, a great businesswoman, ate from a vessel from which a cat had eaten. According to Islamic lore, cats close their eyes when they drink. That way, if Allah asks them if they have had their milk, they can honestly answer that they have not seen any and thus may receive a second saucer. (My gluttonous Pasha would surely have appreciated such a clever ruse.) In still another charming legend about the Prophet, one day his favorite cat Muezza bowed to thank him for some kind favor and, by this story, Muhammad then passed his hand three times down the length of the animal's back, giving to it—and to all cats evermore—the enviable capacity always to land squarely on their feet.

"The Egyptians kept the best place in their house for the cat: He was the

Household God," Gillette Grilhe wrote in *The Cat and the Man,* his excellent book. "They watched unceasingly over the animal's well-being, and if by any chance a cat died under its master's roof, all the members of the household shaved their eyebrows in mourning." But on a happier note, the author continued, "Bastet was also called the Goddess of Love in Egypt. Lovers invoked her aid; women with the appearance and graceful movements of a cat were much sought and admired. It was said that Cleopatra's irresistible charm came from her resemblance to a cat."

The next morning I walked over from the hotel to find the director of the Egyptian Museum. There, under coats of modern and ancient dust, lay the most priceless, beautiful objects from the tombs. Huge wooden and gilded carved figures of gods, exquisite religious wall carvings from the temples, and tens of thousands of small bronze and wood figurines of royal creatures such as Bastet were all piled upon one another like cordwood before a cold winter. The unmarked director's office just off the main entranceway could rather easily have been mistaken for a storage bin. But this subterfuge was a typically elliptical Egyptian exercise. The Egyptians care obsessively about position and prestige, but they believe you will actually think their position higher if it is not precisely marked.

Right inside the office and atop the weathered bookcases sat a small statue of Bastet! In fact, she was the only decoration in the director's office. She was sitting in her accustomed composed position, resting on supple haunches with her legs pulled prudently together, her long and languorous body poised but purposeful, her ears pricked up and her delicate little nose pointed just enough to give her an air of controlled brightness. For a moment, the breath caught in my throat—she looked so like Pasha that I could *see* Pasha leaping with his masterful style to the top of that dusty bookcase and then licking his paws carefully to clean himself up! Doubtless to Bastet's surprise and probable annoyance, I pictured Pasha rolling around next to her and nuzzling this very proper and well-mannered goddess!

There was no hint of animal abandon in her character. Indeed, she properly wore earrings. Cat goddesses almost always wear earrings, and I wondered whether Pasha's love of hats reflected this predilection—the love of decoration.

As I sat in front of the handsome, serious museum director's desk, sipping Egyptian tea, I asked Dr. Mohamed Hassan Saleh, a man who obviously adored the magical world surrounding him, "Is it true that the ancient Egyptians made the cat into a god because the little creatures emerged suddenly out of the desert at the dawn of history and destroyed the rats?"

He noticeably cringed. His visage darkened and he took a deep breath. It was as if such a vulgar suggestion was simply too much to bear.

"Oh no, oh no," he protested. "They made them gods because they were so beautiful!"

Then he began to explain, firmly and thoughtfully. "The cat was worshiped because it brought joy and peace to people. It was a beautiful animal and so they connected it symbolically with beauty. The Greek historian Herodotus said that the people thought that the cat was a spirit and that it was friendly—that was contrary to the dog, or to the jackal."

He then paused dramatically. "The cat," he said slowly and soberly, "was commonly—but also historically—called Miou in Egypt." And I wondered how on earth *that* could have happened.

Before I left, I asked him if they knew what actual color the Egyptian cats had been. "Oh, brown," he said absentmindedly, "surely brown."

———

I pause here for a guidepost on the road of our journey. The poets like to say that, to truly understand something, you first must know its name—and already I was getting the names of cat, which provided some initial order for me. Across the world, cats are called by their utterances: there are *mews, myaus, mios, mauos, maus,* or *meows.* In Egypt alone, the miou is spelled in thirty-one different ways, including *maeow, me-ow, mieaou, mouw,* and *murr-raow.* Domestic cats are capable of coming forth with seventeen different sounds of three distinct types: purring and murmurs; vowels or variations of the traditional (although, in fact, seldom heard, "meow"); and what the cat show officials call "strained intensity" sounds like hisses and screams. Cat sounds consist of nine consonants and five vowels. All versions, of course, came originally from that sweet, cherished, demanding sound of the cat. As the prominent cat show judge and writer Roger Caras concluded in his fine book, *A Celebration of Cats,* the question of language becomes ever more complicated since the original word for meow came originally from the hieroglyphics, probably passing through Greek Orthodox, the high and low Latin of Rome, and very likely Hebrew, Aramaic, or Syriac.

It is whispered in the inner corridors of the FBI, the CIA, the Pakistani ISI, the Israeli Shin Beit, the souks of Cairo and Damascus, as well as in England's Scotland Yard that there is a "Miou connection" or a "Maew file" on all the conspiratorial shenanigans of cats across the globe. But I never was able actually to confirm the existence of such a dossier.

It is further believed that "puss" and "pussy" originally came from one of the versions of the Bastet name Pasht. Some also say that is derived, in the vernacular, from the *psst* sound you say, in Egypt and elsewhere, when you call your cat. But the word "tabby," that's something else again!

To call a cat a tabby has become so common that many tend, understandably, to think of the tabby as a breed of itself, but the word only designates a coat common to many cats and breeds. This name for the gray or yellow striped favored cat of hearth and home today in the West, as well as one of the major type cats from the tombs, had its beginning in the name of a striped fabric first manufactured in the twelfth century. Named after Attab, an Umayyid prince who had ordered the special striped fabric, it was produced in a quarter of old Baghdad. The richly hued coat of the tabby cat today surely resembles "attab."

As Julie Clutton-Brock explained in her beautiful book *Cats: Ancient and Modern:*

Most domestic cats throughout the world today still have coats that are variations on the tabby, either striped or blotched. Besides being nearest to the wild species in pattern, the striped tabby is also a coat that is typical of many wild mammalian carnivores and rodents. The pattern is called by biologists "agouti," because it is exemplified by the South American rodent of this name. Each hair of the coat has a brindled gray, black and white appearance which is due to the uneven distribution of melanin (the dark pigment) throughout its length. The overall appearance of the coat is striped or banded with "salt and pepper" flecks as a result of the distribution of the agouti hairs.

Tabbies are more than a breed; they are the mark of a classic and beloved cat; they are a mark that transcend breeds. Ancient seafarers often selected tabby cats with the most unique and unusual blotched markings to travel with them on their ships because they considered them lucky. They left the more common striped tabbies at home with the family.

Now you might well suppose that my voyage of discovery in Egypt would be easy. The reigning position of the Egyptian god cats, after all, foreswore any question of competition: they were the sovereign monarchs of the entire cat god spectrum—they were the Supremes, the Beatles, the Bolshoi, the Met, the Kirov, and the Beijing Opera all in one. I would actually find that historically no other related royal felines ever rose close to their position of being *gods!* In fact, the very first cat name in recorded history was carved on the pharaonic Hana's tomb in the Necropolis of Thebes, where in the carving an ancient cat named Bouhaki (the first actual name of a cat that we know) sits between the feet of his master.

And yet even in Egypt, the great story was not so simple. For one thing, the Egyptian cat shared this royalty with other animals—the crocodile, the mongoose, and the falcon, to cite only a few. But in this ancient society, which above all sought to order the world so as to understand it, these other animals were merely local gods. Only the cat was a god across all of Egypt and, as I was soon to confirm, across the world! And so, from the very start, I was up against the deeper questions—the philosophical, the theological, the sacred—that Pasha had wordlessly presented to me:

What kinds of divinity *were* these animals? What did they really represent in the ancient Egyptian's soul? What did it mean for a cat to be made into a "royal" creature, into a "sacred" creature, into a "god"? Above all, what could this ancient land tell us about *our* relationships with our beautiful and beloved "pets" today—or the extent to which *they* made pets of *us?*

———————

The day after I visited the Egyptian Museum, I was sitting at the gracious, weathered Mahdi Club, with its languorous lawns, in suburban Cairo. There, under the spreading boughs of its ancient trees, with the Egyptian waiters bustling about in their impeccable white robes, I had found waiting for me Dr. Ali Hassan, the respected former head of antiquities for all of Egypt, looking quite the gentleman in his perfect summer suit, despite the insufferable heat. He began by taking out pages of meticulously written notes, all taken down in a neat and cramped hand.

"Oh yes, I made the notes for you," he responded, a slight smile playing about his lips. "It is one way for me to learn. I have to use every opportunity to put the information in a chronology. Because, in the ancient texts, even to find the word 'cat' is not so easy. For instance, I just now found about the cats nursing the Pharaoh! Believe me, I did not know that before." Then he smiled a truly happy smile, and stated, "I am in love with Egyptology." One of the great joys in my own search was to meet men like these who were so in love with their profession and yet, unlike many lovers, wanted to share that love with all mankind.

Dr. Hassan paused, looked very steadily at me, and began to tell me the story of his own pet cat, who was, like Pasha, obviously a representative of the Egyptian pantheon here on earth. It was a white Persian-style cat that he just adored. "I gave him the name Miou," he said. How original, I thought. Feeling thus encouraged, I told Dr. Hassan that I, too, had a wonderful cat—and began to tell him of finding Pasha in Chicago and of knowing in my heart that he had come from Egypt. I suppose I did go on a bit. And then, of course, I brought out a picture of Pasha—how proudly I proffered it, surely awaiting an appropriate response of awe and approval, something like, "Of course, a true god cat. . . . Look at the resemblance to Bastet." He might even make a joke— "But—no earrings?"

Instead, he looked at the picture without expression and handed it back. "Miou is much more beautiful," was all he said.

Apparently this fine gentleman's eyesight was not as good as his scholarship. He probably didn't realize that his cat, with the ridiculously simple name of Miou, which after all was rather on the level of naming an American dog Woof or Bow-Wow, was not one iota as pretty or sacred as a Pasha.

But I restrained myself as he then began weaving the story of the cat into all of the mysterious religion and rites of his ancient culture, with its risen and fallen kingdoms, its sacred books, and its kings, who turned out to be the consorts of the cat goddesses. He told me how the cat has been known since the Middle Kingdom, around 2000 B.C., how its history is written down in the great books of the ancient Egyptians and how the "Miou" cats are found all over the royal tombs of the Nile Valley. He explained that it was "really amazing" when they discovered through early hieroglyphics that there was not only a connection between cats and the greatest Egyptian god of all, the sun god Ra, but that they had found an "amalgam of personality between the two."

Then an unlikely sly grin—a macho grin—crept over his face as he added, "In fact, the sun god Ra himself was often called the Great Tomcat!"

He paused and began to speak softly about the fact that, to the ancient Egyptians, even the moisture on the nose of the cat was holy. For just a moment I was lost in memories. I thought about the first nights after I had found Pasha in Chicago, and how in the dark early mornings, he would curl up on my chest, bat gently at my cheek with his paw, his claws carefully sheathed, and then nuzzle my nose sweetly with his. I would half awake in the half-light to see his pinched white face close to my face and his bright black eyes staring expectantly into mine. How infinitely sweet was that cool moisture from his nose. I could feel it again, almost like a breeze passing by as Dr. Ali Hassan spoke in almost hallucinatory tones of the Egyptian cats' origins.

"In the Nile Delta, the cat was identified with and worshiped as one of the gods in the sky—Miou was worshiped as the sky! They even called the cat Mistress of the Sky and Eye of the Sun and Eye of the Moon. In the late period, the cat was even shown, as I mentioned before, nursing the pharoah."

The elegant Egyptologist paused here to look around the old club. He seemed to be lost momentarily in his thoughts. Then he suddenly changed his tone and began to speak of the cat not as a god or goddess, not as the guardian of the sun or the representative of the moon, but simply as one's house cat, one's beloved pet cat.

"We can kill any animal in Egypt, or hit it," he said, "but nobody would dare to harm a cat. You ask the poorest peasant, or fellaghin, why he would not kill a cat and he will say, 'No, it is an angel.'" He grimaced, as though in pain. "Oh, I saw them in China eating cats," he exclaimed. "I couldn't bear it."

Before I left, I asked what he thought the usual color of the Egyptian god cats had been?

He thought seriously for a moment. "Black, all black," he answered confidently.

ZAGAZIG

Now I was ready to head straight to the origins of my search, to Bubastis, where surely the secrets of the relationship of mankind to the cat would finally be revealed to me.

The Egyptian embassy in Washington had hesitantly asked the Information Ministry in Cairo to have me taken to the ruins of the cat temple of Tell Basta at Bubastis, northward on the Nile Delta in a small city named Zagazig, which I continuously, despite my best intentions, kept calling Zigazag to myself. The embassy officer was hesitant about the visit, since I was also asking at the same time to see the foreign minister and other notables for my syndicated column, and this might make me look less than 100 percent serious. Finally he resolved it in a typically Egyptian way. "I sent two faxes, two days apart," he said, "the first asking for the foreign minister and the second, for the cat temple." He smiled broadly. "I know my people," he said.

We started out early one Friday morning, my ministry guide, an archaeology student, and I, and we were in high spirits. As we passed by different arms of the Nile, I was amazed and refreshed by the brilliant, almost obscene, green of that long piece of land along the river. I knew how fragile this country was, for in only a matter of miles on either side of the great river begin the awesome and unforgiving deserts, from which Pasha's relatives had escaped in such a timely manner those thousands of years ago. Living in this fragile environment, the Egyptians not unexpectedly created a religion that would beseech the gods for balance in behavior and for moderation in expectation. Thus the Egyptian cat entered into history.

I realized, too, with a sense of awe, that I was entering another world as well: that of the goddess. Anthropologist Joseph Campbell has pointed out that "the basic birth of Western civilization occurred in the great river valleys—the voluptuous Nile in the middle of the harsh and barren deserts, the Tigris-Euphrates, the Indus, and later the Ganges. That was the world of the Goddess." Thus, here the environment, the cat, and the cult of the goddess came together once again.

In only an hour and a half, we came to Zagazig, a pleasant enough industrial city on the Bubastis branch, one of the seven arms of the Nile. Most of the small custodial and archaeological staff at the ruins of Tell Basta were dozing as we arrived, obviously having inbibed some of the qualities of the gods and goddesses they so loyally served. Indeed, they had to shake themselves and stretch—much like Pasha and all sleepy cats stretch and pull themselves together after a nap—to usher us around in the dazzling and dazing sunlight.

For many years the temple had been largely forgotten, just another mélange of half-ruined walls sprawling across a span of the earth, with an occasional carving or statue half buried in the rubble. Then the government became interested in it and sealed it off for archaeological preservation. By this time, visitors had to have passes, carefully sealed and written in Arabic, inscribed with the figure of Bastet.

Bubastis was no slouch of a temple. Herodotus called it the "sacred city" and "Egypt's most beautiful temple." One approached it in those centuries through a wide, beckoning road, and the temple itself seemed like an island, surrounded by broad canals fed by the Nile. The gateway was sixty feet high and richly ornamented. The temple itself was made of blocks of red granite, basalt, and alabaster and the central shrine contained the cult image of the goddess, surrounded by tall trees. Altars where offerings of gold, wine, and beer were made to the cat goddesses were the focus of their great festivals. Ahmed Mohamed Abdel Wahab, the local inspector of antiquities, began solemnly, "The cat was very holy."

How to describe my own feelings, as finally I set foot and laid eyes on the spot where my own Pasha had originated?

By this time the site was merely 238 acres of low, ocher-colored ruins. Walking was dangerous among the great open holes and deceptive, yawning chasms that one could not see until one was hard upon them. (Cats could surely more reliably navigate these stones and rocks than I.) As we walked, I remarked to the archaeology student, "I suppose you think I am a little crazy for wanting to see this." He looked earnest, even disapproving, of my question and he quickly responded in the kinds of words that showed once again the classic Egyptian pride in their heritage: "Oh no, we take all of archaeology very seriously."

Different expeditions had, over the years, uncovered a number of treasures here, all of which had been long removed to the dusty corners of the Egyptian Museum: two hundred gold beads, bronze statuettes of the cat goddesses, the statue of a queen with three kittens. At one place in the ruins, we looked into the walls of a deep hole to see some splendid Egyptian pharaonic paintings. At another spot, we stopped for me to pose between two seated royal figures, one most probably the goddess Bastet. (I tried, without much success, I'm sorry to say, to read some of Pasha's characteristics into her.)

I thought back on these kingdoms that emerged out of the darkness of history beginning in 5000 B.C., of the fine-featured and brown-skinned people who traded and planted like other peoples. Yet Egyptians seemed to be uniquely uneasy, always searching for order and for the principles underlying order, in awe of their universe, yet driven to find explanations for everything about them, most often in their great, gray temples. Above all, they always sought harmony: in nature, in culture, and in their gods.

Thus they studied the animals around them to help explain that world to themselves. Surely it was better to placate the crocodile, the falcon, and the mongoose, not to speak of the agile and beautiful cat, and to woo them with godly titles, than to take the chance of cutting out any real or potential god! The traditional religion of Egypt was polytheistic, so anyone with any sense would know that gods could appear both in human and in animal form!

By the year 2000 B.C., the world's first domesticated cat—the sweet home cat, the pet cat, the loving companion cat—made its appearance when Egypt, then at its height, had a population of 8 million people and twenty great cities along the Nile, nourishing a dazzling culture. Just as I was thinking about all of this that day, I stopped in my tracks. I was standing in the middle of the ocher ruins and suddenly the world in the books began to come to life around me. It seemed mysteriously to be explaining itself to me, as though a voice from the past were speaking to me—but in truth, it was *my* own voice reliving what had happened here, and it was as if I were actually there.

Cats live right in the temples, tended by phalanxes of priests and custodians. In the temple itself, the high priests guard the temple cats day and night—they watch for omens and for prophecies which are spelled out for them by how the cats sleep and even how they stretch, hold their tails, and tweak their whiskers. Cat symbols are everywhere, even in cat amulets to ward off evil spirits. Newborn infants are dedicated to [Bastet], then the child's head is shaved and the hair placed on a balance and weighed against pieces of gold.

By 950 B.C. The Cat becomes one of the most popular goddesses of the land, a deity that seems to speak on uniquely personal and intimate terms to the masses of the people. This deity is usually portrayed as a cat-headed woman depicted standing gracefully and elegantly, holding a sistrum or ancient form of Egyptian musical instrument which is a stringed rattle used to worship the goddess, Isis. Even the beauteous Cleopatra models her style after that of the cat goddess.

Thus the Egyptians have little trouble embracing and integrating into themselves, in ways that modern man has never understood, both the awe inspiring and supernatural goddess of their temples and the charming little housecat of their kitchen and hearth. Unlike in the Hebrew faith and later in Christianity, deities are not centralized deities in Egypt, and so religion is flexible and its symbols, expansive.

But it is in the spring—oh yes, it is in the glorious hope and in the sensuous celebration of the beginning of life!—that Bubastis truly comes to life! For the spring festivals link her worship, if not herself, with sensuality, with musicality, and above all with sexuality. Herodotus visits in 450 B.C. and breathlessly describes the behavior of the pilgrims as they float down the Nile to Bubastis: "Whenever they pass a town, they bring the boats close in shore and then, while some of the women continue (playing instruments, dancing, and clapping their hands), others shout and jeer at the townswomen, while still others dance, stand upright, pulling up their skirts."

Women, it is said and written, could on the occasion of that festival, have sexual relations with anyone. Thus, they said, was ensured the fertility of the river villages. (And might there not be other reasons?)

Finally, Egyptians from all over the realm bring their cats here to be mummified. Some of the cat bodies wear turquoise collars around their necks, while those of rich men are elegantly preserved in bronze caskets with bronze statues of themselves resting gracefully on top, like the deceased monarchs of modern Britain or France in their great cathedrals. But always, the Egyptian embalmers use as their trademark the figure of a scarab, the sacred beetle which even today in Egypt signifies eternal life.

So it was that they embalmed the illustrious among men and the loved and sacred among animals, believing that the souls might one day return to the bodies, that the bodies might thus be revived and that poor and limited humans also might learn from all creatures.

Long after I left Bubastis, I could still feel the pull of the dusty and magical air of that day.

The morning after the trip to Bubastis I was sitting in the coffee shop at the Nile Hilton when an old friend of mine Mohamed Hakki, a talented Egyptian journalist, joined me for a coffee. "You do know," he began, "that there *is* another cat goddess besides Bastet—and a not very nice one. Sekhmet. She's the lion goddess of war and of conflict, but also of the protection of the home."

At first I didn't have the faintest idea who she was. But then I remembered that we had stopped at one of the largest rocks at Bubastis, where we found one of the clearest and finest carvings on the side of the rock. At first, we thought it was Bastet because the profile looked so like Pasha—with a delicate, pugged nose. Then we believed it might be Horus, the Falcon. Finally, one of the men awoke from his semiperpetual snooze, which he had continued even while walking right alongside me, and exclaimed, with passion, "No, no! That is Sekhmet!" For some reason, I just let it go at that.

EGYPTIAN MYSTERY NUMBER ONE:
WHO THE DEVIL *WAS* SEKHMET?

At the Egyptian Museum, I learned that Sekhmet, the lioness goddess, was considered to be the divine mother of the divine concept of pharaoh and that she was not to be taken for granted—not when she was known as the Powerful, and the Dismemberer, and the Mangler! (Mookie's dark hand, this time risen from the Underworld!)

Another director of the museum, Mahdouh Aldamati, tried to explain patiently to me that Bastet was the goddess of the "east of the Nile," while Sekhmet was the goddess of the "west of the Nile." "In these hybrid figures and in these contrapuntal figures, the ancient Egyptians could make it very easy for people to understand," he said. "They are a mixture of the qualities of human beings and animals. The changes of face make us confused, but this was not confusing for the ancient Egyptians."

I studied the pictures of Sekhmet. Her personifications were fierce, and yet somehow sad. Her face was rough and jowly, but usually a tear was shown rolling down tenderly onto her cheek, which was another example of the special ability of the Egyptians to personalize, to humanize, to bring together opposites. Perhaps Bastet was from Venus and Sekhmet from Mars? Were they trying to integrate the contradictions in their own personalities in the two "persons" of these feline characters?

I found still other Egyptian sacred cats: the "hunting cat," the "cat-as-state-god," and even an Egyptian "wildcat," the creature that many feel personifies the soul of wildness that still exists in every cat. As well, there were a number of physical styles of cat. The commonly accepted "Egyptian cat" can be a cat like Pasha or like today's American or British Shorthairs or ticked brown or gray, or even red or silver like today's Abyssinian breed with its amazing hairs, each one of which reflect many colors; the Egyptian tombs also had many tabbies. Because of the extravagant designs in their furs, Egyptians described their tabbies as wearing necklaces, lockets, chains, and bracelets, flaunting butterflies on their shoulders, rings on their tails, waistcoat buttons on their tummies, and kohl around their eyes. But the tabby is a coat pattern, remember, one found in many breeds of cat—it is not a breed in itself.

And so, as the inventive Egyptians struggled to make sense of their world, all these emanations of the cat blended naturally into one creature. Somehow the combination of these characteristics gave the people a unified sense of command of nature and knowledge of psychology and of personality—and these cats were *always* beautiful.

Before I left that day, I asked Mahdouh Aldamati, "And what was the color of the ancient Egyptian cat?"

"Well, surely white and gray," he said assuredly, "and, oh yes, occasionally yellow."

EGYPTIAN MYSTERY NUMBER TWO:
WHY WAS THERE NO SEXUAL REPRESENTATION OF THE CAT GODS AND GODDESSES IN EGYPTIAN ART AND LORE?

Everyone knows the often unspeakable sexual antics of the cat, anywhere and everywhere. So it was strange to find no portrait in Egypt of the, to put it more nicely, "romantic" cat. These ancient and wise people, who could adore cats and know them philosophically like no other men and women throughout history—priests spent days and weeks mummifying tiny cat bodies for the trip to the underworld—a culture that fit cats into every instant of its being—never ever seemed to see them as sexual or sensuous creatures.

Ladies and gentlemen ought, of course, to be reluctant and even embarrassed to discuss the ardent, and often reprehensible sexual lives of our beautiful but unabashed friends. We all know that our decorous and delicate pets fling all propriety to the wind when they fall in love. Yowling, fighting, arching their backs . . . No need to shock ourselves with all the voluptuous extremes of their erotic lives! Still, the historical silence was strange.

In the end, we can say that Bastet was always portrayed in an absolutely proper manner and that is the way we must always think of her. She obviously chose to be the perfect "keep-your-paws-to-yourself" lady.

In fact, not only was Bastet untouchable, she was so holy that she had ties to the Virgin birth and perhaps, in the long scale of things, even to the Virgin Mary! My Egyptologists assured me that the mother of Christ had indeed visited Bubastis—certainly, she had visited Cairo, as still today there is a famous Coptic Christian church marking her steps—although the meaning of such a visit remains at best ambiguous. In short, Bastet was not only goddess of sexuality festivals but she was also the embodiment of the idea of "virgin motherhood," which has appeared with such startling regularity in cultures far removed from one another across the globe.

"Like other cat goddesses in other countries," Roger Caras has written of this little-known relationship, "Bastet was worshiped as a virgin! And when Christianity rolled upward into Europe, collapsing whole systems of belief, other pagan goddesses eventually took the form of Mary as the divine Virgin Mother."

This "conflictedness" of males about these supposed "dual" natures of females did not strike me as terribly new—but I had not heard about in with regard to cats before!

EGYPTIAN MYSTERY NUMBER THREE:
HOW DID THE EGYPTIAN CAT CULT SPREAD AROUND THE WORLD?

I started out believing that the Bastet cult was unique to Egypt. But as I dug deeper, I discovered that the cult of Bastet was later found by archaeologists to be present in ancient Pompeii, in pre-Roman and Greek cities, and in Rome itself. (There were even diplomatic "incidents" when the Egyptians tried to get their beloved god cats returned from the catnappers of other, naturally jealous lands.) Obviously, the cats had been carried out by smugglers or by the Romans after they dominated Egypt in the centuries just before and after the birth of Christ. Thus, the cat cult was carried far and wide by its adepts and believers.

Indeed, in supposedly unlike societies across the globe, from the hot jungles of central Africa to the cool Andes of South America to Palestine to the frigid land of Norway, there was the cat! One of the very earliest clues to the cat's evolution was found in Lachish, in what was historically known as Palestine, in an ivory carving of a cat, probably dating from the year 2700 B.C. In the frozen Nordic world, the cat goddess of love and beauty, Freyja, swept across the gleaming evening sky in a sled drawn by two other cats! (And exactly *where* were the reindeer?) Even more eerily revealing, Freyja was originally a three-way goddess, in charge of that odd, old trinity of sex, motherhood, and destruction.

The cat cult in Egypt began to decline in about 350 B.C., and was finally banned in A.D. 390 by imperial Roman decree. Egyptian-style cats began to spread in all directions—a sad, but true, di*cat*spora. Taken aboard commercial ships across the world to strange ports where they would jump ship and engage in some of their unseemly mating, they would soon start another kindle of kittens, and in a little while a new family of cats would appear! As with their human counterparts, as they moved away from their cosseted world in their homeland, their style and manners changed as well. They adapted to climate, to mountain and desert, to Northern fogs and to Southern summers. Some of those who traveled to the Orient eventually lost their tails. (How embarrassing that must have been for them.) Those who traveled northward became stocky, with dense, insulating undercoats and a layer of weatherproof down-type hair, while those who stayed or went southward became thinner with sparser coats and smaller bodies to help them lose the excess heat. It is said that the long, lean cats were likely to have more gregarious, outgoing personalities (like Pasha!) than their more stolid and squat cousins; the long, lean ones were also said to be more vocal, demonstrative, and protective of their home territories (like Pasha!).

A new map was beginning to form in my mind that might answer some of my core questions about the human-cat relationship: Humans had created and populated the world in ever-widening circles of emigration, settlement, and acculturation; and just as tribes and clans of humans had mixed with one another to create new societies, so had cats! Moreover, with a little effort, one could plot on this map the movements, the centuries, and the kingdoms of cat!

EGYPTIAN MYSTERY NUMBER FOUR:
WHY WERE NO SLEEPING CATS SHOWN ANYWHERE IN EGYPTIAN LORE?

In all of the dazzling cities of the Nile, in those austere gray temples, in the hundreds and even thousands of representations of exquisite cat carvings and statues and whatnot, there is almost every type of cat: strolling cats, singing cats, cats serving mice, cats ruling the state, mice laughing at the cats, cats eating fish. But there is no sleeping cat! Oh, there is the stone statue of one recumbent cat from the Bubastis ruins, now in the Egyptian Museum. But when I asked the museum directors about it, they corrected their counterparts at the site. "No," they agreed, "it is not sleeping, it is only lying."

The ancient Egyptian declared himself to know his dear companion, the cat, so profoundly, so wisely, so totally, that he could make of this family icons of virginity, symbols of the sun, and purveyors of the weather's warnings. He could know what the glow of the light in the cat's eyes meant and he could devise libidinous festivals to celebrate in the name of the cat what he dared not celebrate merely for himself. But—not even one sleeping cat? Was it perhaps another animal he was talking, writing, caricaturing, worshiping, adoring, wondering about? Did he really know his Miou at all?

As anyone who has ever cohabited with one of these creatures indubitably knows, the cat sleeps at least twenty hours a day, maybe more when he's just tired out (as, for instance, after having eaten breakfast, lunch, or dinner). Cats dream in a semiconscious state, which is why they are always crying out in the night, probably dreaming of the old days in Thebes and Luxor, like Pasha. Writer Joseph Wood Krutch once wrote famously that he had known cats with many maladies but that he never knew one to suffer from insomnia. In fact, cats spend twice as much time asleep as most other mammals, and no one has the faintest idea why, except perhaps that they are such expert hunters that they often have time on their paws.

One school of thought is that, since the cats were regarded and portrayed as symbols of wisdom and guardians of the state, they were incongruously never to be shown in a sleeping position (the "wise cat never sleeps" school). A second school avers that showing them dozed off would harm their image as the god-protector of the state (the "watch cat, always on duty!" school). Still a third asserts that the ancient Egyptians did not depict the cat sleeping because they did not want to be awakened at three in the morning to have to play with him (the "Hey, let *me* sleep, will you?" school). Although all of these schools of thought may be attributed to me, I refrain from revealing my own predilection.

EGYPTIAN MYSTERY NUMBER FIVE:
WHAT REALLY WAS THE COLOR OF THE EGYPTIAN CATS?

One Egyptologist said they were brown; another said they were black; and still another asserted they were white and gray or perhaps yellow. One can only speculate that even these fine scholars are not perfect; but that if the descendant cats alive today may be my guide, they would probably be all of these colors. In fact, from what we know about the most direct descendants of those original

Egyptian cats, the closest "relatives" are the Abyssinians or "Abys," the Egyptian Maus, and the various cats with the tabby coat, all of whom can come in many colors.

EGYPTIAN MYSTERY NUMBER SIX:
WHY *DID* THE ANCIENT EGYPTIANS WORSHIP THEIR CATS AND MAKE THEM INTO GODS?

To start with the physical aspects that are often behind elements of worship, particularly in ancient days, cats have wonderful eyesight and can see up to 130 feet away, while their peripheral vision of 185 degrees gives them an abnormally wide field of sight. Their eyes glow in the dark, shamanistically, reminding us poor humans of "seers" in the occult sense. So the ancients believed that cats' eyes glowed at night because they harbored the reflection of the sun long after it was hidden from man. Could it possibly be an accident that cats' eyes shone more brightly at full moon and grew dimmer at its disappearance; or that, in their widening and closing, their eyes reflected the waxing and waning of the moon?

The great Greek philosopher and essayist Plutarch wrote poetically of the cat that "the pupils of her eyes seem to fill up and grow large upon the full of the moon and to decrease again and diminish in brightness on its waning." The ancient Greeks also believed that the shuffling gray clouds of early evening were mice being flicked and chased off by the paws of the shining cat of the moon as night moved in.

The scientific fact that the eerie glow in the cats' eyes comes from a "mirror" behind the retina, which reflects the maximum available light and thus makes the cats' eyes appear to glow with their own exquisite light, may not be enough for modern, scientifically oriented Westerners, but it is doubtful it would have been for the ancient Egyptians. After all, is it not more wondrous to think of the clouds as mice being chased off by the cat of the moon? To see these little creatures as the sacred accomplices of light?

The seemingly magical combination of strength, agility, and night vision—contrasted so strongly with the daytime activities of comparatively weaker humans—created the singularly powerful image implanted in the consciousness of our early ancestors. They were, after all, primitive peoples who believed that by transposing animal qualities onto the realm of the royal, the sacred, and the godlike, they would themselves experience and understand more. This is why the sun god Ra, when he was fighting the evil power of darkness, was sometimes depicted even as the prepotent tomcat. When a solar eclipse occurred, something that frightens men and women still today, the Egyptians ran around shaking rattles to waken the cat god in the heavens.

Then there was the excellent physical coordination and muscular control of cats. Could anyone truly think, in those early but seeking days of mankind, that these creatures could so famously survive dangerous falls if there were not something magical about them? In addition, cats are notoriously sensitive to changes in the weather: their hair often stands up on end if a lightning storm is approaching. They are frisky before the first snowfall, grow restless in early spring, and become languid and lazy in midsummer.

I shall always remember the first spring I had Pasha, the lovely, happy spring of 1976. He was still a young cat, barely a year old, and he was kittenish (what a charming word!). He was often into his twenty hours a day of sleep when suddenly, spring came! It was as if a whiff of world-class catnip overtook him. He leapt about on his hindfeet; he attacked the drapes starting with a long run across the room; and at every turn I would find him nipping at my ankles or clawing at the hems of my dresses. I believe that he did not sleep for four days, and barely did I. He was a rocket of a cat that spring. By midsummer, he grew more calm. I don't ever remember, however, his hair standing on end.

Still, these physical qualities alone are hardly enough to explain the Egyptians' devotion to their cats, a devotion that extends deeply into human philosophy, theology, and spirituality and that profoundly involves the human soul, spirit, and psychology.

In the fifth century B.C., Herodotus wrote that the Egyptian priests had told him that the immortality of the soul was a doctrine that came to them today from ancient times. When the body died, the soul could enter the body of another creature then about to be born—an animal, a cat perhaps. Before I had left those dusty ocher-colored ruins of Bubastis, I sat down on a rock and pondered. My readings about the cat in Egypt had already introduced me to a concept that soon enough I would find to be common across the cultures that worshiped and adored cats—the concept of the transmigration of souls, or the passing of the individual soul at death into a new body or new form of life, usually human or animal. Indeed, one of the reasons for the deification of the cat in ancient Egypt was the idea that at death the human's soul might pass it into an animal who would carry it to the next world. That idea was embedded in virtually all the historical cultures that deified or worshiped cats.

But the Egyptians have a wonderful and creative sense of humor, and they also worshiped their animals because they found them so exceedingly lovable and amusing. They luxuriated in the sheer joy of the animals that, together with them, populated the earth—and thus they lovingly depicted them in their paintings. Papyrus drawings show animals with musical instruments—a donkey playing a harp, a lion plunking a lyre, a baboon tuning a double flute, and a crocodile beating time with a long-necked stringed instrument draped over one arm; meanwhile, a cat is attacked by a duck and a blackbird climbs a ladder to steal fruit from a tree, only to find a miniature hippopotamus waiting for it.

Henri Frankfort, a famous American archaeologist, said that these animals were "alive as humans were alive, but differently; in an animal the human being recognized an *otherness*. Moreover, animals do not change. Generation after generation, they are the same. The first wearer of the double crown of Egypt in 3000 B.C. would see the 'same' duck that Ramses II saw more than a millennium and a half afterwards."

Oh, people can love other animals; people can adore and personally "worship," in literature and prose and psychology, dogs. I am myself most fond of dogs, but dogs ever and always represented the physical being of man. But there is something deeply special about the cat—why else would mankind have carried on so about her all these years? You might appreciate a cat that caught mice, but you would surely never worship her.

———

Before leaving Egypt, I went to do an interview with Egypt's charming Foreign Minister Ahmed Maher El Sayed. As we talked about war and peace, about the Israelis and the Palestinians battling it out, about terrorist cells forming across the world, I could see that we both were getting depressed. Then this charming man asked me what else I was writing about?

Hesitantly, I told him. "I was out at Bubastis only yesterday," I said, "looking into my study of your sacred cats."

"Oh, that's wonderful," he repeated several times, as I told him of my admittedly odd search. "Oh, that's just wonderful . . . I can't wait to tell my wife and my mother." He paused and a devilish look came into his eyes. "And there are no Palestinian cats, right?"

"No, Mr. Minister," I assured him with a smile, "there are no Palestinian cats." I am at a loss to tell you how wonderfully relieved he was.

WASHINGTON, D.C.

En route home, I picked up a *Wall Street Journal* on the plane and found an article about a man named R. J. Sorensen who made "Movies That Only Cats Are Expected to Enjoy." This South Carolina man would retreat behind his camera, waiting for his "case of grackles and cowbirds to arrive." Then he would take pictures sure to delight and excite cats. His first movie, *Kitty Show,* which took four years and half a million dollars to make, featured a cast of bugs and fiddler crabs and sold 100,000 copies. He was quoted as saying of his films, "If I was a cat, I'd tear the hell out of the TV."

When I finally arrived home that night, after being away for so long, Pasha was at the door crying for me. Once inside, I eagerly picked him up and cuddled him and he fell into my arms just as he had that first day on Barry Avenue. But after a few minutes, he leapt away, then crouched down on the floor in his *"I am a very angry cat!"* crouch, and closed in again and again to nip at my ankles. But as soon as he got his anger and jealousy out of his soul, he was up in my lap, purring his head off and welcoming me home. I got his little hat out—the one with the brim that made him look so rakishly cosmopolitan. But when as a joke I tried to put a necklace on him, he balked, hissed slightly, and immediately jumped away. (In fact, even with the hat, he looked more like an Irish saloon keeper from the South Side of Chicago than an Egyptian god cat—he was just not going to accoutre himself like his cousin Bastet.)

So it was that I put all my pictures together, with words and music in a video, just like Mr. Sorenson from the *Wall Street Journal,* and played it for a while every night for Pasha. He had always liked television, and at first he pretended not to notice anything different. He perched on the pillows atop the couch, his legs awry, pretending to be asleep. One eye opened, then the other—and back to sleep again. Eventually, he would actually lie in front of the TV and watch the video. By the time it all really took root in him, he was back atop the television smacking his paws on moving figures of the Egyptian past. I particularly liked it when I showed pictures of Tell Basta and he gently patted my image as I posed before the very same statue of Bastet that I insisted was Pasha himself.

From my first researches and historical mappings, it was abundantly clear to me that Pasha had indeed come from Egypt. I had been right in my intuitions and he had not misrepresented himself a bit. But it wasn't really so tough to figure out—after all, all cats originated in Egypt!

I will never know exactly why he healed so beautifully from his liver operation, but from that moment on he made an unprecedented recovery. He was not only his old self, he was a wonderful, lively, somehow infinitely more sophisticated and secure new self. When we went to sleep that night after the video, Pasha curled up, as good cats inevitably do, in some ridiculous position that only true gods can afford without looking totally ridiculous. I realized that, although I had met many males who thought they were gods, I was for the first time sleeping with one.

From that moment onward, my life was to be filled with reigning cats.

CHAPTER THREE

LIFE AFTER PASHA: MY NIKKO AND JAPAN'S "NEKO"

Cat you went and you didn't come back—
You were like a son to me!
Loving you so, how could we forget you?
FROM "FAREWELL POEM FOR A DECEASED CAT,"
BY IBN AL-MU'TAZZ, AN ABBASID PRINCE
WHO WAS CALIPH OF BAGHDAD FOR ONE DAY
AND WHO DIED IN A.D. 908

WASHINGTON, D.C.

In our last happy years together, Pasha sat at my side or on the corner of my desk or played and scampered about under my feet while I wrote. And of course, he slept by my side.

When I was working on my biography of Fidel Castro, I would suddenly sense a strange silence. Then, although I would not actually see Pasha in the room, I could feel him there—somewhere. Like a sudden hurricane, Pasha would leap onto the desk. Every single paper, pen, clip, stapler, and notepad would spin up off the desk as in the spiral of a tornado, only to crash and scatter all over the floor! By the time I could see anything, the perpetrator of this

despicable act would be scampering away to his hiding place in the closet somewhere, to emerge at suppertime with a look of postured innocence.

That biography of Castro took me seven years, and Pasha saw me through
all the terrible periods—the long hours of research, the frustration—and the
final victory of seeing the book published and successful. I felt then that he
enjoyed the limited celebrity even more than I. (And why, I ask you, would not
an Egyptian god cat enjoy celebrity?) Once as we both sat there during those
companionable hours of work, I remembered how Harriet Beecher Stowe's
beloved Maltese cat, Calvin, had sat with her during the long hours of writing
Uncle Tom's Cabin. He "radiated calm during hours of frenzied writing," she
said later. Of course, it wasn't so hard for Pasha to radiate calm because he was
asleep most of the time that I was writing—and I'll bet you any money that's
why Calvin was radiating all that time, too.

At night, being abnormally long-legged, a veritable Fred Astaire of cats,
Pasha would stretch out, and strettccchh out, until he was nearly four feet long
as he lay beside me, curled up so cozily and sweetly, purring his Egyptian head
off and consoling me for the trials of the day.

In the last eight or nine months that I was writing *Guerrilla Prince,* I began
to have a frightful presentiment that when the Castro book was finally finished,
other things precious to me would end, too. I began to fear that Pasha, whose
health once again was becoming fragile, was going to pass out of my life.

Only a month before he died that spring of 1991, I was taking an afternoon
nap, a custom I embraced when I first lived in Latin America as a foreign correspondent. Pasha would often curl up on my chest and gently nuzzle my nose
with his, and I would feel again the "sacred moisture" on the cat's nose. It was
always a sweet moment, but this day when Pasha curled up on my chest, it was
different. He put his paws around my neck almost tenderly, and then he not
only rubbed my nose with his but he gently moved one of his cheeks against
mine, then the other, and finally, he put his forehead against mine and rubbed
it with his own.

It was intimately otherworldly—and terrifyingly purposeful—and he cried
when he did it. It was not a meow, which he was not given to making anyway.
Rather, it was a series of mournful little cries that penetrated to the depths of

my being and frightened me terribly. I knew full well that it was an omen, and from that moment on my life and his were going to change in an awful way.

A few weeks later, I awoke in the middle of the night and realized Pasha was not there. I supposed that he was just napping somewhere else—although he almost always cuddled up on the bed. Finally I found him in the kitchen, lying on the top of the table with that perfect inertness mastered first by the Egyptian "hunting cat" and memorialized in some of the tombs. But now Pasha was staring fixedly at the floor—and at one specific spot.

He was staring fixedly at a beetle—a rather large and black beetle. I knew then that this was where he had been all night.

My mother, who was artistic about life but highly unsentimental about bugs of any kind, had taught me well. I took a piece of toweling, killed the bug, and put it down the toilet. Pasha took a vast, deep breath, pulled his back up momentarily into one of his "Halloween Cat" stretches, but only a halfhearted one, and came directly into bed. There he slept the sleep of the gallant and successful cat guardian of man, not even awakening for his beloved breakfast. I knew that he had been protecting me.

It also had not escaped me that the creature invading us was a beetle. It was, in fact, a direct relative of the ancient scarab of Egypt, the sign of eternal life which appears throughout Egyptian lore, particularly in the mummification of god cats at Bubastis on the Nile. This strange sign in the middle of the night had a profound meaning for our lives.

Soon after that, I was sitting quietly in my chair reading when I watched him walk into the living room, swaggering and swiggling just a little, his luxuriant tail swishing back and forth with its accustomed "Don't-you-recognize-the-cat-that-nursed-the-pharaoh?" sense of himself, when suddenly his left hind leg gave out. He swayed to the side, unable to balance or to keep himself up, and fell. Even the thrashing about of his long black tail could not help him. In my heart I knew that his time would soon be upon us. That night I put some of the couch cushions on the floor so I could be down there next to him. He cuddled for a while but, when I finally woke up, he was sleeping up on the couch. I had to smile when I woke up to find him up there above me.

The leg weakness was apparently due to a blood clot on his spine, and for two days he went through the strange and in some ways wondrous last minuet of his life. Dragging his back leg, he circled the apartment, going to each of his favorite places, as though somehow looking over his life and making these beloved surroundings his one last time.

Finally there was nothing to do but put the Egyptian god cat to sleep. My last sight of Pasha was at the clinic. He was in Dr. Bayles's arms, being carried lovingly downstairs. Dr. Barbara Stein, my dear friend, one of the first woman vets in the country, who became a world specialist on cats, had told me not to stay with him while he was put to sleep, for that was the way I would always remember him. But I'm not sure she was right. I believe that I let my friend down by not being with him at the end and have always felt guilty.

When Dr. Bayles had, with his ineffable kindness and care, put Pasha to sleep that June 12, I had my old friend cremated, mummification not really being a choice in Washington or its environs. Still, Pasha was surely on a royal golden boat to the Egyptian underworld, having so successfully made his journey from Egypt to the New World and having left so many centuries of wondrous memories behind him. Finally, late in the summer I took his ashes to the house in Wisconsin, site of so many wonderful years of my life, and we buried him in the backyard in the same corner where mother's lilac bushes always bloomed in May.

Like many pet owners, I could only deal with the dull pangs of missing Pasha's royal and mischievous presence by numbing and thus abusing my feelings. He was *only a cat.* "Why are you carrying on so? Is there perhaps something wrong with you? You should have had children—you should not have had pets at all! You should have done this, you should have done that . . . You are a fool." And perhaps I *was* a fool, for such nonsense only made the pain worse.

There are people who say that losing a beloved pet is as bad as losing a beloved person. Actually, it can be much worse. Pets are with you all the time. They never ask anything, except a shrimp here and a pat there. They are unswervingly loyal and true in a world of artifice and perfidy and they share everything in their lives with you, including their spirits and souls.

But I was also beginning to feel something else that went far beyond my own personal feelings of loss and emptiness. For with Pasha's death I began to feel ever more deeply the relatedness of animals to us. True, they can't speak, they have no written language, and they have no "culture," at least as we think of it. Yet, I had been to Egypt and to Bubastis; I had stood on my balcony in Cairo and breathed the wondrous air of the cat's ancient world. Now I began to read systematically about cats as a kind of family—not only as our friends and pets but as political and cultural creatures in themselves, different from us but surely related. True, I had rescued Pasha from the streets; I had salved his voyager's wounds and given him a good home; but Pasha had also left me a wondrous legacy, and now I was determined to extend it beyond him and to share my life with another cat. How amazing it was that, without my actually trying, my new cat would fall into the same pattern of royal search—and royal findings—that Pasha did! It might seem somehow providential or even normal—if, of course, one were a normal human being or if cats were normal for that matter, either.

I believe in connections and ties. I found Nikko through the cat magazine *Cat Fancy,* given to me a year before as a gift by my inseparable childhood friend, Georgia Lengerich, from our old Chicago neighborhood. Later I would discover that my new kitten had been born on May 28, 1991, exactly the same day that Pasha became so ill during the night!

One day, leafing through a copy of the magazine, I found my eye drifting over and over to the pictures of the Japanese Bobtails. They are small, lean cats with beautiful bodies, all of them white with spots of black, gray, or caramel color. (In the cat world, gray is actually called blue and caramel is professionally called red, but, for clarity's sake, I will use the colors as they actually appear to us.) The bobtails have tiny pinched faces with conspicuous high cheekbones, slanted almond eyes, and very big ears. Everyone says they look Japanese, and in fact, they do. Among bobtails, the "tricolor" of white, black, and caramel is considered the most precious and is an impishly cute cat. And there was a breeder on a farm not far away, in Lynchburg in southern Virginia. This would be a perfect change from and foil for my memories of regal Pasha from Luxor: I would get a simple little cat from Virginia with a Japanese accent! Little did I dream what I was getting into.

My friend Elise McCormick and I set out that day in October 1991 for the five-hour drive south through the verdant hills and valleys of historic Virginia to find the Cheval Cattery just outside of Lynchburg. I was deeply excited and found myself taking deep breaths and worrying. Worrying? Yes. After all, *Pasha* had rather conspicuously found me . . . What if I made a mistake? Did the act of actually choosing a cat—of *buying* a cat, as though he were some kind of product or some kind of interchangeable and renewable part of one's life— somehow vulgarize the whole process? Must not a cat, exercising its ancient will, choose *you*? Would I mistakenly choose a cat with personality problems?

Most of all, could any cat be as wonderful as the Egyptian god cat who came to me that day out of history's mists? During the drive, I pondered those questions.

Eventually we found Mr. and Mrs. Marsh in a concrete and brick ranch house deep in the woods. It was a paradise for animals, and the grounds were filled with exotic-looking miniature horses and Shih Tzu dogs, while the cats were kept inside. But could such a setting be a respectable home for a Japanese Bobtail—so close to the Bible Belt and the Elvis center of the world and so far away from the Japanese emperor's palace and the sorrows of the samurai? That night, Elise and I had trouble even getting a drink in town, so much does the Reverend Jerry Falwell dominate the social protocols of Lynchburg! I could not help but wonder whether a cat from such a setting would exactly fit in with the active social life and lively friends I had in Washington—or socialize in the way Pasha had.

Yet, right away there were warnings that these pets might not be as simple as they seemed. Mrs. Marsh, for instance, was a homey woman and she and her lovely, animal-adoring daughter, Michelle, welcomed us inside, where there were tiny cats running about all through the halls—all without tails! Then they took us into a room that was like the formal reception room of a very nice hotel or club with sofas covered in white brocade. Once we were seated on the couch in front of the coffee table, we sipped the duly offered tea, as we waited for the show to start. Michelle brought out one or two cats at a time. First, she would hold the little fellow up in front of us so we could look him over. Then she would let the kitty try to settle in my lap. Finally, there was a little drama when she put several cats and kitties on the floor so that we could watch their interplay, the better to get to know their psychology.

The one that immediately took my eye was a four-month-old bobtail kitten, white with charming gray markings. The little fellow looked like nothing so much as a pirate, because one of his gray spots came right down over his right eye like the the patch of some seventeenth-century rapscallion riding the waves of the Caribbean and "rescuing" gold bound for Spain from Cartagena and the Andes.

Pasha had been a truly beautiful kitten, with his long legs, his lean and slim body, and that arresting black spot right on the end of his nose. This kitten was, well, chubby, with short, chunky baby-fat legs, a tiny triangular face set off by a very pink nose, and absolutely huge ears that made him look as though he were wearing one of the Queen Mum's hats or as though he might simply set sail all by himself across the room at any moment.

And then there was the tail. Pasha had a beauteous long tail, as sinuous and suggestive as a snake, which he waved and twisted like a banner when he walked, like some gorgeous blonde waving her hips in shameless provocation. All this kitty had was a tiny, stumpy, kinky tail of fur. In truth, he looked like a small cat with the rear quarters of a bunny. When he grew stressed or became nervous, the bunny tail trembled with excitement and, as it twitched, waves of movement flowed across his entire back, like a small sea of fur suddenly agitated by a waterspout. At one point, I carefully felt the spot, and I found that it was a tiny remnant of a tail, hooked in two places under the fur. He purred when I gently touched it.

When Michelle put him down in my lap, he did not hesitate for a moment. He cuddled in my arms as though he had been there all his life and then pointedly put his tiny snout down on my hand, where he seemed pleased to leave it—and I, surely, was more than pleased to have it.

Michelle, our Lynchburg impresario, opened the curtains still wider on the true nature and drama of the lives of her cats. She brought out an older Japanese Bobtail, a beauteous caramel and white female who was the Marlene Dietrich of the cattery, and carefully placed her next to the younger cat on the floor. The temperament of Gorgeous Girl did not, however, meet her physical beauty. Though at least twice as big as the little white and blue male, who would soon become Nikko, she growled and hissed and threatened him, circling around him shamelessly like a shark in water. The poor little guy, his eyes huge and glittering like black olives, unashamedly terrified, hid awkwardly behind one of the Marshes' rather large ferns and gingerly peeked around it.

The picture stays in my mind even today of the fat little fella, his ears sticking out like little sails and giving him away, trying to make himself disappear behind that fern while Shameless Hussy accosted him, circling him with her vicious war cries. That's good, I thought of *my* cat. A coward!

One could only describe me as dim-witted because I waited until the next afternoon, when I was five hours away back in Washington and had to make special arrangements to transport him to Washington, to *know* that I had to have him. To make it worse, for several long days the Marshes didn't answer my calls. I was frantic. Most of us know that kittens should not be taken away from their mothers for at least twelve to sixteen weeks. Research in the 1930s proved that kittens handled lovingly between the ages of three and fourteen weeks grew up infinitely better socialized than those who were not—and the finding revolutionized kitten care. (Dire word has spread across the veterinary society that, for lack of such socialization, more cats could turn out like Mookie!) But it was my understanding from the Marshes that these kittens were already close to four months old, so what could be the problem?

Later, I discovered that what often happened to sensitive breeders was that just when the new "owner" was thrilled and ready, the breeders couldn't bear to part with the animals and thus kind of disappeared for a time.

Finally, on a Sunday, I signed my life away for my new "pedigreed" farm pet in the papers of adoption when I promised, among other responsible things, that I would have him neutered at nine months, that I would care for him all of my natural life, and that I would return him to the Marshes if ever I intended to sell him. And when the white and gray bobtail was carried across my welcoming front doorstep, the moment was magical.

Oh, it was love for me, but it took a bit longer for the kitty. Doubtless frightened by the car drive and the separation from everything he had known—his mother, the farm, the other tailless cats—he was carsick. So I let him sit on the pillow on my chair for many hours, looking out at this new world through vague and disoriented eyes while I slept on the couch that night to be near him—but not too near. Once he came and cuddled for just a minute at the back of my neck. The second night, he joined me in bed for an hour, and then, it was love ever after.

Because the Japanese Bobtails were a recognized and popular breed in America, my kitten already had a name. This kitty's name was Furrfayar's Too. His sire was Furrfayar's Pink Lee San of Cheval, and his dam was Takashi's Aoi

Onna No Ko of Cheval. But somehow I didn't think he looked like a Furrfayar's Too who was the son of a sire and of a dam from Lynchburg, Virginia.

So I decided to name him Nikko after the beautiful Shinto and Buddhist shrine I had read about in the high mountains of central Japan. *Nikko,* when said to children in Japan, also means, "Smile, smile." And Nikko does indeed make one smile. Within days he was answering to his name, fetching toys, and showing a discipline, modesty, and thoughtfulness that I had learned in my trips to the Orient was also very Japanese. Nikko never took Pasha's place; but together we made a new place, one in which Pasha seemed to be ever with us as well, instructing Nikko on how to behave in Washington, playing in the shadows, trying to catch the mirrored reflections of the sunlight outside, and moving in and out of my memory with his black tail swishing, while little Nikko was busy fetching his toys, cautiously exploring the world, and proceeding to pour out love at a perfectly extraordinary pace.

I admit that I had certain prejudices about the royal "Mious" of the world. I had this picture in my mind of cat royalty being like Bastet: surely a royal cat must be lean, lithe, and elegant, long-legged like a fashion model, and with the high cheekbones of a princess of the realm. No, I never for a moment in those days confused Nikko with an Egyptian god cat. No, there was no question about it, god cats were not short, pudgy, stumpy-tailed kids like Nikko. Yet I found that knowledge comforting at the time: each of my beloved cats had its place and there was no need to confuse their personalities or to make of one what he was not. In fact, both Nikko and Pasha were infinitely more precious to me because of the clear separation and I never dreamed—then—that Nikko had been sent into my life to broaden the royal and sacred horizon of cats still further.

Pasha was your classic rogue operator, but Nikko could not dream of playing tricks. He was too needy to take the risk of harming his relationship with any possible fount of his needs. Even after he did, I think, feel secure with me, he would sit and wait, a strained look on his tiny pinched face, to jump in my lap with a sweet sigh of relief the moment I gave any signal that I was about to sit down. Once he misjudged and jumped too soon, before I had fully sat down, and he fell ignominiously to the floor, his legs all askew. But even this did not upset him, as it would have most proud cats. Instead, he simply judged again, and this time landed right square in my lap, where of course he *stayed.*

Pasha adored shrimp; Nikko would not go near shrimp. He would eat only his dry and damp special veterinarians' special prescription food on his cat mat in his corner of the kitchen, where I had his bulletin board hanging on the wall with cat postcards, notes to him from attentive friends as well as his carefully displayed medical record (just in case health inspectors happened to stop by unexpectedly). If I placed his bowl of food on the counter in the morning, he would sit there looking at it but would not touch it until it was properly placed on his mat. (Only once did he display a truly vulgar gourmand side of his sweet nature. I was frying liver, and he came running out of the bedroom with piteous cries as though the very world were ending, his short bunny tail quivering in excitement. After I gave him a small plate, on his special mat in his special corner, of course, and after he had eaten it, it seemed that he was still looking to me for forgiveness.)

Pasha, with his incredibly long legs and sinuous black tail, would see a bird on my balcony and leap up and down before the locked glass door until his head would literally hit the ceiling. He would come racing out of the bedroom like a prince of the realm, ready for the attack. Nikko was utterly terrified of birds, as indeed he was of everything. When even a small bird dared to rise from the Washington streets and rest on our balcony, this cat-of-the-people would dissemble himself into a crouch, hiding his head between his paws, barely moving, breathing almost imperceptibly, wanting seemingly not to exist at all, with only the slightest quiver of his short bobtail to bear witness to his inner passions.

Pasha always looked guilty—indeed, because there was plenty for him to feel guilty about, as he was always stealing hors d'oeuvres and playing his endless tricks on all comers. But Nikko was too frightened to feel guilty. In lighter moments, when his spirit was momentarily free, or when my watch would reflect across the ceiling, he would frolic charmingly like a child and run crazily from invisible enemies who were obviously chasing him—or perhaps from foes, or specters, or spirits that only he could see. Nikko, one of Kipling's "cats that walked alone"? Never! Nikko didn't want to walk at all. He wanted to ride through life, on someone's lap, preferably, protected, cosseted, and cared for and never having to be jarred by a telephone or an airplane or even a whistle or an alarm clock, all of which utterly terrified him and sometimes caused him to jump a full foot into the air.

We have already noted that Nikko never showed any aggression against birds—they were, after all, most of them bigger than he was. But he, too, could occasionally find his macho moment, usually coming to the fore at those unusual times when some ill-begotten bug dared to fly up against the balcony window. Then he and the bug, each in its own milieu, and unable to engage, would proceed with the strangest Kabuki dance of thrust and counterthrust, of attack and retreat, of pose and depose, all through the window, which protected each one splendidly. Being unusually clever with his paws, Nikko once actually did catch a wayward fly, which had somehow intruded into our private world. I came into the room some time after the "hunt" was over to find him sitting there looking quizically at the dead fly. He did not have the faintest idea what to do with it.

Nor could Nikko bite you. Sometimes, in a faux display of aggressiveness, he would make a great show of trying to bite my hand with those tiny teeth, but somehow he never could get them lined up straight on my hand. He would move his jaw one way and then the other, and inevitably the whole drama would end up with his licking my hand with his tiny scratchy tongue. It soon became clear to me that if Nikko were any example, the Japanese had definitely missed the hunting-and-gathering stage.

Pasha and Nikko even spoke different languages. Pasha spoke, not unexpectedly, in pharaonic dialect: his rather lengthy gurgled sentences wove up and down the musical scale, a *rerrrrerrreerre* in fluctuating octaves. (In Egypt I was told on good authority that this was the accent of Upper Egypt around Luxor.) Nikko spoke in quick starts and in vowels—*aii, eeo, oou*—all sputtered out so that, if you did not know him well, you would think he was angry. (I was reliably informed in Japan that these vowels were the sign of an upper-class Japanese upbringing in the old capital of Kyoto.) His cries were not an expression of anger, for he was too afraid to be angry. Instead, they were designed to awaken you, to alert you, to force you to attend to the fact that there he was and that he needed still more love!

Pawnote: Speaking of language, I have long wondered: Are there really cats who meow? I personally have heard many cat languages, but never a classic and bell-clear *meoww*. Not that it's all that important in the royal scheme of things.

The two cats even walked and ran differently. One ran like a languid royal; the other, like a hip street cat. Pasha, with his long legs and long black tail, would slink into the room, his tail moving back and forth as if to balance every step; all the while, his shoulders were moving forward and back rhythmically, like a sensuous woman performing a mating dance. Nikko, having no tail, ran like a too-eager puppy, and that was one reason he always looked so young and kittylike. It was all a matter of animal aeronautics.

In short, relatively soon after Pasha came to me as a kitten, he was looking masterful, as befitted an Egyptian god cat lost on the streets of Chicago. Nikko looked kittenish and vulnerable and scared, as could be expected of a farm kitty uprooted overnight from a place where you couldn't even get a drink and cat-napped to our nation's capital. Yet despite his real attempts at sophistication, all his life he would always seem to remain a kitten.

Pasha was a great cat from the minute he was born, the seasoned Egyptian cat who had walked across centuries and time zones and never let you forget it. Nikko remained always the sweet and unassuming puss that kindly GIs carried away from wartime Japan to grow up safely in America.

Although it seems contradictory to his personality, Nikko was a great traveler.

When I was gone only a few days I asked either my assistant or a friend to come in once a day to feed him, pet him, and, most important, to make sure no freak accident might have befallen him. But when I was going to be gone more than a week, I took first Pasha and later Nikko to my brother, Glen's, in Chicago for a little vacation.

Pasha was, not surprisingly of course, a sophisticated traveler. Contrary to his behavior with the veterinarians, when he would howl without ceasing until he was taken home, he seemed to realize that this was cosmopolitan living when I would place him in is little cat traveling case and carry him on the plane and that it was a whole lot better to travel this way than the way (whatever that was) that he had come from Egypt. The flight attendants always loved him, because he would stick his little head—with the black spot on the end of the nose and the black toupee on his head, parted in the middle—out of the small hatch on his cat carrier. He would look at the attendants soulfully. One day, as we flew above the clouds between Washington and Chicago, this obvious ploy was so successful that a stewardess surreptitiously brought him a saucer of shrimp from the first-class cabin, which of course he loved. At another point, there were three stewardesses crouched on the floor, oohing and ahhing and purring to him. In fact, after a few trips between Washington and Chicago, flight attendants knew both my cats so well that they would often ask about Pasha and later Nikko when I traveled alone. (It is always nice to have "children" who are appreciated—I attribute this to their good upbringing.)

But what was surprising was that Nikko, for all his shyness and modesty, was calm, seemingly content, and never said a word when traveling. Not surprisingly, he looked around a lot, with some sense of wonder at times since he had been inside all of this life. Then one day after I had finagled and upgraded from coach to first class, and duly paid the $50 to allow Nikko to travel with me, I settled down in my seat when I realized that Nikko and I were, amazingly, alone in first class. Nikko was in his traveling case, secured (as airline regulations require) under the seat in front of me. Even before we took off, I noticed that our flight attendant had hurried to the back of the plane and indeed spent some time there. Some urgent business, perhaps? Then a short time later, she reemerged in first class with an oddly knowing little smile.

"I'm sorry I neglected you," she said, "but I had a problem to take care of."

"I hope it didn't have to do with the cat," I said, concerned.

She smiled even more broadly now. "Actually, it did," she said. "Those people back there said they were allergic to cats, and what would I do about this cat in the plane?"

Since we had not even taken off yet, I was a little worried. Would Nikko and I be unceremoniously bundled off the plane because some cat-hating bozos dozens of yards away from us imagined my little friend was threatening them with the saliva on his fur? Apparently I also looked concerned, for the flight attendant added immediately: "I just told them our policy. If you have problems with an animal aboard the flight, you are most welcome to take the next flight."

I looked down at Nikko. He seemed to be smiling.

Yet, despite all our good times together and despite his darling personality, I soon began to realize that Nikko had a complex, too, which increasingly revealed itself. From the beginning, people would come up to him and say, "What a cute little cat—but where's your tail gone?" Others would ask if his tail had been cut off (a hideous thought!). Many would take one look at him and say, not how sweet he was, but "What kind of Manx is he?"

Think of how these words from writer Wendy Christensen in the December 2001 issue of *Cat Fancy* might affect a cat like Nikko: "Although many animals communicate with their tails, this expressive ability achieves its full glory in cats. With elegance and economy of expression, your cat's tail can coax, flatter, tease, beguile, lead, demand, amuse, warn, manipulate and charm."

And what about the cat skeleton? We know it has 244 bones, more than an adult human, and that most of the extra bones are in the spine and tail. We know that the cat's tail is an integral part of the spine and, in all cats except the tailless, accounts for about one third of its length. Indeed, this being true, how could Nikko not feel that he was not only disabled but actually deformed? Nikko had a problem, and it was a problem that all the world could clearly see: *he had no tail!*

It was not something you could attempt to deny. You could not hide it with makeup, like a blotched skin; you could praise it and think how cute it was, you could extoll to the end of your days how it made him exotically "different" from every other breed of cat in the world, but always underneath lay the nagging doubts: "Why am I not like other cats?"

The constant comparison with the English Manx also made things only worse. Yes, it is true that the Manx are short-tailed or tailless. Yes, it is true that the Manx also has strong backquarters. Yet, these two cats are not actually related in any sense other than that all cats are related. The Manx cat has a less obstinate tailless gene and probably got ashore off the west coast of England, perhaps in 1588 from galleons of the shattered Spanish Armada as it sailed aimlessly round the English Isles. In fact, the Manx come in the forms of stumpy, stubby, rumpy, and cymric, which sounds rather like a vaudeville act but in truth refers to the type, size, and configuration of the cat's tail—or lack of it. They are for the most part essentially "tailless" having lost their tails, like the bobtails of Asia, due to a mutant gene. Once again, the isolation of the island, as I would later discover with the bobtails and the Malay Peninsula, allowed the tailless trait or the bobtail trait to be perpetuated.

Indeed, how would *you* feel if you constantly were forced to hear one of the proudest parts of your anatomy described as "rumpy . . . stubby . . . longie . . . powderpuff . . . bunny-rabbit type . . . corkscrew . . . and pom-pom"? How would you like to hear your breed referred to as "tailless" or "stumpy-tailed" when you saw the cats of the world running around wagging and swaying their proud and plumed rear ends while their long, luxuriant tails waved like banners of superiority and elegance?

Think about it: it is well known that the cat's tail supplies and aids balance during movement, that the tail provides a complement to its nervous system, giving cats the sense of balance that ballet dancers yearn for. But poor little commoner Nikko was denied that range of expression.

Some months into our relationship, much the same thing happened with Nikko as had happened with Pasha. I awoke with a start in one of those three A.M. dark nights of the soul to find him not curled up against my side or sleeping peacefully at the end of the bed, as he always did, ever on the lookout for burglars and murderers (or bugs small enough not to frighten him). Instead, he was sitting in an unusually poised and alert position right next to me and staring at me with almost a magical intensity. Though there was no light on in the room nor even in the hallway, I could feel and even see the glow of his eyes, gleaming yellow in the lostness and anomie of the early morning, very much like the Egyptians with the moon reflected in their cats' eyes. But could the Egyptian moon reflect in the eyes of a commoner cat?

Eventually, by the time the winter sun began rising over Washington, he was fast asleep. I, of course, was fast awake.

Over a period of months and after this and other portents, an idea began to seize me: Perhaps Nikko was asking me to help him, also, to uncover his roots and to know his history. It occurred to me that Nikko might even know about my wondrous search for Pasha's roots in ancient Egypt. Perhaps when I was out of the apartment, he had surreptitiously looked at my scrapbooks from Egypt. Perhaps he dreamed that he could be the descendant of god cats too?

Starting very hesitantly because I fully expected failure, I began to build a family tree for Nikko. First I looked up information on the Japanese Bobtail and searched early Japanese history for some honorable mention of them but at first had little success. Constantly I reminded myself that I was dealing personally with a sweet but emotionally needy pet, and that I must walk a fine line between consolidating his ego and raising his expectations too high.

But once again, in beginning this search, I was also embarking on my own private investigation into the secret of my own relationship to my cats, and into the secret of the relationship of all humans to all felines.

To my amazement, I soon found my bobtails in the fascinating and glorious realm of Japanese art, where I saw with immense gratification that the bobtails had frolicked, danced, growled, scowled, washed clothes, wiped their brows, fought with mice, cuddled with children, and (of course!) slept their way across centuries of Japanese history.

From at least a thousand years ago, I found everywhere these charming tricolor creatures with their spots and perky ears—and, most of all, their sporty, sassy tails. One famous triptych, *Fifty-three Post-stations of the Tokaido Road,* by the famous nineteenth-century artist Utagawa Kuniyoshi, is an utterly charming exposition of twenty or more cats arranged in every possible position: curled up on their backs sleeping, glowering at one another, playing with fish and being (in paintings startlingly like the Egyptians' caricatures) tormented by mice. In *Mother,* the eighteenth-century artist Utamaro Kitagawa depicts a boy holding a wriggling little bobtail, to his delight. Some Japanese artists have bobtails dancing gaily, like impish devils. In *Cat Washing,* by Ando Hiroshige, a spotted cat with a winsome face is delicately wiping her brow as she washes clothes in a basin. (Of course it is a "she," to be washing clothes in that era!) One print in the beloved Hiroshige's woodblock series *One Hundred Views of Edo,* now in the British Museum and called *Cat Looking at Fields at Asakusa,* shows a lovely bobtail curled up fast asleep at the window with Mount Fuji spread out before him. So like Nikko, only centuries earlier.

In a haunting premonition of what was to come, I read about the primary period of these artworks, the Tokugawa Shogunate, which ruled Japan for 250 years and secured peace and stability by both ruthless controls and suppression and by fostering remarkable artistic achievements, patient intellectual progress, and commercial development. In *Our Oriental History,* historian Will Durant wrote that the life of the Japanese people in this era, which would turn out to be so critical to the history of Nikko that I would uncover, was characterized by "the neatness of their homes, the beauty of their clothing, the refinement of their ornaments, and their spontaneous addiction to song and dance. . . . [Japan's] artists labored with self-effacing devotion and only the artist-artisans of ancient Egypt and Greece, or of medieval China, could rival their industry, taste and skill."

It was during this period that the bobtail cats began to come into their own, even occupying a notable position in Japan that bordered always on both the royal and the sacred, just as in ancient Egypt.

Ahhh, but I had another potential ace up my sleeve. In the sparse literature that I had been able to find on the bobtails themselves, I had several times come across obscure but persistent references to a cat temple in Tokyo! *A Japanese cat temple?* The materials were notably imprecise, but I began to dream . . . After all, we knew that the Egyptian cats had traveled down the Silk Road to Asia after their di*cat*spora from Egypt in the fourth century A.D. Was it possible that there could also be chubby, and, yes, even tailless royal cats from Asia?

In the winter of 1996, when Nikko was five years old, I decided to plan a trip to Japan and southeast Asia, and possibly even China, ostensibly for my column. Nikko could not go with me, of course, but I knew that he would psychically know everything about the trip when I returned. Still, I wanted to plant in his tiny mind before I went the real intentions behind the journey. And so I sat in my favorite chair in the living room and put him on the matching stool. He was not an apt pupil that day, and the first thing he tried to do was go to sleep.

"Now, Nikko," I remonstrated, "this is important. Please be vigilant. I have something to tell you that will affect your entire life."

At this, he half rolled over and began to lick his tail.

"Now, just stop it," I cried. "I have something artistic to tell you—something spiritual—something that I think could be beautiful—"

At this, he lifted his head for a moment, looked me right in the eye with the most disbelieving look, and went on considering his tail. I decided to start, despite his egregiously bad manners.

"What I am looking for is your family," I began softly but, I thought, persuasively. "I'm going to find out where the bobtails came from, how you lost your tail all those centuries ago, and—Nikko, hear this!—who you really are!"

At this, probably because my voice had risen, he looked at me, and his eyes widened for just a moment. Then he decided to wash up some more, and this time he started licking himself all over, using his all-white paw to clean the rest of him—and making me feel as though I were indeed intruding upon his boudoir.

"You'll be sorry you didn't pay attention," said I, the Family of Cats' new schoolmarm. "Someday." But he didn't look sorry at all.

So it was that once again I had become a kind of intellectually indentured servant, traveling abroad in large part because of my supposedly "dependent" pet. If there were royal and sacred cats of Asia, as well as Egyptian cats, they would not have a chance to escape under my purposeful intentions and gaze! Life deals us strange paws, I've always said.

Just as I had always done in my journalistic work, I would begin at the peripheries and close in on my subject, because it is on the outskirts of problems, of conflicts, and even of psychologies that you can most often find the reflection of your search and let it lead you to the hidden center of the tale. (You can always tell more about a man from how he treats his mistress than how he treats his wife.) Start with the reflection and it will lead you to the reality!

And so, on this trip, I would begin in Southeast Asia, in Burma and Thailand, both of whom legendarily had sublime royal and sacred cats, and close in on the northern Asian countries, armed with the wisdom of the borderlands. Our next journey had begun.

CHAPTER FOUR

BURMA'S SACRED CAT IS LOST—WHERE COULD IT HAVE GONE?

Sinh placed his paws on his dying master and faced the golden goddess. His white fur took on a golden hue. His yellow eyes became a deep blue, and his face, tail, and legs turned to the colour of the earth, but the part of his paws that touched the dead priest remained white, the symbol of purity.

RICHARD H. GEBHARDT,
STANDARD GUIDE TO CAT BREEDS

For some reason, all across the Atlantic, the Mediterranean, and the Red Sea, and even after my plane had swept down over the rice fields and the somnolent monsoon plains of Southeast Asia en route to historic Burma, today's Thailand, and finally to Japan on my search for Nikko's roots, I kept having a strange dream about my young cat. I would start to fall asleep on the crowded plane, and then I would "awake" in one of those half-worlds that dreamers seem destined to inhabit, and I would see Nikko trying, trying, and trying again to leap to the top of the Biedermeier chest, which once belonged to my grandmother Oma Geyer. It was a small but poignant study in failure, and yet, in a way, it thrilled me. For I could see clearly that Nikko was no quitter! I saw his attempts to leap as reassuringly noble.

True, his courage was focused on a small mission—leaping to the top of the chest. It was hardly to be compared to Teddy Roosevelt's assault on San Juan Hill or to the raising of the flag over Iwo Jima, and yet in my own mind I rather imagined that, in cat years, his attempts did equal those brave acts.

Now, this Biedermeier is a large gray wooden hutch, which originally came from Germany. It is light brown in color and elegant in style, but is rather simple for its times. The Biedermeier came into mode between 1825 and 1835 in Germany, Austria, northern Italy, and Scandinavia and was known for its lightness, utility, and individuality among the more romantic of the bourgeoisie; finally its popularity was renewed in America in the 1960s. I brought it from Chicago when I moved to Washington in 1975, and I treasure it in my apartment there. It is about seven feet high and it has a large section for serving bowls on the bottom, then a useful wide ledge where you can set out things like mail-to-go and shopping lists, and finally a beautifully glassed-in top section and another small ledge on the very top.

Once again, my two cats seemed in a strange way to be vying with each other across their very different histories with regard to this noble chest. How proudly Pasha, with his long, skinny legs and his strong haunches, would pull himself back into a crouch, pause for a dramatic moment, and then leap in one fell swoop all the way to the top! In only one grand gesture, there he would be, calmly and munificently overseeing us all and surveying his domain; from there, he would stare down upon us with a truly haughty mien, his legs pulled together as charmingly as were Bastet's on her ancient Nile barge. Thus empowered, he would then try (without result, I am pleased to report) to go through the ceiling, scratching at the walls frenetically and theatrically, often enough bumping his head against the ceiling.

I had placed atop the Biedermeier a crouching, sleeping cat figure made of gray stone from England, which looked as though it might just pounce upon anyone or anything that happened to err and come its way. It never occurred to me, the cat being of stone and thus utterly without warmth of flesh or smell, that any real cat would ever go near it. But Pasha loved it and apparently recognized its form as an otherworld compadre. Strangely enough, Pasha behaved just as though the faux cat were a cat of flesh and blood: he loved to cuddle it and would rub his cheek against its cheek and try to roll up beside it before trying once again to go through the ceiling. Friends would gather at my parties and take bets on his behavior.

"Do you think he'll land in the hors d'oeuvres this time?" then beloved *Washington Week in Review* moderator Paul Duke bet once. And analysts like the historian Michael Beschloss, forgetting their serious thoughts and betting on whether Pasha would "do it" again while they were there, would shake their heads in wonderment at this strange leaping cat. At one party, Pasha leapt up there right over the hors d'oeuvres (without touching them, for once) and then hung over the food during the entire party.

Eventually, he would decide he had had enough—only *he*, of course, could decide that precise moment—and simply leap down again in one great swoop. Then he would swagger away, an arrogant little sway in his gait, and go for a rest somewhere back in the closet in his yet unknown (even today) hiding place. One could not escape the impression that he was mightily proud of himself.

As for little Nikko, with his short, fat legs and his adorable, but limiting bunny tail, he never knew that sense of flying at all. He was too needy to nurse such grandiose ambitions. He lived literally hugging the earth (and me, whenever possible) for warmth and sustenance, fearful to stir. Occasionally, he would stand on his hind legs—enlivened by something like the reflection of the sun on my watch, which he of course took for a shining bird—and leap forward on his back two legs. It was so charmingly unexpected and so seemingly outside his personality that it was as if a tiger suddenly served you tea, or a wolf suddenly purred. And yet, as all humans who have and love house cats know, they often do things like that—perhaps to surprise and delight *us*.

Then one afternoon, when Nikko was several years old, that tiny, but active, brain of his apparently got to thinking and decided that the time had come to assault Oma Geyer's Biedermeier hutch. I was sitting reading in my usual chair when I saw Nikko suddenly start to circle, and circle, and circle the chest. His head was down, his thin shoulders slightly arched. He reminded me for a moment of those skinny and ridiculous neighborhood boys who were always making passes at you when you were a teenager and you could not even be insulted but were simply overcome with laughter. What could the docile little cat be up to as he circled about like some pitiful land-locked ersatz shark? I momentarily put down my paper.

After some time—quite a long time, actually—he tried to jump. He scrambled all over himself and fell back. He tried again and could not even make the bottom ledge, much less the top one. A somersault, this time! I stifled a chuckle. But he only continued at his self-appointed task. Each time he tried to leap, it became clearer that his little legs were so fat and so short—and he had no tail to whooossshh him along, like an ordinary cat's tail, or perhaps like a kite's tail—that he would never make it. And then a truly terrible thing happened: he gave one more try and almost made it to the first ledge—but then he fell back, and . . . well . . . he fell right into the wastebasket next to the Biedermeier. There he sat, limbs askew, trying to compose himself, with little wastepapers all over his head.

It was so humiliating—and he, like all cats, knows when he has been humiliated—that for some time he could not even leap out. I picked him up and whispered something endearing about how some of the most noble cats in the world never leap at all but only stay all their lives, resting regally on altars, being adored, but he would not hear me. Finally he just slunk away as fast as his legs would carry him and hid in *his* still unknown hiding place in the closet until the next morning, when we both pretended that nothing had happened. And yet we both always *knew*.

The next morning, not surprisingly, as compensation for his failure, he rather overdid the one really naughty thing that he does: after breakfast, he leapt upon my small brocade couch and just scratched the very devil out of it. He performed almost a dance, with his little legs going and his small body crouched down threateningly—always looking directly at me. In fact, it was a game, but it was also his way of aggravating me so much that I would madly chase him off the couch and around the apartment. I have analyzed Nikko as passive-aggressive, and I do believe that to be true.

So on that long plane ride carrying me forward to Nikko's own past in Southeast Asia, my subconscious kept offering me up equally troubling variations on that theme of the little cat's aborted assault on Oma Geyer's Biedermeier. Nikko would try, and try, and try, but never ever make it to the top. Then he would try again. I would awake with a start, and I would think of where *I* was going. Was it some leap of faith that I was taking this distinctly odd trip? What was I really doing going to Burma? Although I could and would write columns about the country's awful, heinous, abysmal military dictatorship, in truth I would not be going there except for my special royal and sacred "cat itinerary."

I was going there because the country and its cat lore could, would, or should represent the very synthesis and symbol of the history of the sacred cats that I was seeking. Perhaps my dream was a premonition that in Burma I might even find the secret of Nikko's inability to leap.

Rangoon

As a child, I had loved to pore over maps, to find unknown places and to try to absorb their wondrous mysteries. I wanted to know where everything was. To me, finding lost peoples, lost tribes, and lost kingdoms was particularly beguiling. I so loved the Wizard of Oz books, that one day I sat down and determinedly made a map of the kingdoms of Oz. The data and details were right there in all Frank Baum's Oz books, but I had never seen anyone put them together into a map before. That was exactly the type of work that I had long done in my adult life as a foreign correspondent, putting together the hidden internal maps of the worlds-within-worlds that most people could not see. But there were no maps of the geographic kingdoms of cat. Now, I would make one for Nikko, but also for me and for all the cats and for all of those who love them.

Once I arrived in Rangoon, Burma (now Myanmar), the mysteries I began to uncover came, not in the smooth flow I had expected but in what seemed like unrelated spurts and gushes, some of them fully misleading . . .

On the night of my arrival in Rangoon, I was staying at the Strand, the legendary hundred-year-old hotel and watering hole that had long been the glittering center for British colonial social life. One of the Strand's elegant hotel cars (at $60 an hour, thank you!) had picked me up at the run-down, crowded, cacophonous Rangoon airport, and the driver was far more elegant, in dress and in manner, than most of the ambassadors in the capital. He immediately handed me some damp perfumed towelettes for my poor little hands, which might actually have touched something in the airport, God forbid!

Of course, I immediately asked him what temples I would find the Burmese cats in.

"Oh no," the driver answered simply, "you won't find cats in the temples— *nobody* stays in the temples overnight. But you will find some in the monasteries. And, of course, you will find them at Inle Lake. But the Inle cats are getting lazy," he went on, in an oddly revelatory tone, as if he were letting me in on a secret. "They only jump till eleven o'clock in the morning now. The monks have learned that the cats need to go to sleep the rest of the day."

I understood, of course, the part about sleeping when it came to any cats, but as for the rest, I had not the slightest idea of what he was talking about. However, I filed his comments away in my journalist's cluttered file cabinet of a mind for further reference, little guessing how important it would be.

My first morning in Rangoon, I asked Sally Baughen, the charming, blonde New Zealander who managed the Strand, about the Burmese cats. "Cats?" she said, shaking her head, "I've never heard of any Burmese cats."

That night at dinner at the beautiful lakeside home of the acting American ambassador, Priscilla Clapp, I was introduced to Ma Thanegi, a journalist they called the "cat lady" because she often wrote whimsical stories and often featured cats. But this writer, an attractive, small and dainty woman who looked as if she could have been a sacred priestess in another life, only wrinkled her brow and eyes when I mentioned the stories about temples and sacred cats and even the idea of any "lamas," which were Tibetan-style Buddhist priests.

"No, we do not have spirit houses like that in Burma," she said. "No, we don't have lamas, either. No, we don't have anything under those names."

The second day in Rangoon, I was talking to Patrick, a highly intelligent Burmese who worked for the United Nations Development Program, one of the few international organizations still allowed to function in Burma. (Patrick, like many Burmese, used only one name.)

"I remember that when I was little, somebody was buying some cats and taking them away to England," he recounted ruminatively. "They were brown, but they must have had a white belly and paws . . ." Then he added, "There are some cats in Shan State in a monastery in Inle Lake."

This was at a time when the Burmese military regime had been insulting Burma's pleasant and peaceable neighbor Thailand (ancient Siam), clearly as a way to divert Burma's miserable people's attention from their own rulers' depredations and cruelty. At this point, Patrick, with an unmistakable gleam of humor in his eye, said, "They say here that Siamese cats are very aggressive and that Burmese cats are very kind." He smiled, but his smile was not complete but only muted, like so many things in Burma.

I went out that same afternoon with a sense of urgency to find the "Pagan Bookstore," which I eventually discovered on a very small and very crowded and dirty byway. An elderly oriental gentleman, unsmiling and suspicious, such as one would have expected to find in the conspiratorial days of Shanghai during World War II, reached silently back into his store of ancient books and drew out *the* book that everyone says is the number-one must-read on Burma, *The Burman: His Life and Notions,* by a British civil servant in Burma of the nineteenth century, whose real name was Sir George P. Scott but who took the name Shway Yoe to write his classic.

How eagerly I carried the little book back to the Strand, where in the privacy of my room I closed the blinds and opened the volume and immediately looked up "cats" in the glossary. But there were only two references.

In the first, the author asserts that the "harmless, necessary cat is not so abundant. There are, however, few villages without one or two of them." In the second, he makes fun of the "Malay congenitor who does not possess a tail but only a horny hook." He called it the "Straitstabby."

I shuddered. It was too cruel. What would Nikko think, were he to hear such words? Of course, I would never, ever dream of repeating this to sweet, vulnerable Nikko. In addition to all the other brutish words about the tailless cats, they were now cursed with a "horny hook"!

Yet, although I did not realize it at the time, I had inadvertently stumbled upon a rich clue to Nikko's birthright—the fact that the tailless cats originally came from the Malay Peninsula. I knew by now that my Nikko's little kinked tail definitely had roots in Southeast Asia. I was getting ever deeper into my search for the Holy Tail.

The country itself, although piteously poor and oppressed, was also truly wondrous, with its gorgeous, gold-covered Buddhist shrines, temples, and pagodas. The historic Shwedagon pagoda that reigns over Rangoon is ten stories high and 2,600 years old, is covered with sixty tons of gold, and has an exquisite headpiece inlaid with 4,353 diamonds. The pagoda is "protected" by giant stone lions, elephants, dragons, and crocodiles, but there are no cats there. The dreamlike Valley of Pagan to the north of the country has five thousand pagodas. The Lord Buddha, or Siddhartha, came here when he traveled across Southwest and then Southeast Asia nearly five hundred years before the birth of Christ, almost exactly at the time of the high point of the worship of the cat in Egypt. With him, "he who has attained his goals" brought the enlightened and kindly religion of Buddhism, with its search for the truth of the inner life and the true human and spiritual consciousness.

In fact, in studying the Buddha and making comparisons between him and Jesus Christ, one comes across some parallels that, incredibly, have a bearing on our studies of the sacred cats. Both men are strikingly similar savior figures who go through three temptations before setting out to save their people, illustrating once again the degree to which differing societies share a commonality of cultures and call forth out of themselves analogous figures, cultural expressions, and lessons, even among animals. It was very similar to what I had uncovered between Egyptian and Middle Eastern religious stories of a sacred virgin birth. But that was only the beginning.

What I was looking for in Burma had seemed to be quite simple at first. There are myriad stories about the "sacred" qualities of the Burmese cats and, after all, the Burmese breed was for many years the most popular cat family and breed in the world. The Burmese cats had such charming ways, such loyalty, and such an unusual capacity for obedience that they were often called "dog cats." (Nobody's perfect.) They have a neat and oddly stolid appearance for a small cat and have been described as "bricks wrapped in silk." No one who has seen them can forget their exquisite colors, with their chartreuse eyes and the sleek coats that range from the most common brown to chocolate, sable, blue, lilac, red, cream, brown tortie, blue tortie, chocolate tortie, and lilac tortie. Altogether, they sound rather like a delicate table of French ice creams or the colors of the beautiful dresses we so loved as little girls.

But in addition, there was and is the Birman breed, obviously related to the Burmese *in some way*—but exactly how? No one really knows. The Birman is a big, gray furry cat with Siamese markings, an exquisite, furry face, and the pure white paws that are supposed to be its special mark of majesty.

All of the books that I had carefully read before I left agreed that one or both of the two historic cats of Burma were the country's "sacred temple cats," or sometimes sacred temple "guard cats," honored and venerated by one and all. Some are so elegant that they sometimes have been called "rajahs," and both cats seemed involved in that same Egyptian-style "transmigration of souls" that Herodotus had noticed in the Nile Valley five hundred years before Christ. Indeed, the idea that the individual soul at death passes into a new body or new form of life, human or animal, sometimes permanently and sometimes for a time before the soul passes on to the other world, was one I was to find across virtually every single society that elevated cats to sacred or royal status.

There were offshoots of the Burmese line, kinds of breeds-in-waiting: pert little Burmillas, the outcome of a furtive and unapproved love affair between a lovelorn Chinchilla and a Burmese; the Bombay, a black-as-night breed whose fur has the sheen of patent leather and which came out of the union of a Burmese and a black American Shorthair; the Tiffany, a luxurious long-haired mix of Burmese and Persian whose coat resembles an Indian black leopard's; and the little-known Himbur, a mixture of Burmese and Himalayan. Somewhere in here, the modern Ragdoll breed might have fallen into these breed categories as well, but don't, please, ask me exactly where or when.

In all of these stories about the sacredness of the Burmese cats before the great Buddha spread his loving religion to Asia in the fifth century B.C., we are told that there lived beautiful white cats with golden eyes who were the devoted companions of pagan priests in the Lao-Tsun temple, probably in what is today northwestern Burma. Then, one fateful night, a bunch of marauders from nearby Siam burst cruelly into this happy scene; and they killed the high monk, or high lama, known as Mun-ha. As the priest lay dying, Mun-ha's companion cat, Sinh, climbed on him. With her sapphire eyes and golden hair, she faced the goddess Tsun Kyan-Kse and appealed for the transmutation of Mun-ha's soul. As the monk expired, his soul entered Sinh's body and the cat's body began to transform itself, as the paw of the god reached down and took the monk to heaven. When the cat died seven days later, Sinh dutifully carried the soul of Mun-ha to paradise. Richard H. Gebhardt, who was for many years a famous judge at cat shows, states that legend thus has it that the mysteriously blue-eyed Tsun-Kyan-Kse thus presided over the transmigration of souls.

Sometimes, the origins of the Birmans are placed in the high mountains of Tibet, where Buddhist lamas kept them. Some say that after the soul of Mun-ha had moved to heaven under the aura of his beloved cat, the next morning all the other white cats of the temple had undergone the same transformation as Sinh. From then on, the priests guarded their sacred golden cats, believing them to have custody of the souls of the priests. Other versions say that the temple had exactly one hundred pure white cats! The white cat has had a unique, if religiously equivocal place, from Siam to Burma to faraway Turkey.

With the British forces in Burma in 1944 fighting the Japanese, the Burmese cats even came to have their own place in World War II mythology. One British officer in Burma painted cats on army vehicles and kept only pure white cats on the military base. Supposedly the Burmese believed that the sacred spirits must be with the British and thus adjusted their loyalties!

And lest anyone think that these are all tales of yesteryear, he or she need only look today on the Internet to the actual Web site of the Temple of the Sacred Cat, put out by Katascali Cattery, breeder of Birmans in the United States, which begins: "Welcome to the Temple of the Sacred Cat." There is the picture of a beautiful Birman posed on the steps of an Oriental temple or pagoda. The Birman stares very intensely at you as if it were indeed a god and you were about to have your soul invaded!

I should really have had my suspicions about the stories. One located the Lao-Tsun temple in the mountains of Tibet; another in China; and another in northwestern Burma. There were simply too many contradictions—too many mysteries, even for Burma!

Still, on a deeper level, I was beginning to pin down the differences in these stories of cats between the concepts of the sacred and the royal. Burma, like Egypt, was to exemplify for me the sacred: "holy or hallowed, especially by association with the divine or consecrated, worthy of religious veneration." Royal would come to be personified by historic Siam or today's Thailand, and, to a lesser degree, by Japan, where cats were merely "indicative of royalty, reserved for the sovereign or being in the crown's service." One designation had to do with the splendors of eternity and one had to do with service to or identification with a royal crown. I was beginning, but only beginning, to understand.

INLE LAKE, BURMA

The one place where everyone told me that I would incongruously find cats, if not exactly the Burmese cats that I was searching for, was in the remote and mysterious mountainous Shan State in the rugged and, until recently, inaccessible northeast of the country, on a remote lake and in an even more remote Buddhist monastery. There lived monks who had taught their little cats to actually *leap through hoops!* I was excited—I could only think of Nikko, and his, shall we say "difficulty," getting himself even a few inches off the floor. Could I find something here to salve his inner wounds, to refresh his hurt spirit? Could there be some meaning in my journeying to the famous leaping cats of Burma, just as there had clearly been meaning that dark, early morning in Washington when Pasha had lain on the kitchen table guarding the scarab/beetle? Or was I dreaming of worlds that did not exist?

In addition to those doubts, everyone knew that cats, royal or not, were not exactly good at performing on command, so the very idea of "hoop-leaping cats," as they were called, was extraordinary in itself. It was a little like asking an elephant to waltz or a sewer rat to sip martinis through a straw or a giraffe to peek into a keyhole. In fact, cats would not even perform for food. All of that was *for dogs,* who represented that world of servant of man, not the spirit of man.

Oh, there had been one Italian trainer in the nineteenth century, Pietro Capalli, who had a troupe of cats who balanced on high wires, performed trapeze acts, and juggled with their hind legs. And his successor today can be found in Yuri Kuklachev's famous Moscow Cat Theater, where the former circus clown has trained his beloved 120 cats to leap through hoops, walk tightropes, dance to music, and balance balls on their noses. The imaginative Kuklachev was once quoted revealingly as saying, "I'd like to create a cat 'temple,' with at least a thousand cats. It would be like a living museum of cats, with every kind of cat in the world represented." I knew I would like that man! I eventually went to Moscow to see Kuklachev's wondrous cats—and they were splendid.

As several of us left beautiful but downtrodden Rangoon that early morning, I felt deeply confident. This would be the first step toward finding the roots of the Burmese breed, which would lead me, geographically and tail-wise as well, to Nikko's true history and, most important, to a greater understanding of our own relationships with our own cats.

We headed north by two short plane rides, first to the valley of the five thousand pagodas at Pagan, then northeast to Mandalay. Finally, we traveled by car to Inle Lake. Surrounded by low, languorous mountains, the lake has about it the same mystical beauty as has so much of Burma. Strange floating islands, half-drifting and half tethered, form pathways for big canoes with outboard motors to speed you to every corner of the water. A few excellent and even elegant hotels surprisingly dot the shoreline.

Called the "children of the lake," most of the Shan tribespeople lived in simple teak houses hovering above the water, set on piles dug into the mud of the lake. Like all of the Burmese and the tribes in Burma, they were highly superstitious and astrology informed their daily lives. In Rangoon, the officers of the brutal Burmese military, whose top leaders called themselves simply, but clearly, "One, Two, and Three" and who all slept at the same military compound every night to keep an (open) eye on the others, always consulted astrologers. In earlier years, the ruler, General Ne Win acquiesced in his own downfall by declaring most of the Burmese currency worthless and replacing it with bank notes in denominations divisible by his lucky number, nine. At the

Right: The author with a young, affectionate Pasha in Chicago in 1977.

Below: Pasha was fascinated by water of any kind and obviously did not realize how his taste even for toilet water diminished his royal status in the eyes of some purist observers.

Above: With his long athletic legs, Pasha was always taking great—and successful—leaps around the house. A minute after this photo was taken, he made the jump and cuddled up to a porcelain cat on the bookcase.

Left: The author poses in the ruins of Bubastis, the great temple of the beloved cat goddess Bastet north of Cairo. These ancient stone figures once had cat faces.

Top: Nikko at about nine months, his evocative eyes typically balanced between mischief and timidity.
Bottom: Nikko sleeping in his favorite basket, his short bunny tail protected from the breeze.

Above: One of the strangely ethereal diamond-eyes cats of ancient Siam, with eyes of different colors, usually blue and yellow.

Top: The author and Buddhist monk Father U Wai Leinda at the Nga Phe Kyaung monastery in northeastern Burma with his favorite old gray cat Nicholas, whose legs were bad.

Bottom: The author's trusted guide from the Foreign Press Center at the entrance to the Jiseiin or cat temple in Tokyo. The stone Maneki Neko, paw raised in greeting and welcome, guards the temple.

Above, right: The leaping cats of Nga Phe Kyaung monastery in northeastern Burma. (PHOTOS BY AIVI COUTIN, INLE LAKE, BURMA)

Top: The granite stone cat atop the altar of Jiseiin temple, with its bright red cape, furry hat, and barely distinguishable features, weather-worn from five hundred years of noble existence.

Bottom: The handsome priest of Jiseiin temple, Eichi Osawa, and his wonderful scrapbook with pictures of cat events at the temple.

lake, superstition reigned; to take a bath or even to choose days to cut your nails meant choosing the date carefully and cats soon entered this world.

Field workers often tell time by the contraction or dilation of a cat's pupils, the contraction keeping out bright light and dilation letting it in. (Thus, the cat's eyes are narrowest at the time of the moon, when there is light at night.) One can imagine, then, the networks of belief and superstition that would be interjected into every political decision—or into the legends about cats. Indeed, they stand at the most intimate intersection of superstition and practical knowledge.

———————

The Nga Phe Kyaung monastery was founded by one of the Shan chiefs with the aid of Buddhist missionaries from India one hundred years ago. Built entirely of the rich local teak wood, it is large and graceful in appearance, weathered rather like a very good captain's house on the sea in New England. It seems to float above the exquisite lake and this troubled country like a mirage of peace and serenity. The monastery is filled with golden Buddhas that no one now pays any attention to at all—not since the famous celebrity cats entered the story.

The lake, blue when we had first arrived in the morning, now had turned a misty white-gray. It was midafternoon, and a torpid white heat hung over everything and everyone. Indeed, one could barely see across the water as it reflected the terrible heat of the white sky. We breathed heavily. Our boatman moored us at the monastery's little pier, and we walked carefully up the rickety and weathered teak stairs. The whole building seemed to creak with age and memories. What would we find?

In the rather large central room of the monastery, the floor was covered with multicolored and flowered linoleum, reminding me incongruously—and surely sentimentally—of the linoleum in my grandmother's kitchen. The beams were dotted with the calling cards of people from around the world. Beautiful big Buddhas sat by the sides of the room, surrounded by small fencelike partitions. And in this entire milieu, the cats roamed free, although, like all cats, and surely like Nikko, they seemed to have a special fondness for naptime. Every few yards lay very small cats. Very small. I would judge they weighed only about four or five pounds, or about half of Nikko's weight and a third of

Pasha's. Black-and-white cats, gray cats, brown cats, even a few yellow cats! (I could not help but notice that they about encompassed the same color range as Egyptian cats.)

They were curled up in those little balls that cats create so beautifully with their loose and willing vertebrae, all snoozing away in those wonderful sinuous little curves, across my grandmother's linoleum! We came upon most of them, indeed, in the middle of a very sound asleep, their thin little legs stretched out as though the heat from their tiny bodies could pass out through their toes. Just plain exhausted, perhaps from all the world's attention—another opening, another show, every day! (Perhaps they had been performing late the night before.)

In fact, a wondrous, sleepy, consoling calm hung over the entire picture, and if I had not been so interested in the whole thing, frankly I would have just taken a deep breath and taken a little nap as well. I felt unusually at peace, as if I had been foreordained to come here—nor had it escaped my attention that most of the cats looked very much like both Pasha and Nikko, although all had tails.

I found the head monk, Father U Wai Leinda, in his room off to the side of the main hall, as he had been ill. I could rather easily imagine being ill there, for it was so hot and the air so stagnant and the image of the lake so eternally a place of no escape that good health seemed clearly elusive. But he kindly invited me in to talk. It seemed that he had been apparently a very successful business-man in Rangoon before deciding, as many Burman Buddhist men do, to become a monk for an indeterminate time. He was a well-built man, with the golden-brown skin of the Burmese and tribal people and a clear, handsome face. As he sat there before an open window, his deep red robe draped over one shoulder and his bare feet curled up under him, the lake shimmering and shining over his shoulder, I realized I was surprised to find a genuinely sophisticated man, an ele-gant and naturally worldly man, in such a remote spot. We spoke not of Bud-dhism, but of cats, and of course, we laughed about that fact as I asked him how they train cats to leap.

"This is how we trained them in the beginning," the monk began to tell me, as he gently picked up one of the little black-and-white cats with one hand under the animal's chin and the other under his belly. He picked the cat up three times, only a few inches from the floor, then set it down with just the slightest jar. He thinks that originally, just to get away, the cats simply started . . . leaping . . . through . . . hoops as the priests held the hoops two or three feet above the floor. "I got the technique," he went on. "It was very easy to train them first like this"—he made his arms into a hoop—"then, I would throw a plastic fish. Soon it became one of my ideas, that we could train them to jump through hoops. It takes three days to train them, no more.

"All of the tourists like this," he said with a big smile. Then he pointed to his head—it had been his idea after all, he was saying.

In the larger room the real theatrical drama began, with other monks and at least a dozen of the cats easily taking part in the play. When the monks gently awoke their pets from their midafternoon siesta, the little cats of Nga Phe Kyaung came immediately and effortlessly to life. Without the slightest prodding, they would squat down and then spring gracefully from the floor, leaping directly and without fail through the small hoops that the monks held casually about three feet in the air. And when they landed, they pulled themselves together and sauntered away, with the aristocratic air and assumed casual gait of elite athletes who knew they had had a good day and who were just darned pleased with themselves.

The moment when they actually leapt through the hoop remains etched in my mind. At that instant they looked for all the world more like racehorses than cats, racing across the finishing line with little heads held up gallantly and spirits flying. There was something so wonderful and so incongruous about those poor little cats, secluded in that strange inland sea and seemingly destined to a life of unchanging dreariness, yet leaping and leaping and leaping, so grandly and so spontaneously. It was as if they were truly escaping from the miseries of their part of the world, having to live to defy human gravity with their human sense and their cockeyed charm.

Later, back home in Washington, as I studied the photos of the cats, poring over them in the weeks to come, I could see that the force of the leap came completely from the cats' back legs; as they were actually going through the hoops, they held their front paws and legs close to their bellies; then they would instantaneously extend all four legs and paws in the very moment that they moved out of the hoop; finally they landed with all four legs out, before they would walk away with a slight rhythmic movement, much like tumblers who landed squarely on their toes and then swaggered insouciantly away. The only thing that was missing was the towel that the trainer would bring after a victory—but the monks did give them victory hugs.

In short, there was something just *grand* about these little creatures, these true celebrity cosmo*cats,* leaping and leaping and leaping, as they transformed themselves into something far beyond their supposed destiny.

I must admit that, at one point, they did remind me a little of the young Pasha with his immensely long legs, going in one leap to the top of my mother's doors in Chicago, his legs hanging out, like a falcon's wings. And surely it made me think of Nikko, with his patent inability to jump even a couple of feet in the air. Those poor and ill-fed little cats of Inle had this incredible talent! And Nikko in Washington, had everything in the world, except their ability. There must be a moral—and there was. It showed that the spirit of determination, of talent, and of nobility can live in even the poorest creature on earth—and that something can enlighten him to cause him to have to overcome.

That day, I did not want the cats to stop leaping—and neither did they seem to want to.

"Today we have twenty-four cats here," Father U Wai Leinda was saying. "We have a new generation, too. In the season, we have two hundred tourists a day. We had to ask them not to come until after noon because it was getting to a point where we could not run the monastery. Now tourists have seen the cats on TV—and on the Internet . . . For dinner, the cats eat fish curry and some chili. Tourists have brought them foreign cat food, but that spoils them for the reality here. One big cat food company in Germany uses them on its packages—they send us food, too. This generation of cats has already been here twenty-three years now."

At this, he petted his favorite cat, Nicholas, eleven years old and a neat and handsome gray who was asleep on the arm of the head monk's chair. "He is retired now," the monk said tenderly and he smiled again. "His legs were too tired. . . . He never eats without waiting for me," he continued. "Most of us love the cats too much," he added softly.

Then he called them by name and most of them came: Ricky Martin, Leonardo DiCaprio, Marilyn Monroe . . . Through these evocative names, he had brought the outside world to this closed one. After all, they were celebrity cats—why should they not have names from celebrities in that big world so far away? Were they not, indeed, at least the equal of the Egyptian cats who had nursed the Pharaoh?

That magical afternoon, I was so involved in the spirit of their movements—and in the sense of their incongruous performance in this unlikely part of the world—that I almost forgot about the true "royal cats" of Burma.

While it was clear that these cats were intelligent and even noble—assuredly more worthy than any "sacred cats" who might for all we know just lie around all day on some altar making snippy judgments about humankind—still my duty and mission was to track down the true temple cats, the genuine royal cats. And so, I had pressed the head monk about the Burmese and the Birman cats—and about the stories.

"No, no," he answered immediately, "these are not the Burmese cats. Those are burly and they have big heads. Their color is usually gray, dark gray." For a moment, he looked puzzled. "I don't know much about cat history," he went on, "but I am sure that it is Kachin State where the real Burmese cats come from. They have one eye yellow and one blue. There are really beautiful Burmese cats there, with big bodies." But, sacred? He wrinkled his lip and shook his expressive head. "No."

"No, no," he went on. "Six years ago when I went to the northern part of Burma," he went on, " I stopped in Kachin in some villages. They had the real Burmese there. There are also legends in Kachin, where an animal can take over the qualities of the king. They have those ideas of the transmigration of souls up there."

I felt something slipping away, a little like a love one no longer can hold in one's hand. The actual address of the legend seemed to be moving ever farther and farther from me, receding like a dream or a mirage dissolving. Indeed, a fleeting and ominous idea suddenly gripped my mind, although only for a moment: Were these little cats somehow protecting those sacred cats from discovery by diverting attention away from them in this secretive part of the world? Were these charming celebrities actually only shills perhaps for the true sacred cats? Were the truly sacred cats perhaps hiding out in those caves?

Or was *I* going a little crazy?

No, as it turned out, I was not. But I did need to begin to remind myself that Burmese cats *would* be mysterious and lost, if only because Burma itself was so mysterious and lost. The cats of Burma represented and symbolized this deceptive part of Asia. And yet, despite all of this, I had found in this misbegotten land, tiny, hungry cats who would grandly leap through hoops for hours just because they wanted to. That was the way cats were and that was part of the tie between us and them.

The way Nikko looked at me—could anyone be so dumb as not to see it? We pretend it is the moon in the cats' eyes, but in reality it is their soul. They fulfill our mysteries, they are part of us and part of something else. We could reach out to other worlds through them, and they implant themselves in ours in part in order to inspire us. And only cats can do this—not dogs, not bunnies, not ferrets, not chipmunks, not chameleons, as charming as all of them can be. Only cats were chosen by humans across history for this special and wondrous task of representing to us our own souls and spirits through all the wondrous stories that have been passed down to us as myth and legend, they answered our own deepest spiritual yearnings.

Why had I insisted before that everything be made clear?

That night on the lake, after we had left behind our wonderful monks and their brave little cats, our group was in high spirits, invigorated by theirs. For a moment we could put aside the cruelty we'd witnessed in this country and simply think of what we had seen. I, for one, had a great sense of victory. My two delightful friends from Washington, Esther Coopersmith, an extraordinary woman who was the American representative to UNESCO and who is the Perle Mesta of her time, noted for her friendships everywhere in the world and for her magnificent parties for kings, queens, presidents, and the rest of us, and Ina Ginsburg, a longtime editor of *Interview Magazine*—had in the beginning, despite their better selves, rather mocked me. After hearing me ask so many people in Rangoon about the "sacred cats" and after having so many people look at me with baffled wonder, this was not a surprise.

But this night at dinner at our hotel at Inle, after our magical afternoon with the hoop-leaping cats, Esther began telling us about the little cat she and her late husband Jack had had when her husband was alive. "He was a wonderful cat," she said, "and when Jack was dying, that cat never left his side. For eighteen months, he stayed right there in bed with him all the time."

Now it was I who smiled, although in fact it took great effort on my part not to mention that her story bore just a little likeness to that of the dying Munha and the loyal Sinh. Then I asked her, innocently, "What was the cat's name?"

She hesitated. "Pharaoh," she finally answered, at first plaintively but then with a kind of sick smile as she realized what she had said. "Pharaoh."

Later, when we were all safely back home, I read that Edgar Allen Poe was equally devoted to his tortoiseshell cat, Catarina. When his wife was dying and he himself was poverty-stricken and unable to afford sufficient heat for his direly suffering mate, Poe placed Catarina on the bed to keep his wife warm. It was in honor of the cat who stayed with his sick wife that, inspired by such fidelity and loyalty, Poe was moved to write one of his most famous tales, "The Black Cat."

As for me, I did notice that after that both of my good traveling companions were considerably more respectful of my search. *Pharoah,* indeed!

———

I continued my search, through phone calls and e-mails, when I was home. I found Professor Richard Cooler at Northern Illinois University, another specialist on Burma, and, while he did not know anything about cats there, he did tell me the curious story of how, one afternoon just after he and his wife had lost a beloved cat, a beautiful brown cat wandered right off the street and into their house—and stayed. "You know," he said with some wonder, "it was actually a full Burmese cat."

All *I* wondered was how many centuries it had been en route?

———

Next, Sally Baughen, the charming manager of the Strand, wrote to me about a friend. "She had just returned for a second visit to Burma," she wrote. "Last year she visited the 'Leaping Cat Monastery' and told me about how, walking inside, she was overcome with sadness and tears! She wasn't quite sure why this was at the time, but upon return to her home in Bali she discovered that her aging and ailing cat had actually died on the very same day that she had visited the monastery! Those cats have obviously infused the spirit of everyone who visits them."

All I could think of was, why should anyone even have been surprised?

Of course, I never did get to Kachin (pronounced with the emphasis on the "in" rather like a sneeze's kachoo), where there were close to six hundred thousand Tibeto-Burman tribespeople—or, thus, to the square-faced cats of our good monk's remembrances near the Yunnan-Tibetan region of China. The region was long totally closed by the military to foreigners. But I did attempt to discover still more about the Burmese and Birman cats' legends.

In Dallas at the Wycliffe Bible Translators, I located Paulette Hopple, an anthropologist-missionary who had worked with the Kachin and who had done a study for the University of London in 1978 on the Burmese word for "cat." She found that, in all the languages in Burma and among the hill tribes, as in Egypt, the word coincided with the actual sound of the cat, like "meow." (It was almost as if, because we say "Hello," we would then be named Hello, or if we sneezed, we would be called Sneezy. Say, didn't that happen somewhere?) Scholar Dau May Kyi Win at Northern Illinois University at Carbondale searched through the Burmese encyclopedia and said that "Only the characteristics of the cats, including cats in other parts of the world are mentioned, but not any Burmese cat." I asked Professor Saw Tun, an associate professor at Northern Illinois University, about the transmigration of souls, the underground cave, and the name Lao-Tsun. He had come across none of these in any historical record of Burma. I then asked my respected friend and colleague, our former ambassador to China James Lilley, about the Lao-Tsun name. "It's almost definitely Chinese," he said.

What I finally came to believe, especially through the intercessions of Daphne Negus, an elderly Englishwoman in Utah known as Ancient Aunt Daphne in international cat circles for her exceptional work and her editing of *Cat World International,* was that all the tales about the Burmese cat saving the monk and carrying it to heaven were probably made up by cat fanciers in Europe, probably two little old ladies in Marseilles, who wanted to bless their kittens with a great biography. Speaking to me by phone, Daphne said, "It was a pretty story, and it just grew." This kind of creative imagining had happened before in the hothouse schemings and conspiracies of the cat world, commonly called *Cat Fancy.*

Then she stopped talking, but within seconds, her voice came back. "Oh, it's just one of the pussycats walking across the phone," she said. "You know"—and now her voice took on a certain sadness—"after a certain age, it's not a good idea to take on new pussycats." I found that an unhappy conclusion, but I surely understood its poignancy: nobody ever wants to die before his or her cat.

What is known is that the ancestor of the Burmese breed in the West was a square-faced, sable-brown cat ultimately named Wong Mau, which was apparently adopted by a sailor in Burma and carried to the States in the 1930s. There he was bred with a Siamese by Dr. Joseph Thompson in San Francisco. The rest of the saga, we will just have to enjoy, but we are wise enough to see that even the most preposterous stories about the cat lend true light on its character and soul—it *would* have saved the monk in the Lao-Tsun temple.

———

For the moment, I had to deal with still more dreams. The last night in Rangoon, I had another compelling, if time-disordered dream, which is the way dreams are but which may explain about as much as anything about all the mysteries and contradictions of the legends. It was one of those nights where you simply sail along all night, half awake and half asleep, dipping into many worlds.

I saw, first, Pasha, as a kitten, starting off from the Sphinx in Egypt, with his knapsack on his little back and his small brimmed hat on his head, just as the Roman troops appeared on the horizon off Alexandria. He was walking, walking, walking down the many routes, sometimes getting so tired that even his strong long legs and haunches gave out and his beautiful tail sagged and dragged on the road—first along part of the Silk Road, then down across Pakistan and finally to the Kachin people's Bhamo Pass between China and Burma. But as he approached China and then Burma, he became transmogrified into a sturdy little brown cat—half Pasha/Egyptian and half Burmese—who was carried away from Ayudha—the ancient capital of Siam—by all those heartless Burmese marauders.

Then I saw this new cat, which was of course not only part of Pasha but an incarnation of all the cats that had traveled those long roads over the centuries, living for decades with the Kachin in northern Burma, where the cat had bravely helped the British OSS defeat the Japanese by riding along on the Jeeps with the British soldiers. For a time, the Burmese cat fell in love with one of the pure white cats in the temple, but it turned out not to be a serious attachment but only kitty-love and so eventually they parted. One day he had a terrifying experience—marauders attacked the temple where he had been happily renting a room with the good monks and, as the blue-eyed head monk died, our Burmese cat had jumped on his chest and in a fleeting second took on the soul of the priest. This was a deep duty and he bore it pluckily for a week before the soul of the monk left his weary little cat's body and passed to heaven.

At that, he saw that he must move on, and so he started walking over the mountains—across whole magical valleys filled with temples—and then finally he arrived in Rangoon, wading across the shallow Irrawaddy River at sunset. After a stay in the kitchen of the Strand, where he made many friends and enjoyed leftovers of curried fish and rice, he learned to curl up silently under the beds of the guests who were paying $360 a night.

This brave little cat then took a side trip to Malaysia, on the straits from which it is said the Straits tabby came—and there he actually *became* Nikko. It was in Singapore that he lost his tail and, according to the old legends by which the cats' tails that were marred in the making grew into cattails and pussy willows, his original tail was used for cat's tail decorations at a modern hotel. This pert, new little bobtail cat, direct descendant of Pasha and the little brown Burmese, then eventually made his way to China and finally to his true home in Japan, where he gained prestige in the Buddhist temples before coming to America in 1946 and finding a home in Lynchburg, Virginia.

All right, it might not hold up in court, but that's my story and I intend to stick to it.

CHAPTER FIVE

In Siam, a Cat's Home is His Palace

One called the jewel cat, of white body, with eyes like gems
Four black feet, ears and tail black as if ink applied
Has incalculable value, will bring great gain, more property
Who raises it will gain power, retainers and all good things
THE "TAMRA MAEW," THE FIFTEENTH-CENTURY
CAT-BOOK POEMS OR *CAT TREATISES* IN THE
NATIONAL LIBRARY OF THAILAND

BANGKOK, THAILAND

As brilliant a cat as I had known Pasha to be—and as smart as I knew Nikko was, even despite all his occasional displays of modesty—I was never so unrealistic nor so romantic to think that either of them could create works of art. (Although I certainly knew that, given their eternal self-absorption, all cats were first-drawer inspirers of all kinds of art works about *themselves*.) Oh, I did know that the great eighteenth-century Italian composer Domenico Scarlatti had written of his pet cat: "One evening while dozing in my armchair, I was roused by the sound of the harpsichord. My cat had started his musical stroll, and he was picking out a melodic phrase. I had a sheet of paper to hand, and transcribed his composition."

Still.

Perhaps in my heart of hearts, I saw my cats as pet versions of the classic "dumb blonds," who across history (and for reasons that jealous women preferred not to understand) could inspire men to such heights simply by their beauty and the excitement they engender. And in fact, when Nikko's "creativity" was indeed loosed in an unlikely fashion one morning, I cannot really say that I considered it to be a notable success.

———

It was a mid-morning one day in 1996 and Nikko was five years old. I had just read the early papers sitting in my favorite armchair, and I was preparing my mind for what I was going modestly to tell everybody in the world exactly to think on that particular day! But after a few minutes, I was distracted by an odd tap-tap-tap, followed by a loud buzz . . . and another a tap-tap-tap-TAP—TAPP—TAPPPPP!!! Then a kind of dim clanging! I hurried to the scene just in time to see sweet, modest, nonexhibitionist Nikko tapping away like a fiendish little imp, right on those innocent computer keys, which are far more sensitive to "gentle" cat's paws than you might think. In fact, Nikko was dancing!

Oh, not Fred Astaire–dancing or Gene Kelly–dancing, but more like southern Wisconsin polka dancing or Italian grape stomping. He would lift his paws and then throw his tiny head back, all the while actually jumping up and down and turning in circles—and in the very center of the keyboard. If Guy Lombardo had only been playing the background!

Before I could grab for him, the machine itsself responded. Indeed, I soon realized that I had not only a crazy cat on my hands but a crazy computer as well! It kept "shouting" in type on the screen: "ILLEGAL MOVE . . . ILLEGAL MOVE . . . ILLEGAL MOVE . . ." Oh, for heaven's sake, I thought to myself, it's surely stupid to have your cat behaving like this, but, come on, it's certainly not illegal!

But before calling my lawyer, I had to calm Nikko down and remove him from the occasion for sin, for his eyes seemed as big and black as billiard balls, so excited was he! When I put him down on the floor, he ran around in circles for quite some time, his bunny tail quivering with excitement, his tiny ears nearly flat back on his head. There, he crouched down to challenge me, grab-

———

bing his stuffed toy made to mimic a veterinarian and shaking his "vet" relentlessly (showing what he really thought about the "establishment," surely!). Finally when I chased him, as I often did, crying out like a crazy person myself, "I'm gonna get you, I'm gonna get you," he ran under the bed and stayed there for many hours. Doubtless he was in hiding from the sheriff's office, while I . . . was left to address the computer, which, not surprisingly, was sorely pissed off, its screen still flashing an ominous black picture at me.

Would my fate be the federal pen? Or would my case against my cat perhaps rather be a local "domestic court" matter, seeing as how the whole dispute began between me and Nikko in our very own home? Might he be taken away from me by one of those self-righteous, damnable, busybody "child welfare" agencies? Would I have to go to jail, as the keeper of the house, or should the vile perpetrator of the crime himself be put away for nine lives? Immediately I thought with a heavy sacrificial sigh, forgiving him already, "No, I will go."

I called my very able computer man. He came over and turned the computer on—only, it didn't turn on. He officially turned the whole system off for ten minutes, while we nervously waited. He took some parts out and fiddled around with them—but still it didn't work. "The computer has an office called Intensive Care," he said finally, giving Nikko a weary look. And that's where it went. But in fact, the whole drama seemed to remain a huge mystery even to those experts, and when, eyebrows screwed in amazement at such a curiously destroyed machine, they asked me how this on earth had happened, I didn't think I ought to answer. In the end, it was sent to San Diego for repair and eventually came back workable, but never again really its sassy old self. However, I don't think it ever snapped "ILLEGAL" at me again.

Nikko, meanwhile, quickly reverted to his dear modest self and harmed no one and nothing so seriously ever again. Apparently he got something out of his system, but, as one so often had to wonder with cats, *exactly what*?

One morning several days later, I sat down with Nikko to have a serious face-to-whisker talk. Surely he didn't have a winning paw—I mean hand—but still he acted as though he did.

"All right, Nikko," I demanded, very seriously, "I need some answers. Now, exactly *why* did you do this?" He looked at me with the most insincerely innocent look that I have ever seen, which of course irritated me intensely.

Finally, he sat there and licked his tiny tail rather more assiduously—and insultingly—than usual, and then he stared at me with the most engrossing gaze, as if he were trying to figure out what exactly it was that was upsetting me so much when he was clearly so relishing life. And, of course, the fault was mine. Would any true cat lover ungraciously balk at paying $755 to fix the computer that her cat had so embarrassingly destroyed?

As I proceeded on my trip, Nikko's destruction of my computer would also come to symbolize something besides the harmony of our home. It came to symbolize for me personally the destruction of so many of my own suppositions— and surely many of the most accepted myths—about the royal and sacred cats of the world.

For now I was moving on, and perhaps backwards in time at the same time, and, of course, to ancient Siam—today's modern Thailand—to further test all of my findings and suppositions and to continue my search for answers to my two major questions: Why had so many ancient societies made cats, and cats alone, into royal and sacred creatures? And what could my findings on those questions tell us about our own mysterious relations with our own cats—and perhaps about ourselves, as well?

———————

Siam, as I shall call the country from here on in deference to those wondrous days when cats were next to kings there, was my next way station on my journey into Nikko's past: from Egypt and Burma, down to the Malay Peninsula, and finally to Japan itself. I knew I was "on the trail" of the royals and sacreds in the family of felines, and also on the trail of one branch of the family's tail. Indeed, I could already begin to chart historically how the different original clans of cat or tribes of cat over the centuries became the huge Family of Cat and, finally subdivided into cat breeds. Here, too, in this pleasant country, I would gather information and impressions that I could eventually put together in that larger map of the world of cats that I was beginning to create. And at each stop, I was smitten ever more hopelessly with an insatiable curiosity that only seemed to grow . . . and grow . . . and grow.

Now, Siam was obviously home to the great Siamese cat, long considered the most elegant of those in the Family of Cat—and once again, I had many well-established "facts" at my fingertips. Things that I just *knew!* The Burmese cat story, after all, had been tricky from the beginning. But—the Siamese? The search for this part of the family would be a cakewalk (or perhaps a *cat*walk). We knew that Siamese cats were the most royal cats of all! They lived in the temples and in the royal palaces, where they were exquisitely spoiled! The Siamese were the most proper prince and princess of all of the breeds, being always perfectly coiffed and beautifully behaved! There was only one type of Siamese cat: the cross-eyed ones we know, with their luxuriant fur with the color that flows like waves of definition out to the ends of the tails, snout, ears, and paws—those were called the "points." These true Siamese were the undimmable stars of the international cat shows; and being such a good product and advertisement for their country, the Siamese breed was being reproduced in Thailand and the cats were greatly beloved by all Thais!

With those articles of faith in my heart and in my hands, I set out for the next chapter of our journey.

It was the second day in Bangkok and I was lunching with a group of Thai diplomats and officials in a handsome downtown hotel. I was delighted to be sitting next to the governor of Bangkok, Samak Sundaravej. A big and impressive man, he was himself a renowned cat lover and, in matter of fact, had eleven cats!

But when I pressed him at some length about the sacred Siamese cats—eager to know exactly what temples I should immediately go to in order to find them—he only wrinkled his brow and seemed to think carefully. "Temple cats?" asked this man, elegantly dressed like so many prosperous Thais and obviously at ease with himself. "Actually," he began, "the ones we have in the temples are only stray cats, only leftover cats." He paused. A long pause. "But there was a cat that stayed by King Rama the Fifth," he went on, "and it was white. So far as I know, the relationship was not documented—it was only said that he kept a white cat with two different colors of eyes."

Stray cats? . . . Leftover cats? Was any of this in the history books? I pressed.

"No," he answered. "But there are some temples where there are engravings about the cats. But—Siamese cats? There are actually very few in the country. We have some 'copper cats'—you know the 'coppers,' they are those all-brown cats that one finds across Southeast Asia and especially in Burma, but also here. Then there are the Siamese Korats—they are all gray." He smiled. "They say that, if you own a Korat cat, every day you must give him a hug—every day—or he will soon die."

Coppers? All-brown cats found especially in Burma, but *also in Siam?* I filed that away for future reference and, as it would turn out, fruitful use.

When I then mentioned that I usually wrote not about cats but about politics, he smiled again. "Well, cats and politics are a little bit similar, aren't they?" he mused. I thought that I knew what he meant: both engross you, both reward you, and, most of all, both endlessly confuse you with their labyrinthian historic mysteries, tricks, and appearing disappearing acts.

So—no cats in the temples? Well, okay. My mother would only have said that sacred cats, since they obviously must have beautiful manners, could live anywhere.

———

The next day, I was by accident having lunch with a group of very elegant and cultured women from the palace. We were in the tearoom of the Teak Palace, where King Rama V was supposed to have kept his beloved and unforgettable white cat, and I, of course, asked them about the famous, internationally known, royal cat of Siam. The group stilled for a moment. "Thais don't keep Siamese cats because they're very ferocious, very nervous," the delicately lovely and intelligent lady at the table, who was actually the private secretary to Queen Sirikit, interjected. "They're not like ordinary cats. They're overbred. And they're also very hard to find." I found it momentarily hard to breathe. "Oh, Thais like Siamese cats," she went on, perhaps sensing my dismay, "but they think they're hard to raise and need special care. In the old days, the people believed, too, that the Siamese would bring good or bad luck—they also thought that the diamond-eyes cat, which is another kind of Siamese cat, when he died would leave you a diamond ring." She paused again, a worried look on her delicate face. "Whenever I have seen Siamese cats, it was when I was abroad," she added. "Never have I seen any here. Among my friends, they only have normal cats."

Normal cats? Could it be possible that she does not know that there are no "normal cats"at all—anywhere? And surely not among the royal Siamese? But how admirably I controlled myself!

Then she brightened. "I do know of one friend who has a lovely Korat—you know, the gray cat from northern Siam—and she loves him very much. She got him from the States," she added matter-of-factly.

But my quest received an even worse blow when I was speaking the next day with a former Thai ambassador to Washington. When I told him of my royal quest, his expression noticably darkened. Then he told me of this, the newest royal "scandal" for cat lovers, saying, "The king . . . has no cats." He paused, as if for sad emphasis, then added, "but he has thirty-six dogs."

I was silent. Leftover cats? Abnormal cats? Siamese cats, so ferocious and nervous, not like ordinary cats, overbred and hard to find? *Dogs* having been given the cats' favored historic place in the royal palace, when everyone knows that dogs should do the dirty work, protecting the ramparts of the castle and getting the sheep in line, while delicate and manipulative cats should rule and reign? I truly admired the Thai royal family, and I understood all too well from my love of history that, with societies, or humans or even cats, lives rose and fell, and courts and systems waxed and waned, much like the moon in the cats' eyes—but this? Shock and dismay nearly overcame me. I could only wonder how such a fine family could decline so precipitously—and all in the sphere of only a couple of generations.

Getting a bit tricky, wasn't it?

To follow my quest for the roots of the Siamese cat—and particularly, this special white cat—I decided to go to the beautiful Victorian Teak Palace of King Chulalongkorn, commonly known as Rama V. This was the king with the palace of seventy-two rooms who reigned so wisely and successfully from 1873, when he turned twenty, to 1910 and the king who had the famous *beloved white cat* in his extraordinarily delicate and exquisite wooden palace.

This son of the reformer and educator King Mongkut, or Rama IV, who became immortalized in the West as the monarch-subject of *The King and I,* constantly endeared himself to his subjects. Indeed, his popularity peaked when he announced at his second coronation in 1873, when he officially came of age, that henceforth there would be no prostration before the king—then, in one great moment of history, the entire court rose to its feet as one in gratitude and Siam was never the same again! I also discovered that Rama V had introduced a system of diminishing hereditary aristocracy, by which the king's heirs go down one step in rank each generation, so eventually a royal descendent is addressed only as a plain *nai* or "mister," while others in the kingdom rise on merit. This is a process, I would soon find, that would turn out to be common among the Family of Cat as well—royalties fell and new breeds arose as they were created by former "commoner cats"; the concept of "breed" took the place of the royal and the sacred.

But sadly, I was unable to learn anything about the king's famous "beloved white cat" anywhere in the Teak Palace. In all of those family and royal photographs—pictures of oriental splendor and of trips to England, where he was also beloved and known to be of good kingship—there was not one single photograph or even mention of his *beloved white cat!*

Perhaps, like difficult little Nikko, the beloved little white cat hated cameras! Over the years, I had tried repeatedly to take pictures of Nikko, but it was almost as if he could actually hear the confrontation coming. It seemed that he could anticipate, almost as a kind of stirring, when there was a camera somewhere in the house, anywhere in the house. Maybe, like many superstitious tribespeople across the globe, he and the beloved white cat feared that the camera would take their souls. I know this speculation is far from adequate, yet in fact I have no other real answer for the mystery as to why there was no space in that vast palace for even one picture of Rama V's beloved white cat.

As so often happens, just at this moment of true desperation in my quest I began to encounter some luck. The other interviews I had requested came through and, one beautiful, sunny mid-morning, I found myself at a gorgeous home, surrounded by lazy oriental gardens on a meandering canal, at the home of the famous Pichai.

Now everyone knew Pichai, whose "last name" was Vasnasong, a name seldom used in Thailand, where last names are artificially created. He was not only a prominent legislator and thinker, he was the determined leader of Thailand's energetic family planning program. In fact, it was his program that had kept the population at reasonable levels and thus allowed the country to thrive: his message about family planning, pure Thai, was that you, and your family, will be "happier" if you can give more to a small family. But he did not apply that wisdom to his love for animals, for Pichai was also a great cat lover, and he once had had forty-eight cats.

Both of my cats were—of course—altered and I could only think of all those poor cats across the world who were not, and who were thus in part doomed to live short, brutish, and cruel lives, out in the open, surrounded by disease and wild animals and wanton humans.

Handsome, portly Pichai, by then in his early seventies, began his speech that day by saying, "All Thais love cats. Historically we have used cats as a symbol of rain. The other thing is that cats were always related to stories about the royal family. We're not sure they are all true, but we know that Rama V loved his cats. The Siamese cat and the Egyptian cat are very similar. But the Siamese, sacred? No. Related to the temples? Yes. But that is because people would leave them at the temples. Then, besides the regular Siamese, there are the white, diamond-eyes cats. People hoped that their eyes would turn to diamonds: they look very precious and the idea was that they would bring luck to anyone who owned them."

At that moment, as we sat sipping cool drinks in his exquisite garden, one of Pichai's maids delicately carried out to us a little basket with a webbed covering and in it were four squirming, adorable, classically Siamese kittens. They were probably about a month old and they were all mewing their heads off as they wound themselves around one another just like balls of yarn all tangled up together. One kept pushing a little dark paw out of the top of the basket, as though hitting at the wind, which of course kittens do so very well. Three were classic Siamese, with the dark nose and paws and the bodies that would obviously become the long, elegant body of the breed; the fourth was a gray tabby that looked just like gray tabbies anywhere—and reminded me immediately not only of the many tabbies in American homes, but of the royal tabbies from the Egyptian temples—and once again, I realized that the so-called "common" tabby had always been right there, in the bloodstream of the royals and the sacreds. Pichai smiled broadly at this revealing "discrepancy."

"That is the way life happens," he said.

Mark Twain had said once: "A house without a cat, a well-fed, well-petted, and properly revered cat, may be a perfect house, perhaps, but how can it prove its title?" Surely with Pichai and in his loving home, that title was secure. And, seemingly with the blessing of this remarkable man, my luck was beginning to turn—but first, I had to absorb some new shocks.

———

The fact that the regular, real, royal Siamese, with its crossed blue eyes and with its color dispersed to the "ends" of its body, was not the only Siamese cat in Siam was my next shock; there were several other very famous types within Siam—and there were still other revelations, shocking in their nature, yet to come.

One of these cats could not possibly be more different from the traditional Siamese. The Korat, often called by its native name, *Si-Sawat,* is round, muscular, and very gray. In contrast to the traditional Siamese, there is something very clear and simple about the Korat. It is as if the animal itself, with its single color, were making a bold, simple statement, its stunning yellow-green eyes gazing at you with their riveting stare.

I am unhappy to have to report here that social class prejudices in cat circles raised its unfortunate head with the Korat, for purists among the Siamese breeders used to scoff at any claims from Korat lovers that *their* cat is also a cat of true breed—it is, Siamese breeders point out, *only* the "village cat" of Siam! But we shall ignore such improvident snobbishness, and give the Korats, like all beautiful cats, their due. Note that at least their eyes are not crossed!

"The Korats are the cats of the people," the late Daphne Negus told me when I phoned her about the Korats. A cat expert and a Korat specialist, Daphne continued: "It is said that Thailand's personable and innovative King Rama the Fifth saw the silver-blue, green-eyed cat one day and exclaimed, 'What a pretty cat! Where is it from?' 'From Korat, Your Majesty,' came the answer—and that inspired the king to name the cat after the province in northeastern Thailand."

The Korats are now, of course, a popular breed, but their story goes beyond the virtues of egalitarianism and illustrates dramatically for us how little we also know about the actual *places* on the geographical map that illuminate for us our cats' true history. Roger Tabor, the prominent British cat biologist, noted that, "In talking with some Korat breeders in America, I was amazed to hear them say, 'What a pity there is no such place as Korat!' They were so wrapped up in breeding and showing their cats they had not even bothered to look at a map! I was able to tell them that not only was there a city called Korat in which I had seen Korats but that a huge area called the Korat Plateau made up a large part of northeastern Thailand."

And one more shock! It is the homey Korat and not the exotic Siamese that is considered the "classic Thai cat"! The Siamese people have for centuries revered the Korat, not for being royal or sacred, but, as with the Egyptians, for being something more important: auspicious and beautiful!

Although I could not exactly put it together yet, the Korats had already given me still another valuable clue to their relationship to Nikko and his Family of Cat, for the pretty gray Korats were not royal cats like the regular Siamese, but they were rather the cats representing good fortune and good luck—I was very soon indeed to find how closely that appellation approximated Nikko's position in the family pantheon.

Meanwhile, I did not need to be reminded that virtually nothing in my search for the Siamese cats was turning out as I had expected. I was surely finding that one has to remain open-minded when doing research on royal and sacred cats.

But in order for me to really put Pasha's and Nikko's family history together, I still had to deal with the third of the traditional cats of ancient Siam. These were the white, ethereal diamond-eyes cats, a kind of lost "Anastasia" cat.

And so it was, on a beautiful spring morning in Bangkok, when, after considerable searching for him, I went out, finally, to see Namdee Witte, the former Bangkok film producer who, apparently alone in the world, had been given the royal "duty" of raising the pure white diamond-eyes cats by the royal family. I had first been alerted to his mission in an article by David Lamb from *The Los*

Angeles Times that was provocatively entitled "So, You Think *Your* Cats Are Spoiled?" The story, from Bangkok, told about "one royal family that lives in splendor and lazes about most of the day . . . the 50 members of the family are white cats of Siam whose ancestors lived at the palace of Thailand's late, beloved king, Rama V . . . at their home—which is actually the home of film producer Namdee Witte—the pure white cats live in teak-paneled rooms, drink bottled spring water from gold- and silver-plated bowls and wear collars embedded with cut glass that resembles diamonds. 'They are princes and princesses, and they deserve the best,' Namdee said. 'Their value is beyond price. How valuable? Well, I can tell you six years ago a monk had a Siamese of this breed and he sold it for 150 million baht (about $4 million) to a very wealthy jeweler. The monk built a temple with the money.'"

"Namdee," as he is called by everyone, turned out to be a small man, lean and witty, with a sensitive face. He said he was past seventy, but he surely did not look it, probably because of the elevating spirit of his love for his white cats, and as we sat down in his living room, he began to tell a story every bit as noble as that of the hoop-leaping cats of Burma.

"They used to say that they were as rare as the white elephants," he began, the same ethereal look of the cats' eyes in his own. "King Rama the Fifth had his favorite among the diamond-eye white cats, or the *Khao Manee,* as they are called in Thai. He entrusted one of his sons to preserve them through pure breeding. The responsibility was then handed down to to me. There were three hundred cats three years ago, but many of them died . . . I made a commitment, a verbal commitment, to the princess and to the king to look after this heritage. But when the king gave them to me, he set the rules: they have to mate only among themselves, and they cannot be sold to anyone."

Then the little "show" began, which reminded me for all the world of the day at the Marshes' farm in Lynchburg when I had found Nikko. Namdes carried down eight or ten delicate cages of the cats and set them about the room on the first floor—and in them, were these incredible white, white, and more white cats. They were such fine-looking creatures that they almost reminded me of those delicate Englishwomen who have such pink-pink and more-pink porcelain skin that they stand out like fine roses. The cats had almost transparent ears and long, sinuous white tails and, because of the inbreeding, most of them did indeed have one yellow eye and one blue eye! All had fine collars on, made of shining glass and appearing to reflect the putative "diamonds" in their eyes, and there were ersatz gold or silver dishes with water in their cages, the design of which I recognized from certain human displays at the Teak Palace.

The little creatures lounged languidly in their cages and seemed, as with Nikko sometimes when he was feeling punk or low, beyond playing. They made no sound and they seemed eternally exhausted (they probably they needed some village blood). In truth, they seemed like cats that should be in the court of a king, a sultan, or, perhaps most appropriately, a magician or a shaman—surely not in any normal place or with any of us (more or less) normal people. They were obviously loved and well cared for, but like any inbred creature, human or animal, they had a distinctly otherworldly look about them. In fact, the diamond-eyes seemed like a lost tribe, existing out in nowhere, a living memory of the distant past. They reminded me of nothing so much as some pale and ethereal displaced White Russian princesses in a flat in Shanghai in 1945, with no homeland to return to.

I knew by now that white cats had appeared in the art of many countries— the nineteenth-century French artist and print maker Edward Manet, for instance, loved to paint white cats—as well in poetry. ad-Damiri, an Egyptian theologian and zoologist, wrote in the fourteenth century:

> When sorrows press my heart I say:
> Maybe they'll disappear one day;
> When books will be my friends at night,
> My darling then: the candle light,
> My sweetest friend: a kitten white.

Still, Namdee clearly felt he was dealing with some level of eternity in nurturing these faded little cats with the strange, abstract look in their pink, blue, green, and yellow eyes. "Maybe by the time that this generation grows up," he told me at one point, his voice soft, "the elephants will be gone, but the *Khao Manee* diamond-eyes will still be here."

Slowly, and again thoughtfully, I found myself forced to the realization that perhaps the original Siamese ought not really to be called the "royal" Siamese, but
the "randy" Siamese. But before we address their fall from grace, one has to
look back just a little.

Historically, we knew that the first pure and divine Siamese—with its eyes
so intensely, mystically blue—had first caught the avid attention of the West
when it was bought to America in the 1870s as a gift to President Rutherford
B. Hayes from the American consul in Siam. The president named him Siam,
rather in the same spirit as the Egyptians insisting upon calling their cats
Miou—or Americans calling their dogs Woofer or Doggy. The cats won worldwide acclaim when they were first exhibited at London's Crystal Palace in 1895.
But even then, the praise that the creature first evinced because of its, frankly,
strange and certainly exotic characteristics was qualified. One critic of the time
called the Siamese an "unnatural nightmare of a cat!"

Those original Siamese, then called apple-headed or traditional, were large,
robust cats with round heads, normal-looking ears, and lovely, staring, almost
cross-eyed azure eyes. But as they became the world's most popular cat throughout the middle of the twentieth century, obsessive breeders bred them more and
more into the sleek breed of today, with their painfully thin features and their
fashionable nervousness. The breed standard was rewritten and, by the 1950s
and 1960s, the "new Siamese" had become the reigning star of the increasingly
active and crowded cat breed world, appearing in movies like the popular *Lady
and the Tramp*. The females, meanwhile, were the "Big Mamas" of the designer
cats who eventually dominated cat shows, first in England, then in America,
and finally, internationally in the 1930s and 1940s, when cat clubs, and their
attendant cat shows, were increasing their numbers across the globe.

Such was the perfervidity of the Siamese cat lovers of this era that
Siamophiles would write to one another across the oceans soberly averring that
"if all people loved Siamese as we do, no countries would go to war ever
again!"

This worthy acclaim makes it even more difficult to be forced to consider
something surely better left unnoted, but which must be said, if only for histor-

ical accuracy. Surely the Siamese *looked* royal, with their courtly behavior and prim blue eyes and the suave fur that flowed artistically out to the ends of their noses, ears, and tails, virtual ripples in a sea of ever-darker fur which was called the cats' "points." The Siamese were the most aristocratic-looking of all of the members of the great Family of Cat. They were the heroines, but also the heroes, of feline feminism, for in the Siamese family, the father cats would often remain present at the births, show no aggression—and (sometimes I think we don't really ask enough of males) not eat their kittens.

In short, because of their beauty and bearing, everyone just naturally *thought* them royal, for an *aesthetic aura* seemed to hang over them like a cloud, tossed here and there by the winds of their exotic and sensuous beauty! And so they must also be modest and virginal in their behavior!

We note also that this great Family of Cat was also excitable and demanding and, as rather too many owners would soon somewhat testily remark, they reminded us of many of our own relatives who also always "talked" too much! Indeed, their voices came not even in the form of meows but usually in the form of incessant yowls and gurgles and ERRARARAHHHGURRGLERAHS.

But it was exactly those qualities that also got them into what my beloved mother always referred to, unmistaken in her tone of voice, as "TROUBLE!" (Later I would chide myself for neglecting to take sufficiently into account the fact that Bangkok was notorious as the "fleshpot of Asia.")

And so, let me put it to you with no embellishment . . . Without ever a paw being given in marriage, from those supposedly self-contained and prim Siamese we have: Tonkinese, Himalayas, Havana Browns, Singapuras, Javanese, Oriental Shorthairs, and Balinese. All were "experimental matings" to put it nicely; all were originally offspring of the busy-busy Siamese, clearly the first globalizer sex kittens. Why, there was even a Russian Blue, which emerged from, of all places, Archangel on the northern Arctic Sea of Russia and which is believed to be a rare offspring of the Siamese. Like all cats that settled in the Northern climes, it came to have a heavy—in fact, a double—coat of unrivaled plushness. (One famous Russian Blue was owned by Czar Nicholas II of Russia, assassinated in the cellars of Yekaterinburg during the Russian Revolution—apparently his cat did not bring him much of that old "good luck"!)

And all the while, in the background, I could hear my beloved mother tsk-tsking, as she observed, "You never can tell by looks, can you?"

Now, God knows I do not mean to be judgmental or to jump to conclusions about the roaming and randy Siamese; but the fact is that, despite their proper training in courtly and lady-in-waiting behavior, they emerge clearly as *the* romantic adventurers of the Family of Cat! Indeed—was it the "Sacred Siamese" or the "Sexy Siamese"? One could contend that mixing it up every-where and with apparently every cat, every cute kitty, and every pretty puss was not the way for real royalty to behave. But on the other hand, it was very high-level catting around. The charmingly wayward Siamese certainly created an amazing family of new breeds from one end of the world to the other, and all as beautiful as sin itself!

What's more, by the time I visited their homeland, true Siamese cats were bred only by a few wealthy matrons in Siam—and foreign cat fanciers had actu-ally become so snobbish that they would not recognize a Thai pedigree for a Siamese cat! Although Siamese cats remain a special taste throughout the world, in Siam Siamese cats had almost yowled and preened themselves out of Thai existence, not unlike many of the spoiled princes and princesses across history.

A Pawnote: It is also only fair to remember that those Greek gods and god-desses weren't exactly just reading the Epistles on Mount Olympus.

In the end, however, the important thing is that there is no question that the Siamese cats are indeed royal cats!

They were not sacred, like their Egyptian cousins, because they were neither godlike nor were they the reflection of God; but they were always part of the royal family and, in their sleek and sophisticated persons, they were certainly, even more than decorations, symbols of the royal court. For many centuries they were kept at the palaces of the king; they were a primary representation of royalness, much like royal accoutrements, and present at—and often emblem-atic of—the ebb and flow of the monarchy. They were presented by the king— and only by the king—to special honored guests from abroad and they could also be temple cats set to guard the temples against enemies. (Siamese love high places and riding around on their owners' shoulders, so they would be naturals for the important job of temple guarding.)

Then, in Siamese mythology, there are also stories of black-coated animals with huge golden eyes, kept in cages adorned with gold leaf, resting languidly atop cushions with offerings of incense and food from the priests and the faithful. Sometimes a pure white cat was carried in the procession in a gilded cage, particularly when a new king was crowned. (These were surely royal gestures.)

Still other Siamese legends contend that, when a member of royalty died, his or her cat would be buried with the person—an almost perfect comparison to the entire "transmigration of souls" stories from both Egypt and Burma. But in Siam, in a typically kindly Siamese variation on the theme, the tomb would be pierced with small holes so the cat could free itself—and at that time, the soul passed into the cat's body and the cat was led to the temple with great ceremony. One can almost hear the chirpy Siamese cat, escaping from the tomb in time, letting out a very noisy sigh and a relieved, ERRARARAHHHGURRGLERAH.

Siamese cats are sometimes given names meaning "jewel" or "moon-diamond," thus connecting them to Egyptian moon fantasies. We know that in the north of Thailand some kind of cat played the central role in the famous "rain ceremony"; the animal, believed to have mystical power, is taken around town in a little cage, water is sprinkled on him, and he or she can bring—or not bring—rain. (In Europe in medieval times, cats were blamed for storms, and dogs for high winds, and thus it would be "raining cats and dogs" during a rainy windstorm—you wondered, didn't you? I wanted to see if you'd read this far.)

Cats even figure importantly in traditional Thai interpretations of dreams. Writer Martin Clutterbuck, whose book *The Legend of Siamese Cats*, is a masterpiece of cat writing, states that, in Siam, "it is considered that killing a cat is equivalent to killing a monk or, more usually, a novice." And when I e-mailed Martin Clutterbuck in Bangkok about the "royalty question," I found his e-mail answer to be particularly compelling:

Thai cats are "sacred" inasmuch as they were believed to bring good fortune . . . You can't kill a cat in Thailand. As I said in the book, even vets are reluctant to put them down.

The people of Siam further believed that the shadowy patches on the Siamese cats' necks were thumbprints or shadows of sacred hands, left when a god picked up a cat to admire it—and these stories are so strikingly similar to certain legends about the Burmese cats, as well as those about the Prophet Muhammad and his favorite cat that they could leave one, at the very least, most thoughtful about the role of the cat in history and its curious role in the great subconscious of the human race.

And so, to me, then, despite their unfortunate weakness for adventure and fun in the shadows outside of the palace walls and despite their incessant and distinctly unroyal chatterings, in their beauty and spirit and history and in the many gorgeous breeds of cat that they have left behind, the Siamese cats will always reign as one of the greatest of the royal Family of Cat, if not *the* greatest.

Yet, in fact, my most serious and sobering surprises were yet to come.

In doing my research on Pasha and Nikko, and through them on all the cats of the world, I had often regretted that there were no real historic books from their own early eras. I had to rely on snippets and suggestions and suppositions, on a quote here and a remembrance there. There was no Bible, no Torah, no Koran, no real historical reference or bible of the cat. In Egypt there is a great pictorial representation of the cat, but it is mute. The history—the maps—the congruence of cat myths across the globe—the stories of the di*cat*spora—all are simply legend, many say. But they are wrong.

Indeed, before I had left on my Asian trip, I had sat with Nikko, curled up in my lap, and told him, "I am going to write the book about your history, and then you will know everything about yourself. I will be your historical psychiatrist." I paused, then added, "And thus, perhaps, my own, as well."

But breakthroughs come when you least expect them, because there—in Siam—I found the veritable bible of the Cat, a book that brought together the history and the culture of the cats of Siam, plus even a poignant portrayal of the the cat as moralist. For in the bosom of the National Library of Thailand in Bangkok, there rests today in the precious care of the librarians the *Cat-Book Poems* or the *Cat Treatises,* called in ancient Siamese the *Tamra Maew.* This is a long-preserved manuscript, probably written by anonymous Buddhist monks from the great early city of Ayudha. Like monks in Europe in the monasteries of the Middle Ages, these noble holy men wanted to preserve every precious detail of their culture—and their cats were clearly considered to be a crucial part of it. The manuscripts were written and put together in the years between A.D. 1350 and A.D. 1767 and involved sketches and rich verses and incantations about cats; they were filled with drawings of cats of every form, shape, and demeanor, some looking up in expectation, some standing as if posing for the artist, some staring off the page . . . In fact, almost surely the *Tamra Maew* constitutes the world's oldest breed standards for cats!

The texts essentially describe seventeen types of good cats, including the black cat (today's black cat), the copper (which I would soon find most probably to be today's Burmese breed), the gray cat (today's Siamese Korat), the original yowling Siamese cat (today's Siamese cat) and a whole, whole lot of black-and-white cats (today's American and British Shorthairs), and six types of bad cats.

These perfectly marvelous manuscripts reminded me in many ways of the early texts in America for schoolchildren—perhaps the McGuffy Reader of the Cat, for they were manuscripts of instruction, of moral judgments, and of exhortation. There were careful delineations of "good cats" (Pasha and Nikko, Bastet and *Si-Sawat*) and there were "bad cats" (Mookie and Sekhmet again raise their claws, now in words and pictures from the grave). In fact, there is nothing in the world comparable to these hundreds of pages of sketches, poems, and musings both philosophical and scientific about cats.

Whenever the good and obsessed (and ever-quarreling) people of the international cat shows meet in their shows, whether in London or Tokyo or Phoenix or Chicago, basing the excellence of their cats upon the breed standards of today, the standards of beauty, of form and of behavior of the breed cat actually harken back to these ancient manuscripts, created and pored over so painstakingly and lovingly by those worthy ancient monks.

Most important, here I was, almost exactly halfway around the world from my own home in Washington, D.C., and the pictures of many of these Siamese regional cats, as shown in the manuscripts *look just like both Pasha and Nikko!* The same coloring, the same spots on the top of the heads and over the eyes, the same spots down the backs, and the same pinched little noses! I was so beside myself with joy when I discovered this that I could have leapt to the top of my grandmother Martha "Oma" Geyer's Biedermeier chest and kissed the stone cat myself.

For it confirmed to me that centuries ago in these lush monsoon rice fields and glimmering beaches of Southeast Asia, cats who were direct ancestors of my two pets, albeit then with tails, had lived noble lives, had thrived, and had even been the subject of love and concern on the part of the single most cultured and enlightened group in the entire society!

———

I was on a roll, for soon in Siam I would also even find the roots of the mysterious Burmese cat whose origins had so eluded me in Burma. The difference here lay in the fact that, as the suave governor of Bangkok had alluded to me on those first days in the country, the Siamese "copper" exactly fits the pattern of the Burmese!

Roger Tabor, the prominent British cat biologist and author of *The Wild Life of the Domestic Cat,* after visiting Bangkok and making a famous BBC-TV series on cats, wrote that: "I was able to show full Burmese cats living feral as temple cats in Bangkok. I was delighted to meet my first copper at Ayudha, the ancient capital of Siam." And as early as the 1880s, no one less than Harrison Weir, the British founder of the international cat shows, reported a cat that had a rich, dark brown body and darker paws, ears, and tail, and which had probably come from the peninsula that is today's Singapore. This "chocolate Siamese" appeared to exactly resemble the current Burmese.

But the real key is to be found in the ruins of a once-great city a couple of hours by car north of Bangkok, in the shards and memories of Ayudha. That capital city had been founded in 1350. Its court was brilliant and its monks, who wrote the cat treatises, were dutiful and devoted scholars. Indeed, in this era, the court of Siam was rivaled in Asia only by that of imperial China's, and this part of southeastern Asia soon became the thoroughfare for travelers between Europe and the Orient, a fact that would naturally have facilitated the movement of cats from Egypt to Asia. Indeed, the city was more than four hundred years old when it was leveled by Burmese invaders in 1767 in hand-to-hand and perhaps paw-to-paw combat. Since the Burmese took so much else of Siamese culture back to Burma with them, they surely also took the copper cat, which comes down to us with the Siamese name of *Supalak,* or "copper brown, after its color—and is surely the ancestor of today's Burmese breed.

And so, what we know of today as the Siamese, the Burmese, and the Korats, some tailless varieties and many black-and-white-spotted cats that looked so much like their British and American distant cousins, came together in history on the amenable land mass they called Siam in ancient days—and then moved with the flows of historic circumstance. The cats' movements were simply rather like those of the Celts, the Goths, the Romans, the Vikings, and those of so many other humans, all roaming and roving about Europe in earlier centuries—and finally creating a new European man.

———————

I was about to make still another discovery, the greatest of all.

I have already spoken of Nikko's sensitivity about his tail and its origins, how he surely dreams of having a full, furry tail, just as I dream of having slim, supple hips. I knew it the first time I carefully touched and caressed his little tail, that first day in Lynchburg, Virginia. He always liked to have his tail petted but still, at the same time, he looked at me with such a sad look that I could only believe that he was thinking that perhaps I would not take him because of his kinked tail.

But now, I learned that the real Siamese legend of days of yore also celebrates the story of a beautiful Siamese princess who was washing herself in a rushing stream. She was very frightened about losing her precious rings while she bathed and, as she looked around for some secure place to keep them, her eyes fell upon her favorite cat. By chance, the pet had just crooked his tail up to gain attention from her and so the princess put her rings on her cat's tail for safekeeping; after that, the Siamese cat's tail always had a little kink in it, but only at the very end. In another charming mythological version of this story, Siamese cats guard a royal golden goblet in the jungle and kink their tails to wrap them around the goblet; at the same time, because of the long hours of guard-cat duty, which of course are hard on the eyes of any cat, they squinted their eyes, thus creating the legendary cross-eyes of the traditional Siamese. Far less well known in the West is the fact that the Siamese cats, although of course having long tails, also have a number of kinks carefully hidden inside those apparently straight tails so as not to give away the princess' secret.

In fact, I knew by now that the kinked tail had originally come from the Malay Peninsula and moved up through Siam and China to Japan and sometimes moved in circles. To Martin Clutterbuck, this is natural because geographically "the Southern part of Thailand, Burma and Malaysia form a peninsula, and there is obviously a lack of land borders. Singapore, at the tip of the peninsula, has more short-tailed cats than anywhere else. A peninsula's species, like those of an island, tend to have little input from outside as new animals must be imported by man. The genes from just a pair of short-tailed cats arriving from China, Japan or Korea—where there have been bobtailed cats for centuries—would impart their dominant short-tail feature to almost all of their descendants."

Then, Nikko—here it comes! Even the great Charles Darwin, in his theory of evolution, set his sights on the profound question of the historic loss of your tail! In his *The Variation of Animals and Plants Under Domestication,* published in 1868, he wrote that, "throughout an immense area, namely the Malayan archipelago, Siam, Pegu and Burmah [sic], all the cats have truncated tails about half the proper length, often with a sort of knot at the end."

And so, far from being a disability or some freak of nature, your furry little tail was the blessed container for a beautiful princess of her precious rings, the holder of a royal goblet, and even a subject of most intense interest on the part of the very man who categorized the evolution of all the animals of history. Besides, who really needs such a long tail? It can get caught in the vacuum cleaner!

———

When I finally got home, I sat my pet down in front of me once again and told him the whole story. This time he sat very still, and his ears quivered a little bit, so I knew that he was listening. "You got your darling little tail when a beautiful Siamese princess was going to bathe in a river in the mountains," I began. "She took off her clothes, and . . ." At this, his little nose trembled and he started licking his paw uncontrollably.

Ignoring this typical male response, I soldiered on. "But she needed some-where to put her rings . . ." At this he looked oddly expectant. Finally, I finished up with, "There, hidden in the long, swishing tail of the sensitive, slinky, sexy Siamese was . . . *your kinked tail* . . . knotted secretively in the luscious tail of the favorite cat of a royal princess of Siam!"

Finally, I took out the atlas and carefully and patiently pointed out to him Darwin's beloved Galápagos Islands in the Pacific Ocean off the coast of Ecuador. At this point, Nikko gave me one of those probing cat stares and then, after a few seconds, lay down exactly on the Galápagos Islands on the map and went to sleep. I understood perfectly how well he understood.

Now there was only one more place that I needed to go on my trip to fin-ish my work—to the Vatican of the Tailless Cat—to Nikko's own Japanese ori-gins. Then I, too, could finally go home again.

CHAPER SIX

JAPAN: MY GOOD FORTUNE WITH THE GOOD-LUCK CAT

Consider the Cat: self-contained, completely its own creature, staking an indisputable claim to any territory it inhabits, and over any action, or inaction, it takes. Serene. Living in the moment. Existing in harmony with its surroundings—which, in Zen terminology, are qualities of the enlightened. If so, the cat is the embodiment of Zen. But it's an unwitting embodiment, a natural one.

JANA MARTIN IN *ZEN CATS*
WITH PHOTOGRAPHER YOSHIYUKI YAGINUMA

As I approached this last leg of my journey, now heading toward Japan, my mind kept reverting with ever more intensity to a theme that had recurrently haunted me from the first moment I found Pasha on the streets of Chicago. This was the theme of "lostness"—a lostness that, just as it has afflicted human beings in times of affliction and devastation, encompassed almost all cats over the centuries at one time or another. It kept recurring in the recesses of my mind like some revelatory moment that strikes you suddenly and then refuses to leave you in peace.

Pasha, after all, had been totally lost physically, if not spiritually, when I so wondrously discovered him. The Egyptian cats became displaced—and, yes, finally lost, too—when they were so cruelly taken by the Romans and the Greeks and all those other jealous usurpers so far away from their sacred homeland. The Burmese and Birman? Well, we know about *them,* don't we? The origins of those beautiful, sensitive creatures are even today lost in history's unforgiving mists. And no one will probably ever know where those pure white diamond-eyes cats, one of the handful of subgroups of the Siamese family, quite belonged.

Oh, cats, like human beings, have surely had their "golden eras," but even those periods were almost always followed by tragedy. And on a larger scale, until the cat clubs and cat shows rescued them in the nineteenth and twentieth centuries and again gave felines a recognized place and status in civilized society, most of the cat families had been lost for centuries. And then, there *was* the night that Nikko actually did get lost, that awful nightmare night when I thought he was gone forever.

The evening marked a special birthday for my good friend Phyllis Eliot Oakley, a talented diplomat who had been the spokesman for the State Department and its head of research and intelligence but was also (sigh) a big-dog lover. We agreed we would celebrate together with a big party. Like, 250 people! For us, at least, big! There is no need to go into the particular birthday that it was, let us just say that it was in 1995 and that it was a memorable one, with both of us looking tremendously sexy and beautiful. With so many people, we had to have the party on the pretty roof garden of my condominium. Phyllis's husband, Ambassador Robert Oakley, whose only bad trait, as far as I'd been able to discern, was that he liked very big dogs—kindly volunteered to set up a tent on the roof that morning.

Now, I fully admit to having a small obsession about my cats, one that many careless and stupid people, even some who profess fully to like or even love their cats, like to make fun of. My apartment, you see, has a small balcony overlooking Washington to the north and it oversees some sweet little gardens, from which Nikko and I early in the morning can hear the birds singing their hearts out, totally unaware that a "ferocious" cat is listening in on their joy. And I have always been terrified of both Pasha and Nikko getting out on the balcony and falling off. Yes, yes, surely you have heard the *assurances*: "Don't you know, cats never fall off balconies? Don't you *know* that, if they do, no matter how high, they never hurt themselves?"

What crass and ignorant stupidity! Cats fall off high places all the time, as any fireman or policeman, and/or the animal welfare service can tell you, and usually they perish. So I had always assiduously kept the glass doors to the balcony locked and opened them only when I was there myself to monitor any movement. But at this big party, not only would we have to have the balcony open, we would have to have the front door open so guests could mingle and move between the balcony and the roof garden. What, then, to do?

I decided that the safest thing to do was to put Nikko in his little airline carrier. At first a cat doesn't like being confined to the case, but soon he or she finds its close embrace soothing and just goes to sleep until released. So it was that, just before the guests began to arrive, I hugged him—later I would remember in some despair that he gave me the strangest, hurt look—and put him in his case, placing it next to the bed in my bedroom. He cried for just a few minutes and pushed at the case with his paw and claws, but soon he went to sleep, just as he always did on planes.

Now, you have to understand the kind of Walpurgis Night it was to become. That night, the bad gods of memoried Mookie decided to wage a destructive swath of war across all of Washington and northern Virginia. Even as we all assembled on the roof, we could see the storm gathering across the Potomac River, moving toward us with a great black sky that seemed to explode on us in an orgasm of rain and wind. They said afterward that there was even hail that "summer's" night in June, and several people were indeed killed across the river when tents were knocked over by the fearsome winds. Others were actually plucked up off the ground and tossed about like paper dolls. The outcome, of course, was that everyone crowded into my condo and all of our careful planning was gone with the wind, so to speak.

How constantly I reminded myself afterward that, no, I had not forgotten Nikko—not for a moment! I checked him regularly, even while our tent on the roof was blowing over and people were jamming into my apartment. Each time, I found him perfectly safe in his carrier case, and I assured myself that I had done the right thing. In fact, each time I looked in on him, Nikko was sleeping nicely, seemingly totally unaware of the Teutonic War of the Worlds going on outside.

It was about 2 A.M. before the storm cleared. We would not know the full extent of the damage until the morning newspapers came out. Finally—finally—everybody went home. I was exhausted. I cleaned up a bit, reassured myself that the glass doors to the balcony were closed, and then went into the bedroom to free poor Nikko from his confinement. I turned on the light, moved to the side of the bed, and opened the case. I waited for him to jump out and confront me with one of his irked RHHHRHHAGGHS. But the case was open—and *Nikko was not there!*

It is impossible to describe my horror, or the emptiness, or the terror. At first, I tried to assure myself that he was somewhere in the apartment. I looked everywhere. I dug into the closets, thinking he might have fled there out of fear of the storm. I searched, I cried, I was near panic. Finally, I made my way up to the roof in the darkness, although I could not imagine in my wildest dreams how he could have gotten to the roof in all of that chaos. It was 4 A.M. by then and the city was calm. Everything was drenched, the tent had buckled in upon itself, and the whole roof was a shambles. I found nothing.

It was impossible, of course, to sleep. All I could think of was that poor little white-and-gray cat, with his funny tail and his sweet and timid soul, lost here or lost up there or—worst of all—having fallen off the balcony or the roof. I sat up and tried to doze, but I could not: I was only waiting until dawn, when I would begin what I now feared would be a terrible search: looking for his little body on the grounds around the building.

Dawn came, but by then I could barely move out of fear. I thought of phoning someone to help me, but I decided to search alone. And so I began.

Once again, systematically, I looked everywhere around the apartment. I called him—from the time he was that funny kitty who arrived from Lynchburg, he always came when he was called, but now there was no response. Then I decided to search the roof again. In the sad dawn, a kind of half-rain still hung over the city, hot and humid and white as a veil. I noticed that lemon peels and cherries from the glasses and drinks were hanging on some of the little trees, making them look a little like surreal drunken Christmas trees. Still, I found nothing. Then, since the sun was coming up and making its way through the sheet of darkness, pouring a friendly light over the scene, I went to the east side of the building to watch the sun rise. And then I saw *it!*

In the pretty, flowering plants on the east side of the roof garden, I spotted something! A white swath! I think my heart stopped beating. I moved closer, and then I could see—it *was* Nikko! But was he alive? If he was, I didn't want to frighten him, because he might get so scared, he would jump off the roof. I decided to call him. "Neek-koh, Neek-koh," I cried gently, and then I saw him stir. He raised his little head gently and slowly turned it toward me. Then he got up and stretched and then ran—yes, ran—over to me and jumped right up in my arms. I cuddled him with all the passion of a wild and demented witch with her devil cat, and he dug his head into the crutch of my arm. He was soaking wet, but otherwise he was all right. I rushed him downstairs, soothed him, covered him with towels, and gave him food and love. To my surprise, he was not as terrified as I had feared (confirming once again that, just when you think you've got cat psychology down pat, they surprise you), although Nikko did go under the blankets and pretty much stay there for three full days.

I shall never forget the moment I spotted, and then found, my lost pet. He was lying in the midst of some beautiful pink and red azaleas, circled in upon himself in that magic shamanistic circle that cats so well approximate. Later, in Japan, at the shrine of Nikko, I would see the famous *Sleeping Cat* portrait with the cat asleep among very similar flowers. Are these all possibly "accidents"? Perhaps you can tell me.

But first you want to know what happened. How did he get out of his case? How did he get to the roof? How did he survive in that awful storm? I have asked those questions of myself hundreds of times and the only answer is "I don't know." There is always the chance, of course, that, in my rush to get ready for the party, I did not fasten his case as well as I should have and that he got out, although that possibility seems slight to me. Could someone have accidentally let him out—or, I hate to think it—deliberately do so? Once free of the case, frightened, he could have gotten out the door in the chaos of the storm and the party and made his way to the roof on the stairs or in the elevator. As odd as it may seem to think that a cat can walk out and slip through people's feet on the stairs, or when they're standing in an elevator, that is in fact what cats sometimes do.

There is the reality that there are many, many mysteries about cats, and that will always remain so. All *I* know is that first he was lost and then he was found.

TOKYO, JAPAN

And, now, as I headed toward Japan, it seemed to me that the larger lostness I had felt about cats was disintegrating and that everything was gradually, but systematically, coming together for me. Pictures were beginning to form in my mind, no longer merely snapshots or even enlargements, but now larger, integrated photographs of history. Was it possible that Japan, Nikko's forefathers' home, would provide me with answers to more questions?

I had just gotten off the plane at Narita Airport outside Tokyo and was making my way through the bustling, busy building, when I saw it: there, in one of the speciality shops with Japanese goods, was a perfectly beautiful cat statue. It was a large cat, made of plaster, about nine inches high, chubby and full-bodied. It was white with the caramel-and-black spots of the classic and precious tricolor bobtail. Its eyes, yellow with big black pupils, stared at you and indeed seemed to follow you with a strangely knowing look. Its nose was yellow and its whiskers were very black and thin; they were drawn rather poetically on its cheeks, rather like a Salvador Dali line drawing. Its lips were sweet-red. Its nails were neatly painted gold, its inner ears were red, and its pert, pleasant little face was half-smiling, as if to greet you—not in any "Hi-Ho!" way but rather in a sweet, homey everyday "Howdy, fellows!" welcome. Around its neck, the little creature had a red collar, from which hung a gold pendant with black Japanese lettering on it, saying, "Good Luck!" I looked behind it to assure myself that, yes, it had a real black bobtail and not some useless long tail that, after all, only takes up more space in the world.

Then I saw the paws. This charming creature had its right paw neatly positioned in front of him, rather like the Egyptian Bastet's, but its left paw was raised next to its head. It was one of the sweetest and most welcoming things I have ever seen; I stopped dead in my tracks when I came upon it, causing the man who bumped into me to become quite cross.

"What *is* that?" I asked the Japanese saleswoman behind the counter, and she stared at me almost the way that cats stare at you when they just can't figure out what on earth you can be thinking. She stared some more. "Why, everyone knows that," she said, rather curtly. "It is the Maneki Neko. He has his paw held up in welcome. Sometimes he wears a neat little apron around his midsection, but today he only has his collar on." She did not explain the discrepancy in dress.

This was my first confrontation with the fact that my Nikko-type of bobtail cat is the greatest folk culture symbol in Japan!

The Foreign Press Center in Tokyo is a professional office sponsored in part by the government and in part by the major Japanese newspapers. Frankly, the officials there not only know everything about the country, but they can find anything—and they have the Diet National Library, the scholarly repository of the Japanese parliament, at their disposal as well. You'd like to see the medical exam of Hirohito in 1943 and wanted to know how the CIA got it? You needed to know if Douglas MacArthur met with a famed geisha at 8 P.M. on Saturday, August 5, 1948, and why? You were curious about the four kamikaze pilots from World War II who were still alive and living happily ever after in Hokkaido? It might take an hour, two at the most.

And they knew nothing about any cat temple!

It was while I was waiting for them to try to find the temple, if there were a temple, that I decided to send a fax to China, where I happened to be traveling next—not for my cat search but simply for general journalistic work, yet hoping there might be some cat-related revelations. I would just see what they might know about the bobtails since I knew that these cats had originally come to Japan through China.

But apparently this request utterly confounded them, for my journalist/guide, Mr. Liu from the efficient All-China Journalists' Association, asked,

"And—what was that message about . . . CATS?" I tried to explain it to him, and it is not too dramatic to say that he was amazed, if not stupefied, at my answer. "Everyone in the office looked at your message on CATS," he said. "They couldn't figure it out at all. They thought it must be some new UN agency." (The Chinese, as it turned out, did not come up with anything on the historic cats, but I did turn up some history on my own.)

Meanwhile, as my bewildered friends at the Foreign Press Center were now getting deeper into my search, they suggested that, whatever the truth was, not only my own cat's dear name but the very wellsprings of my story were to be found at the beautiful Buddhist/Shinto shrine at Nikko in the Japanese mountains. They wanted me to visit Nikko while they rummaged around for more information. It was only about three hours by fast train from Tokyo and, while I was there for two days, they would be looking into my cat temple search. What a fine idea!

NIKKO, JaPaN

From the moment that you approach the shrine at Nikko, you begin a journey into a wondrous spiritual and aesthetic world.

First you come through three avenues of fifteen thousand Japanese cypress trees. Ancient, elegant, weathered wooden farmhouses line the road. Temples were found in this area as early as A.D. 766, but parts of Nikko as we know it today were built as early as A.D. 1617 by the feudal rulers in honor of Shogun Tokugawa Ieyasu and is a mixture of Buddhism and Shintoism. This syncretism of religions—not only styles and forms but also beliefs—is noticeable in the art and architecture of the twenty-two treasure buildings of Nikko.

But if anyone thinks that these Japanese shrines reflect some of the simple "less-is-less" style of so much modern design in Japan, he or she could not be more mistaken. Nikko is a riot of deep and vivid reds and golds, of colors and feelings that smite instead of console as you walk along its exquisite stone passageways. As I was wandering slowly through the great complex of the shrine, trying to understand a little the meaning of all of this searching, I came upon *it* . . .

On the upper cross timber of the corridor of the main sanctuary is the famous carving of the *Sleeping Cat* or *Sleeping Kitten* of Nikko that I was searching for. It is a brightly painted engraving said to be the work of the artist Hidori Jingogo. Around the recumbent kitten there are beautiful carvings representing red and pink flowers and birds, and they are considered masterpieces of sculpture due to the freedom of their design—they look almost modern, indeed almost postmodern, in their bold simplicity.

And the cat itself? It is a charming little white cat with dark gray spots. It has its head down so that you cannot really see the eyes but only the top of the head, which is dark gray. The cat sleeps peacefully, even as we pilgrims mill around him. It is obviously an ancient bobtail-type cat, curled in upon its being, so warm and cozy that one could think only that it represented something deeply spiritual. I found myself stunned and delighted, seeing the juxtaposition of my Nikko's exact style with the "lying cat" of Bubastis in Egypt. In fact, this famous *Sleeping Cat* of the Nikko shrine *looks exactly like my own Nikko!*

I had found what I had come for—but I was still not exactly sure what that was.

Luck was with me when I returned from the shrine. I was having dinner with an old friend, Professor Sumiko Iwao of Keio University, who presented me with a sheaf of papers: There was a map, and a phone number, and the name of the cat temple right there in Tokyo! (Why couldn't the Foreign Press Center find it? Another one of those mysteries that apparently surrounded cats!) The first day I could go out to find it was Sunday, I had to get a taxi and go alone. But it was then that my adventure into Nikko's family really began.

The temple—the formal name is the Jiseiin Temple—was so beautiful that I could at first barely believe my good luck, aesthetically as well as politically. As with so many areas of Tokyo—which is structurally a mélange of ancient villages spliced together with the city's gleaming skyscrapers when prosperity raised its head in the twentieth century—you had to walk to the temple down a simple narrow path, as though you were indeed still in a village. It was clearly quite new, with exquisite modern lines and small, almost miniature, gardens around it, having been rebuilt several times over the centuries.

A stone cat atop a pillar stood at the entrance to the road and a robust, very furry yellow cat, with wise and gleaming eyes, sat unmoving, as if on watch at the entrance to the garden—an omen? Its eyes followed me, even though the eyes did not move.

Since the doors were open, I walked eagerly inside. It was very quiet, and no one seemed to be about. The temple was clearly Buddhist, another outpost of the Lord Buddha's spiritual empire, and it reminded me oddly enough of the Baptist or Methodist church congregations of my childhood on the South Side of Chicago, with its neat meeting rooms, its poster boards filled with announcements, and its rows of small chairs for children. And then I came to the sanctuary.

I entered hesitantly. Being largely unfamiliar with Buddhist practices and being a respecter of all religions, I was not certain I should be there. But the sanctuary was so bright, so cheerful, so lovely, that one really could not assume that one was "invading." Later, when I diligently did additional research, I would find that Buddhism was a most popular and efficacious religion. By this time, there were 70,000 Buddhist temples in Japan, far more than the 24,000 primary schools and the 25,000 post offices, and that Buddhist priests were much like our beloved old family doctors.

And then I saw it: on the altar, there was not one, but *two cats!* They were carved out of dark stone, perhaps some type of soft granite, and although they were very weathered, one still could see the outline of the cats' faces and paws on the large round stones. On top of that, they were dressed! One had draped around its "shoulders" a red cape made of a velvety material, with white lace trimming and a kind of hat that I could only describe as resembling the dramatic flying hats worn by pirates in the Caribbean in centuries' past. I wondered what on earth I had finally found, but not before trying to figure out if the cats' facial features, so totally blurred over time, bore any resemblance to Nikko's.

While I stood there, the priest, a strikingly handsome slim young man wearing immaculate white robes, entered the sanctuary and smiled benevolently at me. I immediately felt peaceful and welcomed. He did not speak English, nor did I speak Japanese, so we could not really talk, but I managed to point to the cats on the altar and then to draw awkward-looking cats in my notebook—and it was then that he generously ushered me into his study and brought out *the scrapbook!* For more than an hour, we looked at the wonderful little book, pictures of children in the temple, pictures of happy young brides and bridegrooms, the joy of a beautiful faith. And then there were the other pictures:

The two cats on the altar were dressed in bright hats and capes, and always costumed appropriate to the season on hand. The children from the temple were pictured gaily taking part in parades—and they, too, were all dressed in wondrous cat costumes. I was filled with the joy of it, and somehow I got through to this good priest that I would be in touch with him the next week. But before I left, I pondered. Remember, these were *stone cats!* And I, and both Pasha and Nikko, had this strange history of interchange and intercommunication with stone cats, whether the one on top of my big chest or the many stone carvings of cats on the Nile.

I stood there for one last moment and I could see Pasha leaping, fully blown so to speak, to the top of this altar and trying to nuzzle these two dressed-to-kill stone cats—and then the picture changed and there was Nikko trying to leap up to the altar and only falling off and tumbling clumsily into the sanctuary, just as he had when he attacked Oma's Biedermeier chest. For a moment I even thought that I could see the two stone cats on the altar give each other "Who-on-earth-is-*this?*" glances.

As I left, it seemed to me that the big yellow cat, flesh-and-blood guardian of the temple, nodded good-bye. Although his eyes did not actually move, he watched me as I walked out down the same path I'd followed before. Or could I have imagined that?

When I returned to the temple I brought with me a translator to meet with the chief priest of Jiseiin—I was now able to find out that this cultured and elegant young man's name was Eichi Osawa—and as we sat in the pleasant parlor, a cat story far more incredible than any I could have dreamed of wove itself around the three of us, not to speak of my Nikko and indeed all the cats of the world.

The elegant simplicity of Priest Osawa's manner and of his storytelling surely enhanced the moment. Even my translator, a retired Japanese military officer named Seichii Soeda, with whom I had worked for many years, at times during the story showed deep emotion at what we were hearing. Mr. Soeda would shake his head slightly, and then sigh a heavy "Ahh-so," which actually sounded at times amazingly like Nikko's sweet and rueful sighs.

The priest began to tell the story of the two cats on the altar. "Five hundred years ago," he said, in the spirit of telling once again a very old tale that had been told many times before, "Japan was in the middle of a civil war between two feudal lords. There was a terrible battle in this area—the Battle of Ekoda-gahara—and the sun was setting on the battlefield. One of the warriors, the noble Dakon Ota, got lost in the forest as the sun was going down—he feared greatly he would be killed by his enemy, the lord of Toshima Castle.

"But then, just at that moment, a small black cat appeared. He motioned for Dakon Ota to follow him, and the warrior did so. After they wandered through the woods for some time in the darkness, the little cat led the lord to the temple that had once stood on this spot—at least in memory, history, and perhaps past myth. There, the warrior/lord was able to stay overnight, and thus he was saved and was never caught by his enemies. The noble cat stayed around the temple and, some years later, after those wars were over, the cat died. Dakon Ota, wanting to thank his small benefactor, made a grand ceremony in that early temple, which most probably stands on the same site as today's Jiseiin, for the dead cat. But he wanted to do something more, so he had a statue of the cat carved out of a precious local stone and presented it to that early temple." The priest smiled. "After all these years, you can hardly see the whiskers carved in the stone anymore," he added, pointing to the altar cats.

I tried hard, to make out the whiskers, hoping to compare them to Nikko's, but, as in Egypt, the large seated carving of the cat god Bubastis, the stone had become too worn to make out a face.

The second cat statue? It was carved separately in honor of a local woman who was the very quintessence of the good wife and housekeeper—a friend had it created and erected after her death and the cat was chosen as the most worthy creature to represent her goodness.

So it was that when at Jiseiin the little children actually came to the temple dressed as cats, they believed that they were in some way being incarnated, too, into the noble cat that saved and spared Dakon Ota—and that thus they could now somehow share in his valiant and protective spirit.

First we learned that the temple has been called in the vernacular the *Neko Dera,* or "Cat Temple," or *Neko Jizo,* or "Cat Guardian Spirit," and that its particular sect had even had memorial services atop Mount Nikko. The word *neko,* of course, means "cat," although it can also revealingly mean "sleeping young." The common Japanese word *jizo* can be a cat statue or it can be a stone statue of a monk with a shaved head, usually holding gems in his left hand and a staff in his right. Most of these statues are considered to be the Buddhist guardian deity for children, as well as the divine guardians of travelers and of pregnant women.

These engaging stone Buddhas, often with little aprons tied around their necks of the same type that Japan's stylized cats wear, can be found standing along country roads in rural districts, even sometimes touchingly half covered in the deep snows of Japanese winter. They represent only one of those many small human touches that the Japanese are so wise to give to such noble representations of their fields and forests.

Still, the overwhelming role of these little cats was infinitely positive. Through the presence and blessing of these symbolic bobtails, the Japanese believed, and believe today, that they can partake of—what exactly shall we call it?—the magic, the spirit, the aura of the stone *jizos*. But these stone symbols are more than the guardian deities of children; they are animals who, not unlike the lore and beliefs about the Egyptian god cats, come to our world and show great acts of valor. In their beings, they not only embody such acts but they inspire humans to ever greater ones. They actively encourage good conduct and are believed to have power beyond common sense, but they are also looked upon as the carriers of the supreme feudal Japanese Samurai values of loyalty, noble self-sacrifice, and unswerving devotion to duty.

By the time we left the temple that day, I had chills running up and down my spine at the ending of the story. For Dakon Ota did not turn out to be just any man. He was the man who built the famous Edo Castle in Tokyo in 1457, where the rulers first lived and he is considered by Japanese historians to be the true founder of this rich period of Japanese life. As for the castle, it became the official residence of the Tokugawa or Edo rulers in 1590, and was expanded after 1603 into a very large castle. The ruling class lived well, under the military shoganate, alternately called the Tokugawa and the Edo period from 1603 to 1867. In fact, George Sansom writes of our hero, in his *A History of Japan (133–1615),* that "Dokan's own residence was in the centre [of the castle], and included apartments furnished in excellent taste, where he held poetry meetings or gave other elegant entertainments, for in addition to his merits as a general he had a fine literary judgment."

By 1888, that castle, seat of the Edo Shoganate, became the Palace Castle of the Imperial Family and after World War II, in 1949, became the *imperial palace of the Japanese emperors and the most sacred place in the entire imperial nation!*

Today the imperial palace, the home of the emperor of Japan, lies at the heart of Tokyo and is surrounded by stone-walled moats and broad gardens. It marks the very heart, soul, and mind of the Japan that has been democratized since World War II. The emperor's powers were balanced during the MacArthur occupation much as the bobtail cats were democratized when they were brought to the United States after World War II, and all of this was made possible only by that small black cat that Lord Ota met when he was lost in the woods! Surely the lord was saved in order to fulfill his destiny—and he was rescued by the valiant creature that suddenly appeared as if called to perform some great deed! I was quite breathless with this new, wondrous story of the valor of cats and their place in our history!

In other parts of the bobtails' history, we know that the bobtails originally came from China, where they were known as early as the Han era (206 B.C.–A.D. 221), and that the cat was prized at certain times in Chinese history. The ancient Chinese *Book of Rites,* dating from the second century A.D., for instance, advises the continuation of certain sacrificial and theatrical ceremonies performed for a "cat god" because of "services rendered by cats to man."

Across the Orient, cats were appreciated and treasured for many of the same qualities that the Egyptians had prized them for—their beauty, the light of the moon held fast in their eyes, their grace of movement, and their ability to inspire in humans the special qualities that they embodied. They were most likely introduced into Japan in the early sixth century A.D., to protect sacred documents from damage by rodents. (Once again, we find the same pattern across much of the world!)

But Nikko's family did not have an easy time in China, because the Chinese and the Japanese looked at their cats in very different ways. The Chinese were utilitarian and they chose cats that could hunt. Until the beginning of the seventeenth century Japanese, on the other hand, primarily judged their pets for their beauty and personalities and actually revered them. This was in great part because, again like the ancient Egyptians, they believed in a true sense of brotherhood between men and all living things. It was becoming clear to me that when these ancient societies were dealing with the symbolism of their cats, they simply always had to have the cats represent the two polar extremes of morality and power.

Even the wondrous pure white cats, with their special magic—cousins of the white Angoras and the Siamese diamond-eyes?—were to be found in both China and Japan! In the year A.D. 999, for instance, according to the *Classified Annals of Japan,* in the reign of the Emperor Ichijo, by the light of the ninth moon, kittens were born at the imperial palace in Kyoto. In fact, the pure white mother cat gave birth to five absolutely beautiful pure white kittens, a most unusual and auspicious event that, in fact, so enchanted the emperor that he decreed that the animals be brought up with exactly the same care given infant princesses! Indeed, it is written that the ministers of the monarch themselves prepared boxes with delicacies of rice and with clothes as for newborn babes and one lady of the court was actually appointed their wet nurse!

But it was in the Tokugawa or Edo period of the progressive shoguns, when the little cat saved Dakon Ota, that the peaceable and welcoming small bobtailed cat appeared everywhere in Japanese woodcuts, in paintings and in artwork, representing that potentially happy stability of human society. It was then, indeed, that Japan's short-tailed cats became so popular and so beloved that they were the darlings of royal society! They were so spoiled that they were led around on silken cords and the long-tailed cat came to be regarded with such superstition—they were called "cat demons"—that the Japanese began to spread the idea that cats with long tails would take human form and curse people, in part in order to explain why the native cats of Japan had such very short tails.

And, why should the bobtails not have been so beloved? Because they represented a time that, as historian Will Durant writes, "inaugurated one of the longest periods of peace and one of the richest epochs of art in human history."

Given the bobtails' symbolic suzerainty, it was only proper that they should be richly robed and clothed, as were the royal Egyptian cats—and they were! They were properly seen in art, in commerce, and in Japanese mythology wearing at least a collar and a medallion, and sometimes the famous apron, while the Buddha statue that so often accompanied them almost always wore an apron. But in fact, the two costumes are most likely related, because the collar evolved from a red apron that affluent ladies of the Edo period put on their beloved felines (usually with a bell attached) that came out of the Buddhist wish to have a child grow up peacefully.

In at least one earlier period, the Heian period between A.D. 794 and A.D. 1185, when the imperial capital was moved from Nara to Kyoto, cats became so elevated that they were considered to be on the fifth rank of nobility. The bobtails also at times became a kind of metaphoric artistic representation of themselves. Ceramic cat statues, which in their time were the scarecrows of the fields and byways, were used to frighten away mice, with small oil lamps lit behind the statues' hollow eyes so that rodents would think the cats were real.

In fact, as I discovered much later, the Maneki Nekos can be found in large and overwhelming quantities at still another temple, the Gotokuji temple in Tokyo. At the heart of this temple, on the altar, appears a most astonishing assembly of cats, ranging in size from one half inch to three feet tall, sculpted, painted, and carved in relief, crowded all together and effectively mounting guard, each one with its small right paw raised to just the height of its eyes. You can purchase cat effigies there for cats that have passed on, and they are all white. (This is the only place, they say, where it is the right paw of the Maneki Neko that is raised, and not the left. What meaning does that have? I wish I knew.) There is even a rather large cat cemetery within the temple grounds. In this temple, which is about two hundred years old, the cats were believed to have acted as a kind of (another role for the Japanese Bobtail!) "messenger" between Buddha and the 500 million Asians who worship him!

There are other stories about noble cats in Japan. But by far the most sensitive and lyrical stories of all about the Japanese cats—in fact, the bobtails—is British writer Elizabeth Coatsworth's *The Cat Who Went to Heaven,* which deals with still another version of the cat in Buddhism, the legend that Buddhism actually advocated the protection of all animal creatures *except the cat!* Except the cat? How could that be, in this beneficent and loving and transcendent faith? Well, another legend (don't hold me responsible if legends contradict one another, please!) has it that, when the Buddha was being called to Nirvana, the cat *fell asleep* on the way to the funeral and arrived too late for the ceremony. It has the ring of truth.

Anyway, in the story, this poor and disconsolate little Japanese cat yearns to be taken into the Buddha's loving and transformational arms, but now he is once again excluded when the poor artist he lives with is commissioned to do a painting of the Buddha's death and must deal with the question of his own cat, a pretty little white bobtail with two big yellow eyes named (what else?) Good Fortune, and whether he must leave the cat out of the painting, thus dooming Good Fortune. Finally the painter realizes that the Buddha's "love for all the world . . . flowed out even to the smallest grains of sand on the furthest beaches." He puts the little cat into the painting and the cat dies out of sheer joy and is taken directly to heaven. Good Fortune is a small bobtail with "a little tail like a rabbit's and she did everything daintily." In fact, Nikko looks just like Good Fortune, just exactly like her.

But there is something far more important to *this* story: this is the only tale I found where the story of redemption, whether we call it transmigration of souls or however we care to characterize it, was not *through* cat but *of* cat. It was not man who was being redeemed through his cat, but the cat himself who was being redeemed. I had now come upon still another entirely new dimension to the entire question of the royalness and sacredness of the Cat.

A Pawnote: I had returned home soon after these events. At a dinner party, I ran into the former Speaker of the House Tom Foley. He had just come back to the United States after serving as the American ambassador to Japan for several years and I asked him if he had seen any bobtails while he was there. He smiled. "Well, one day, two bobtails just walked into the embassy," he answered. "So my wife and I took them in and we ended up bringing them back home to the States with us. It was a long trip and one of the cats was fine. But the other— well, when we arrived home, he went up the chimney and stayed there for twenty hours until I was able to lure him down with some shrimp."

I nodded sagely. Frankly, I was not at all surprised. I had already learned that, with cats, whether going upward to heaven or eastward to the United States, relocating is very hard to do.

But I also was to find conflicts among the Japanese cats and in their part of the rich philosophical culture of Japan—and in fact many of them turned out to be the self-same black/white, good/evil, light/darkness conflicts, each side represented by cats, that I had found in Egypt and elsewhere. It is believed, for instance, that the Maneki Neko, as with so many other moral and philosophical conflicts and spectrums that the Cat has exemplified in the world, is the outcome of two extremes.

As it happens, Zen Buddhism came to Japan from China and developed and prospered during Dakon Ota's Tokugawa regime between 1603 and 1867, and was always wondrously complicated in its contradictions, at least to the literal Western mind. One quintessential Zen story, for instance, has the Zen master advising, "Make haste, slowly."

As to the feline part in Zen, writer Jana Martin wrote that the cat is "a Zen kind of embodiment . . . Rather than taking an element and adding a physical being, the myth takes the physical and adds the element. This is a great distinguisher. A cat does not flash as if it were lightning. Lighting scratches—as if it were a cat." In her sensitive *Zen Cats,* Martin considers the dualities present in the ethereal form of Buddhism known as Zen in which the characterizations are dramatically similar to the Egyptian ones. "There is the cat god of lightning, a frenzied creature called Raiju, who leaps frantically from tree to tree in a thunderstorm, scratching the trees with its razor-sharp claws and creating the sound of thunder. Then there is the cat god of good luck—Maneki Neko, who sits beneficently with its paw raised . . . In the complex history of this myth, the gesture of the raised paw may be based on images of cats washing their face—an action they sometimes perform in the company of strangers. At some point, a link was made between a cat washing its face and the presence of visitors; as time went on, it became causal—the sight of a cat washing its face could actually mean visitors were coming. From there came the next step: a cat washing its face would invite visitors, much like an inviting hand."

It all seemed clear enough to me on my own homey terms: Pasha was Bastet in Egypt, Nikko was Maneki Neko in Japan, and both were saints on earth; Mookie was Sekhmet in Egypt, Raiju in Japan, and Lucifer in hell. In fact, I found the Cat in Japan, as elsewhere, represented the extremes of ambivalence among men and the most complicated spiritual thinking among theologians and poets.

I began to wonder, what kind of Zen wisdom would Nikko himself tell of, were he able to speak? He might say, "I sleep because I sleep," to be also interpreted as "I sleep because I am," or, "And sometimes I do not will myself to sleep, it just happens." Bordering on the style of my sister advice columnists, this might be: "Always get enough sleep during the daytime while she's away so you'll be fresh to bite her fingers and force her to play between 2 and 4 A.M." At least, this is the way I have interpreted the thoughts that Nikko would put down, if he were writing his *Book of Zen Thought*—from a cat's point of view, of course.

Meanwhile, I was being struck by—and enormously invigorated by—the comparisons I was finding across all the countries I had studied and visited. Those early societies seemed to have a far greater sense of brotherhood between men and living things than we experience today. In Japan as elsewhere, cat's eyes are believed to reflect everything from the time of day to the movements of the moon, and the old idea of a transmigration of souls at death from human to animal is also found there. We see the concept often says Barbara Nixon in her *Cats of China and Japan*. "[It] manifests itself as homage to unseen powers, as in the Japanese veneration of animals after their death . . . Sometimes the soul will go into the animal form briefly until it frees the human soul that was contained within the animal form on earth and allows it to attain eternal perfection."

Above all else, in Japan, the historic bobtail—the inspiration of artwork and of spirit, Dakon Ota's black cat—was a good luck or a good fortune symbol. They were not sacred, as in Egypt, and not royal, as in Siam, but rather had the quality of a good omen, of a medallion of good fortune. All I had to do was look at Nikko to see how true that was.

Then after the great centuries of happiness and recognition in early Japan, once again came disaster and tragedy for cats. Between the thirteenth and fifteenth centuries, the imperial court, not wanting to force its beloved pets to actually *do* something as horrible as catching mice, thought it would be enough for the mice just to know that cats were around. These exercises in unreality, like all illusions, of course only set up their supposed beneficiaries—in this case, the Japanese cat—for a fall, and it was not long in coming. Even after the fawning and adoration, the Japanese cats, rather like the Egyptian cats in Roman captivity, were themselves doomed to suffer direly from such insistence upon delusion.

So it was that on one desperate day early in the otherwise brilliant and humane Tokugawa period—a year that will live in infamy in all cat history—the imperial government passed decrees stating that all cats were to be "set at liberty," which only meant that they were to be thrown out onto the streets. It was forbidden to give, buy, or sell cats. While still prized by artists and others, Japanese cats effectively became a working class; thus, in only one year, Japanese cats went from their pampered lives at court to wandering at large in order to rid the country of vermin! (Sometimes bad things happen to good cats.)

After this perfidy and humiliation, the bobtails remained mostly street cats in Japan until after World War II, when sympathetic GIs brought them to America and the Japanese Bobtail, with all of its ups and downs across history, became one of the great breeds of the cat world, with a most fascinating and little-known history.

When I got home, Nikko was waiting at the door, as my assistant Rita had said he waited every day for me for those long weeks that I was traveling. When she would come in to feed him in the morning, he would be standing there—not sitting or even sleeping, but standing—staring at the door. When she entered instead of me, he would automatically turn around and go into the living room and pose on the little couch he so loves to scratch, his furry little tail twitching with anxiety. But when I came, he would not leave me alone or get off my lap. His damp pink nose rubbed my wrist with that precious moisture of the Cat and his little bunny tail made him seem ever more the personification of the cat in its eternal circle. Nikko looked very peaceful and happy then, so much like the famous sleeping cat of the temple in Nikko.

I felt that Nikko knew his story already, that he was indeed the lost progeny of a great long line of tailless cats—and from Egypt, too, having only stopped off in China and Korea for a while, perhaps to look around. Not only had his great-great-grandparents been led around on silk strands and guarded the great silk fields, but wonder of wonders, he was the offspring of the cat who saved the man who went on to build the greatest palace and inspiration of art and faith in all Japan and was the architectural and artistic midwife for the entire Japanese imperial system! Nikko's family line would never be as regal as the Egyptian family, but his own Family of Cat was interwoven deeply into the religious and spiritual significance of still another great world religion, Buddhism.

And yet, I thought I had to tell him more directly, since he still seemed shy and much too thin and vulnerable.

The week after I came home, I invited my dear friends Mary McDermott Coder and Mary McGuire over to help me. We got together earlier in a coffee shop in Georgetown to go over the "script" and so everyone was ready when we got together that night.

"Oh, Nikko," Mary Coder said first, "look at you, so much prettier and so much more pert than a cat with a long and frivolous tail!"

At these words, Nikko, who had naturally been sleeping, got up and stretched theatrically. I mean, not just stretched, but sttrreeetttchhedd . . . He even held the pose for a full minute before he collected himself, into his usual little bundle of fur. Then he sat there and just looked at her—stared, really—for quite some time.

Then Mary McGuire, looking directly at him, said in a soothing voice, like a doctor's or a psychiatrist's, "And then there was the wondrous story of Dakon

Ota and his heroic cat, the same cat who, through saving the Lord Dakon, was memorialized forever on the altar of a beautiful temple in Tokyo."

By now, Nikko was posed, with quite deliberate dramatic consciousness, on one of the embroidered pillows on my couch, but I knew he was only pretending not to listen, for little ripples of attention, like swirls and waves in a gathering sea, moved from his neck across his fur as Mary spoke.

But it was when I told him the wonderful story of Good Fortune, and how that cat went straight to heaven, that his ears twitched, really quite noticably, in my direction. His eyes also flickered oddly from time to time. And when I opened the book to the page with the charming picture of Good Fortune, who, it did not escape him, looked exactly like his own good self, he got up, stretched again, meandered slowly (surely so as not to reassure us too quickly) over to the open book, sniffed the page carefully, and then lay his whole body down on her page—really for quite a long time—before he went quite soundly to sleep on it. Nikko always slept through the night after that. In his preternaturally perfect circle.

In fact, from the moment of my return, he surely grew into a far more confident cat than ever he had been. He smacked his lips now while purring. He was often ARFFING instead of RRHHHRRRING, a development for which I have no explanation at all. His sweet and modest style never left Nikko, but it did seem to me that he became somewhat more aggressive as he lost a lot of his fear and his excessive vulnerability.

Later on—in 2001—a bobtail actually won the International Cat Show and we were watching television when it was announced. Nikko had been asleep but he suddenly sprang—delicately to be sure, but still sprang—up! His eyes burst open, his tiny crooked tail stood up as straight as ever it could, his eyes gleamed black instead of their accustomed yellow, and there was for a few minutes a certain kamikaze air about him that I had never dreamed he possessed! Another evening, we were watching TV films of World War II and there were dramatic films of Japanese battleships and Zeroes fighting American ships and air support in the Pacific. Again, he seemed suddenly agitated. I wondered for just a moment that night: "Was I sleeping with the enemy?"

But no, he was only exercising a certain confidence that had come to him with the discovery of his noble roots. Each time, he finally only yawned and stretched—and went back to sleep in his sweet half circle, with his little white paws and their very pink cushions carefully pushed together, just exactly as oriental people do when in their traditional costume. Sometimes he stretched his front legs out in front of him and his back legs out behind him. At times like this, he resembled nothing so much as the Egyptian sphinx, instead of the drowsy "let-me-sleep" cat of Nikko or the chubby little "Come-on-in-please" Maneki Neko of Japan. Then, almost always, he would settle into one position in which he looked for all the world just exactly like the sleeping cat of the Nikko temple.

And, indeed, he probably was *all* of these!

CHAPTER SEVEN

COMING TO AMERICA: BECOMING *SOMECAT!*

Every life should have nine cats.

ANONYMOUS

CHANTILLY, VIRGINIA

There are people who love cats but who still don't like cat shows. That's all right, I know some of them myself. My cat-loving German friend Uta's particular aversion to the shows were not that she didn't like all the kvetchy, tchotchke stuff, like the Meow Marts, the Calico Coverings, the socks with little cats embroidered all over them, the Bastet and Sekhmet pens, and even the ice cube trays that produce (my favorites!) perfect cat-shaped cubes for special sunset soirees.

No. She cannot bear to see the little cats from the pounds—HOMELESS signs figuratively hung around their necks—on exhibit. They wait in their small cages and it is sincerely hoped by all that they, too, will be adopted and find happiness. It is just too painful for her to think of them, at the end of the day, being carried back to the pound, another dream burst in their young lives before they have even lived, another travesty of hopes gone awry.

Then there are people, even true cat lovers, who still feel that breed cats— the specific, regulated, interbred *breeds* that today form the international cat world and cat shows—are simply royal fancy cats (or royal fancy-pants), spoiled princes and princesses. Underbrained and underfoot, these precious pusses have been bred far too long away from their original sturdy working-class ancestors across the sea—but still do not have exactly the "class" of their royal ancestor cats, either. (There are as many differences about how many full breeds there really are, and which cat associations recognize them—they can number between forty-one and more than seventy—as there are quarrels about which of our cats is the most perfect!) These people object, for instance, to the fact that some of the cats at the shows are so made up that they sometimes even have sunscreen dabbed on their precious little noses and ears to protect them when they are out in the sun (actually, cats' noses and ears *do* get sunburned!).

But I do not feel this way. I fully enjoy the cat shows, particularly if they are held in big, airy, modern, lighted, and air-conditioned spaces, as you can well understand.

On a beautiful sunny Saturday—September 8, 2001, to be exact, just three days before the terrorist attacks on New York and Washington—I traveled to the national cat show at Chantilly, one of those pretty and prosperous northern Virginia Washington suburbs. This show happened to be in the large and very airy Expo Capital Center, which had lots of space and sunlight between the different cages of the cats and thus presented an unusually attractive spectacle. The cages were expecially roomy and they stood in neat lines. So many of them had beaded or embroidered or sequined coverings that I wondered if they had come from some ancient Egyptian or Greek temple (the cats did not have Bastet's earrings, although the men and women there surely did).

The cat "owners," if we can in truth call them that, for there is always the big question here of who owns whom, usually sat by the cages, politely but often archly answering the questions of strangers and pleased and proud to show their pets (but don't touch, please: diseases spread that way). Cat lovers don't actually laugh a whole lot—in fact, there was an air of dead seriousness about the whole day that I found, oddly enough, to be quite natural and "right." It was a bit like a bookshop, with authors showing and selling their beloved books, or an antique show, except that these books and these antiques were flesh and blood.

After Nikko and I had seen the International Cat Show on television, when the Japanese Bobtail won first prize, I had looked for the winner's "human," and finally I found him in Allen Scruggs, who had had more than fifty winners in various cat shows and on different judging levels with fully fourteen of them being national champions. I reached him at his Nekomo Bobtail Cattery ("Nekomo" means "cat" in Old Japanese) in Winston-Salem, North Carolina, and we agreed to meet at Chantilly.

When I finally did find Allen Scruggs, an attractive, gray-haired man with a nice, friendly air about him, he greeted me in a slightly preoccupied manner. "I am looking for a feather," he announced. Then he just walked away for a while. Once he found the feather, a gray one as I recall, perhaps to match his own hair for his bobtails were white and carmel-colored, we sat down alongside his cages and talked.

"You see, I always liked the Japanese culture and many things about it," he began. "I think the Japanese aesthetic is just wonderful—the tea ceremony, the fine art, the architectural landscape design . . . I was an interior designer and I began to use the Japanese aesthetic in my work. I lived in Manhattan then and I went to a cat show in New Jersey and there was this brown bobtail and I just fell in love with it. I tried to buy him and I couldn't; but the next week, at another show, the man decided to sell him." The cat's name? He shook his head, almost abashedly. "MacGregor, of all things!" he answered. "Well, he won the second-best cat in premiership in the U.S. in 1985, so one thing led to another and I got to know cats all over the country. I collected bobtails from seven different lines, and they're very playful and loving. I've been breeding them ever since."

"Do you want to see my top winner?" he asked. I wondered why he would even ask?

Scruggs had been playing with the most adorable carmel-and-white bobtail kitten, a little sweetheart about four months old, who was scampering about in her cage, enchanted with the gray feather, and then, when he took her out for a moment, licking his face and nuzzling his nose, her entire little body infused with an impish spirit. But then he put the kitten away in one cage (where it promptly went to sleep, a real adult cat in the making) and took out his winner, who was grandly and impressively named Grand Champion Nekomo Bobtail

Junko Yamada 2001. This bobtail was an all-white cat, rather like one of those magical diamond-eyes that I had first laid eyes on in Bangkok but which weave wondrously, always alone and apart, through many "human" histories—and it was exquisite!

In fact, it was your perfect bobtail body, lithe and strong, but it was also tiny, tiny, tiny. Not even two thirds of Nikko's size! In fact, it was so delicate, it almost looked like Dresden china. Scruggs picked up Grand Champion Nekomo Bobtail Junko Yamada 2001 and showed her to me the way the judges do, holding her up in the air carefully, with two steadying hands, spreading out her front and back legs so that the cat seemed to be floating in the air—and I thought I had never seen such a gorgeous sentient creature! All the time, the champ gazed at me with that perfect infinite calm of the true winner who just knew she was the most gorgeous girl in the whole wide world!

"She is named after a real person," he went on with a very sober air. At that, he looked at me and then the cat looked at me, too; in fact, Grand Champion Nekomo Bobtail Junko Yamada 2001 gazed steadily at me, as though she knew something I did not know. (Did she perhaps know where the Lao-Tsun temple was?) "I think they are real people," he added, but really as an aside because, at this show, who was going to contest that?

Later, I paused to wonder: At home, in everyday conversation, when you're just hanging out, perhaps fixing coffee in the morning or getting ready for bed, what do you call a friend with a name like that? In fact, I put that specific question to Allen Scruggs one day. "Junko, I call her Junko," he responded, as though the most dim-witted fool ought to be able to figure that out. "It's just like the first name of a lady. Like Shirley or Mildred . . ."

Just then, a woman from Maryland stopped by who had waited two years for the birth of a bobtail with exactly the spotting that she had dreamed of. Needless to say, the cat was now her most-treasured pet (and no doubt fit right into her home decor and design, as well). "I take her to the senior homes," she said, "and the old folks love her—but many of them can't see, and when they feel her, they think she is a bunny."

At this point, I could not help but notice that the lady with the cage next to Scruggs's who had a very white and very pug-nosed and (what else?) very snippy-looking but gorgeous Persian, was very busy meticulously daubing a fine white powder carefully around the furry cat's bright little eyes. I was aghast—but Allen Scruggs assured me that this was quite in accordance with the rules, and that powdering a cat's upper and lower lids was one of the few "cosmetic" changes people could make on their cats before judging. It reminded me, of course, of Cleopatra and her beautiful eye makeup, which in turn was inspired by the fashion and style of the Egyptian cat goddess, Bastet.

Allen Scruggs had long ago fulfilled all the requirements that the international cat world places on owners: he had been a member of the Japanese breed clubs and councils and even a judge for the Japanese breeds; he met twice a year with the governing council of the Cat Fancy, as the international bodies and people are popularly called, and knew other breeders and exhibitors all across the country. He talked perfect cat show "talk," discussing how, in this distinctive society, one breeder would serve as a "mentor" for another. I realized that day that this is a marvelous and creative community—a little wacko because obsessed people are always a little wacko, and that is also what makes them so arresting.

———

Now, I have to pause here and say that, for much of the rest of the afternoon, I was close to breathless. For as I roamed and roved around the cat show that day in northern Virginia, there before my very eyes I was seeing the real-life descendants of all the cats I had studied—most of whom I had never actually *seen!* Moreover, I quickly understood that when I looked at these beautiful creatures, I was seeing very different things from what the other cat lovers there were seeing. They saw graspable todays and, at most, tomorrows—shows to be won, victories to be grasped—I was seeing centennial and even millennial yesterdays.

By chance, the three cat breeds that *are* today the most direct descendants of the Egyptian god cat were the first I came across in my wanderings.

First of all, I found the pert and alert Abyssinians—their special deep-brown ticked coats, every hair having many colors, so distinctive that they were often called the Hare Cat or the Rabbit Cat or the Bunny Cat, because their coats resembled those animals' coats. These Abys, as they are fondly known, are also often called the "personality cats" of the breeds because they have such cute, and often trickster, manners. They often affectionately greet strangers at the door and even learn quickly how to mischievously open doors in order to let their fellow cats slip through. (Their antics reminded me of Pasha—and brought tears to my eyes, remembering the many tricks he seemed to devise to amuse and bemuse me.)

Others looked at these Abys and saw beautiful and beloved house cats or only pretty accoutrements of civilization (or maybe rabbits or hares or bunnies). But when I looked at them, I saw slim Bastet sitting regally in her poised and posed manner sailing in her barge down the Nile to reign over the raucous spring festivals; I saw the temples at Karnak and Bubastis and the little statues in the Egyptian Museum of the cat goddess so lovingly carrying her market basket for her family; I saw images of eternity and of our curious and unending search for it in these innocent creatures.

In cages next to the brown Abys, I found the silver Abyssinians, known today as Chinchillas, with their shimmering and luminous silvery coats. Next to them were the Somalis. These are one of the "designer breeds"—breeds that are not historically original, or natural, but were created through the specific breeding of specific types of cats. They are wild-looking creatures, often described as having a striking resemblance to the fox because of their large ears, full ruff, and masked faces. In truth, they are gentle, soft-voiced, companionable, and very frisky, taking inordinate joy in playing tricks like running sidewise, holding food in their paws, and even turning on water faucets.

Some people saw these two breeds, deliberately created by human inbreeding, and wondered if they were not too beautiful to get along with the children in the family or whether their unusual colors would match their decor—I saw two cat families created after the di*cat*spora from Egypt through the union of Abys and other cats; I saw the offspring of the cats that nursed the pharaohs, traveling as slave cats to Rome and Pompei and probably across abusive medieval Christian Europe before finding their way to England. There they mated with others creating these lovely breeds. I sighed, pondering for a moment all they had seen and all they had been through.

In the next row of cages, I found the Egyptian Mau, also a direct descendant of the Egyptian god cat, its very name meaning "seeing" or "light" in Arabic. Others that day doubtless thought of these exquisite silver-and-black cats, with their bold stripes, as just beautiful and beloved pets. I looked at them and recalled how the Maus have a perfect M as a dark markings on their foreheads—this mark is alternately said to be that of the sacred scarab beetle, the Egyptian long-life symbol, or, in Italian legend, the mark of the Virgin Mary. In the manger, it is said that a small Mau cat was the only one who could soothe the Infant Jesus, and it was for that reason Mary put the M on his forehead to bless him.

Think of it: only this one beautiful breed of cat is a veritable repository of rich religious imagery. (But don't miss the fact that the Mau's cheeks are artistically decorated with "mascara" line, exactly like Cleopatra's own and that the fur on the head resembles the Egyptian long-life scarab!)

Close by (immigrants always form their own communities), finally and joyfully, I found the third Egyptian cat, a tabby kind of shorthair itself, with its furry gray/black stripes and its charmingly wayward expression. Other people looked at this venerable cat, chubby and gregarious, and saw the homey "common" cat of the fireside and hearth, the cat your daughter picked up, wet and miserable, as a kitten on the street, saved from the alleys of mankind, and nursed back to health. "Alley cats," they used to call them, half out of homey affection and half out of disdain—and few would ever dream that they might ever be found in a starring role at a cat show!

But I looked at the tabby shorthair and remembered all the wonderful pictures of the "spotted cat"—*this* cat, surely!—in Egyptian life and lore. (How could I forget the wall painting from a temple at Thebes, dating from 1400 B.C. showing a spotted cat on a duck-hunting trip, or the papyrus, from about 1100 B.C., showing the sun god Ra in the form of a spotted cat?) Yes, that same playful, cavorting tabby-patterned cat that Americans love so much and that crosses all breeds, while they think of it as everybody's everyday cat or everyone's sweet home cat, actually was just as royal in Egypt as good Bastet or bad Sekhmet!

Still another Pawnote: It must be noted that these modern-day "Egyptian" cats were not upright, proud, and distant like their Egyptian forefathers and foremothers. In fact, they were playing and scampering about and kissing humans and (like all smart cats) catching a snooze whenever an opportunity presented itself before, the wondrous call, "Hey, it's curtain time!" Every cat becomes more relaxed in the New World.

I turned another corner, back by the coffee shop, where I overheard a couple discussing whether the Oriental Shorthair or the Balinese actually had the most luxurious hair. (It seemed a toss-up to me, frankly.) And then I came upon these gorgeous breeds and so many others. The long, lean, thin Siamese were there, as glorious as ever, with some of their many gorgeous offspring, the exotic Javanese, the alluring Tonkinese, and the exquisite Balinese.

Down the lane were the stark black Havana Browns, who surely look as though one had just walked out of a sexy Havana bar in the 1940s on Ernest Hemingway's arm; the adorable American Curls and Scottish Folds, with their sweet and slightly drunken curled ears; the charming American Wirehair; the wild Ocicat; the barely known LaPerm; the cute shorthaired Cornish Rexes, Devon Rexes, and Selkirk Rexes; the odd hairless Sphynx; the European Burmese; the wild Siberian; and the exotic Chartreux and the Exotic; the Himalayan; the Ragdoll; the American Bobtail; and, of course, the popular gray Korat.

Next, I found the sturdy British and American Shorthairs, the Exotic Shorthairs, the Colorpoint Shorthairs, and the elegant Oriental Shorthairs, with their long, slim, and ruminative faces reminiscent of early paintings of Italian Renaissance women; and I paused to remember how my old vet on Clark street in Chicago would, or so I thought, put Pasha down by insisting he was just an "American Shorthair." *Indeed!* Now those "just a shorthairs" were right there in this new "palace" for the modern "royal" cats of the world!

I walked around another corner and there were the charming Birmans, with their chubby gray and white furriness and—of course and above all else!—their pristine white paws.

Some looked at them and saw the most aristocratic of cats, with their stunning beauty and regal manner. I saw mysterious caves, filled with Buddhas in the north of Burma; I could hear the chanting of the monks as the attackers came, and I trembled at that moment of transformation when the sacred cat's paws slowly turned white, hair after hair after hair. One Birman stopped swiggling about in his cage when I walked up. He stopped short, pulled himself up in all his luxuriant furriness, and looked me very squarely in the eye. He held my attention tightly for quite some time, staring at me as though he knew something. (Perhaps *he* knew where the Lao-Tsun temple was.)

Then, the Burmese. After my great search for them in Burma and across Southeast Asia, this was the first time I had actually *seen* them, and I realized immediately why they were so beloved. There is something so small, so square, so playful—so utterly clear and dear about them—that they seem in many ways your Ur-cat, your quintessential cat, your *very essence of cat.* As such, they had none of the mystery of the ethereal Birmans; they did not stare at me but just went about their business, which at the moment was resting, and so I did not have a chance to ask them about the Lao-Tsun temple and the monk.

By accident, I came upon the the Turkish Vans. These lovely cats, which hail from the Eastern part of Turkey are furry white cats usually found with black and gray and caramel spots but also with solid colors. Their story is that when Noah's Ark arrived in the waters at Mount Ararat some five thousand years ago, just about at the beginning of the Egyptian cat saga, two of their ancestors leaped into the water in what was admittedly a certain overzealousness to touch dry land. It was then that the Turkish Vans learned to swim, the only cat in the world to do so. Not the Romans, but the Crusaders carried these beautiful cats to Europe sometime between 1095 and 1272.

Next to the Vans were the related Turkish Angoras, another one of those all-white cats, with one yellow eye and one blue eye that seem to have been left to develop their beautiful selves alone, on isolated islands of civilization all across the world. It turns out that the modern capital of Ankara was originally the old, word-related capital of Angora and that these white cats were born there. The Turks confused them with Persian cats because they had long hair on the neck "like a lion" and carried their tails parallel to their backs. Like the diamond-eyes white cats in Bangkok, they are haughty and more than a little psycho. Yet because of their beauty, the Turkish sultans in days of old presented them to foreign dignitaries, just as the Siamese kings did, and the great Turkish reformer Mustafa Kemal Ataturk is said, in Turkish legend, to be returning some day, reborn in the shape of a white Turkish Angora with one blue and one golden eye.

Turkey gives us a superb example of what countries and governments can do to preserve their precious historical cats.

When I visited there in the spring of 2002, I found that the veterinary school of the university in the Lake Van area had taken as its major task the gathering, caring for, and breeding of the Van cats! Think of what would happen if every country could or would do that!

And then there were, of course, *my* bobtails. Others look at these small, compact, playful cats and see the perfect household pet. A "little person" wrapped in fur! But I looked at them and saw Dakon Ota, lost in the forest on a stormy night, fleeing for his very life; I saw the emperor's palace being painstakingly built in Tokyo; all of this made possible by the black cat that saved Dakon Ota that dark night. And after centuries of misery and sadness out on the streets of Japan, I saw the GIs after World War II, carrying these creatures quite literally in their knapsacks back to America.

Today there is even a still obscure "Kurile Island Bobtail," from the Russian-controlled islands just north of Japan. As far as I can tell, this is the first "Post–Cold War breed" and thus is an important symbol of the twenty-first century.

When I left Chantilly that day, I was grasping many new convictions fully for the first time. Because of the new freedom and the new egalitarianism for cats, and also because of the concerned intervention of man, more new breeds arose in the twentieth century than in the history of domestic cats before the century began. This gives catdom remarkable new reach!

At every turn, one can see the clear overhang of the cat's royal and sacred past, reflecting in and out of the mirrors of this new present. Once their ancestors came to America, and like all immigrants, cats worked hard to become modern cats (insomuch as the word "work" can ever really be applied to them) or at least to put their pasts behind them. In America, the men and women of Germany, Italy, and the Pale of Russia became *somebody*. Once in America, cats too, left behind *their* pasts—in Bubastis and Ayudha, in Nikko and Ankara—and became *somecat!*

And, today, the American Shorthair, with its pert, bright trimness, is right up with the regal Persian; the tabby shorthair with its Liza Minnelli "bob" is there with the Norwegian Forest cat and its long Veronica Lake hair; the shorthair and the bobtail are breeds just as much as the newer and less "in" "designer" fancy-cat Burmillas, Tiffanies, Himalayans, Bombays, and Chin Chillas. At cat shows they not only compete against their own breeds but against all the others: American democracy truly won out in the end, each individual against each individual, because of or perhaps in spite of its good, solid family ties! The royal and sacred cats of old had now become the grand champion breeds of America; my furry little friends had gone from Bastet to the breeds, from royalty to rules and regulations, from shadowy Inle Lake to the brightly sunlit Expo Capital Center in Chantilly, Virginia. These modern breed cats—prized for many of the same qualities as the royals and sacreds—were now the *cool cats* of this new democratic and competitive egalitarian setting, and the cat show was the last act of the long drama for the cats, which had once strode the temples as tiny titans.

I did pause before I left the show to wonder whether—perhaps when their humans are arguing over whether to get the cat boxer shorts to match the cat socks—the felines might whisper across the aisles about the old days in Thebes and Saqqara, in Lao-Tsun and Ayudha, in Nikko and in Persia, or what they had really done at the spring festival on the Nile, or what the Siamese monks didn't get right when they wrote their hoary cat treatises in ancient Siam or, currenty, which breeds today were really only copycats?

But while I strongly suspected that many of these things really did take place in the privacy of their cat conversations, I was never able actually to confirm my suspicions.

When I got home that night, I told Nikko all about the show. He was lying crosswise in my lap as he usually did, with his head down so far on the side and his little rump up in the air, the bunny tail quivering only once in a while in the sheer joy of being so loved, and it was hard for me to tell if he were listening—or dreaming. I told him in some detail what I had found. At one point, his eyes opened and he looked at me, one of those frank-cat looks, as though he wanted to burrow right through to my soul, but on the other hand wasn't quite sure what I was talking about. Then he curled up in my lap again and went to sleep, stretching out his chubby little legs in every direction and frankly looking very funny and even quite undignified (he never did rise or fall on false dignity). I could not help but note that he was purring in his sleep. Probably he was thinking about how smart Allen Scruggs was to raise only "beautiful bobtails."

But where had the idea behind the cat shows, the cat breeds, and the prize cats actually come from? How and where did they come to life en route from the Nile, the Irrawaddy and the Mekong to the Thames, the East River, and the Mississippi?

After the Christian Middle Ages, when cats were too often persecuted as the "consorts" of witches, to their renaissance in the 1800s, the influence of science was rising in the West and it was hardly surprising that science also entered the equation when the cat slinked into it. Instead of being worshiped, the cat now became the subject of scientific research that attempted to understand it in a new, hopeful, and generally refreshing manner.

As early as 1607, the English naturalist Edward Topsell published one of the first books to deal scientifically with cats, *The History of Four-Footed Beasts* (it surely pains me to hear our beautiful cats called "beasts," but there it is!). Far more agreeably, Sir Isaac Newton in those same years is credited with the invention of the cat door or cat flap for his own pets, thus indicating the degree to which people of culture were now learning not only to appreciate feline society but to make it part of the home. At the same time, Louis Pasteur's work on the real causes of disease in the nineteenth century quickly made hygiene into such a "craze" that during this period dogs were touched by fastidious people only with white gloves, but the cat, always licking and cleaning itself and appearing so fastidious (except, one hastens to mention, in its mating habits), was considered a model of cleanliness. Cats fit beautifully into the spirit of the Victorian era with its gingerbread lives and its proper Protestant principles declaring that all were equal if they behaved morally and worked hard. (Although, frankly, the Protestant work ethic never really even came near cracking the hoary nap ethic of the cat.) The early question of Henry David Thoreau—"What sort of philosophers are we, who learn nothing of the origins and destiny of cats?"—seemed to have come full 'round.

The next step was to incorporate cats into the larger culture, with standards of their own, as though they too were a respected family sometimes with an illustrious past. Thus emerged the idea of breeding the cat. It was in England that cats had finally found, not the royal and sacred home of the past in which they reflected the search for god and nobility, but a humanitarian and loving home, in which they reflected the modern satisfaction with the individual human self. Finally, they were to end their wanderings and their often cruel di*cat*spora.

Harrison Weir, the founder of the cat shows, was an archetypal nineteenth-century British gentleman of Victorian times, a big, ruddy Englishman with a rather fearsome, bushy white beard. Weir had the soft sweet soul of a poet and the higher sensibilities of his time. A Fellow of the British Horticultural Society, he was an artist and a passionate and egalitarian cat lover to boot. Because of his kind, idealistic nature, all the Victorian do-gooder dreams of his era became focused for Weir on the idea of breeds and what the cat shows, along with the breed standards that he introduced, would do for all cats.

Weir wrote at the time, "I conceived the idea that it would be well to hold cat shows, so that different breeds, colours, markings, etc., might be more carefully attended to, and the domestic cat sitting in front of the fire would then possess a beauty and an attractiveness to its owner unobserved and unknown because uncultivated heretofore."

Weir organized the first real cat show at London's Crystal Palace in 1871, and thus was born what came to be known as the Cat Fancy, which is simply the popular and fanciful name given to the entire panorama of cat breeds, cat clubs, cat shows, and cat attitudes across the world. His first club's motto was "Beauty Lives by Kindness," but Weir had other "odd" ideas, like insisting upon a special class for "Cats Belonging to Working Men." And what a show that first cat show was! Ladies in long flowered dresses and sweeping hats mixed with elegant gentlemen and, yes, even working men and women, all went to see . . . *little cats,* often reclining gracefully on crimson, gold, or midnight blue pillows and staring curiously at these outrageous creatures who had for so long abandoned and mistreated them and who by now seemed so oddly intent upon once again worshiping *them!*

Indeed, the shows began in the late nineteenth century as a reflection of the reforms going on inside British society and a reflection as well of the importance of individual growth in the Western world. But just at the time that the cat was once again becoming prized, now as a clean and virtuous friend and home companion, and, indeed, symbol of the growing middle class, many of the little creatures were still out on the streets of London, living lives of misery along with the poor British of the early industrial era. Such contradictions were unsustainable for the Victorians, whether with humans or with animals.

In short, these reformers looked at the cat—and found still another "friend" to "save."

No one could escape Weir's hand as a *cat's*-paw of the creatures he had so come to love. One day, as he wrote in his groundbreaking 1889 book, *Our Cats and All About Them,* Weir related how, on the day for judging at Ludgate Hill in London, he ran into a friend who joined him in his railroad car. "How are you?" asked the friend. "Tolerably well," Weir answered. "I am on my way to the Cat Show."

"Well, that surpasses everything!" exclaimed the insensitive friend. "A show of cats! Why, I hate the things; I drive them off my premises when I see them. You'll have a fine bother with them in their cages! Or are they to be tied up . . . ?"

Weir barely tolerated this, finally saying, "I am very, very sorry that you do not like cats. For my part, I think they are extremely beautiful, also very graceful in all their actions, and they are quite as domestic in their habits as the dog, if not more so. They are very useful in catching rats and mice; they are not deficient in any sense; they will jump up at doors to push up latches with their paws . . . They know Sunday from the weekday, and do not go out to wait for the meat barrow on that day . . ."

Finally, Weir summed up: "That is why I instituted this cat show. I wish every one to see how beautiful a well-cared-for cat is, and how docile, gentle, and—may I use the term?—cossetty . . . Now, come with me, my dear old friend, and see the first cat show."

The story, of course, had to have a happy ending—and it did. When the friend saw the beautiful cats reclining on cushions, far from the grimy alleys that had been their home in the past, their only sounds a homely purring as they lap new milk, surrounded by the most fashionable men and women of London, he became interested. "What a beauty this is!" he exclaimed, "and here's another!" And of course, the gentleman ended up with two homey cats, curled up right on the chair next to him at his home, and, of course, he adored them.

In America, the first Cat Fancy was born with a Madison Square Garden cat show on May 8, 1895, the importation of cats into America having been officially approved as early as 1749. With typical American organizing genius, many societies were then formed, celebrating the talents of the cat, such as various librarians' organization and the Cat Library Society in America. From that period onward, both in England and in America (and also now in many other countries, notably Australia and Japan), cat shows became a regular and popular event and, as once again in history, cats became the subjects of works of art, showing clearly their representational importance for their eras.

I mentioned earlier that the great early nineteenth-century Japanese artist Ando Hiroshige had portrayed a lovely cat in an evocative window overlooking Mount Fuji in his woodblock, *Right Cat Looking at Fields at Asakusa,* which hangs in the British Museum, The cat is wound around itself, sound asleep, as though the world were utterly forgotten. It is a typical representation of the earlier cat style of Japan. But symbolically representing the new era, in 1913 the great Russian painter Marc Chagall put an equally charming little cat in his *Paris Through the Window.* In Chagall's equally lovely but spiritually very different painting, the cat is wide-awake, ears perked up and mouth open, as though speaking to the scene, as indeed modern cats had begun to do. No one called them "alley cats" anymore; and while they were no longer the inspiration for godliness and royalty, they were now the force behind the advertising of hundreds of capitalist products and for motivational therapies of all sorts, not to mention the joy of their owners.

Meanwhile, talk about cat fights! There were endless internecine fights within the Fancy—over breeds, over standards, over imagined slights to one's cat's appearance or breed that were often interpreted almost in civil rights terms or egalitarian/legal discrimination terms. Jealousies and ambitions often reigned, impelled by the inspiration of the cats. In fact, Cat Fancy history is dotted with "peace treaties" between clubs, with the formation of new federations and with "ententes" (Metternichian, Kissingerian, Kaiser Wilhelmian?—it is difficult to say). Some contend it is even whispered from cat cage to cat cage that the cats themselves actually see a "Human Fancy" at work in the world about them, that the cats call the fights over the breeds "human fights," and that, when these occur, the animals sit back and pretend to get some shut-eye, preferring not to have to see or hear how their humans choose to embarrass them so. But I could never really confirm this.

And yet, as the cat fully entered American folk culture in the nineteenth century, images and memories of the Egyptian god cats were always there, casting a spell over just about any art or literature about the cat. In her wonderful book, *Cats on Quilts,* Sandi Fox, the former curator of quilts at the Los Angeles County Museum of Art, writes, "When the cat moved to Europe, she took with her an image with which she had been associated in Egypt, the sistrum, a four-stringed instrument; no doubt this led to the medieval portrayal of cats playing fiddles."

> Hey diddle diddle!
> The cat and the fiddle
> The cow jumped over the moon.
> The little dog laughed
> To see such craft.
> And the dish ran away with the spoon!

In this famous nursery rhyme, "The Cat and the Fiddle," which generations of children heard in America, we found again underneath everything the Egyptian cat goddess Bastet, her sistrum instrument now a fiddle, along with the cow goddess Hathor and, always and of course, the moon! Over and over, Bastet and her refined image were gradually reconfigured in America, where she was now newly stylized, more as a tabby but with that same upright and knowing Egyptian mien, especially in American rural folk and decorative art. And this was particularly prevalent on American quilts!

But in contrast to the rigid stylization of most of the sistrum-playing Egyptian cats, these violin-playing American cats-on-quilts were free, modern, curvaceous cats—their figures were liquid and moving. And, because of the modern cat's sinuous, curving lines—unsquared and fluid as flowing water—the cat figures were often thus appliquéd on quilts.

———————

I had started out with essentially three questions. Now it was time to answer them.

What could and should human beings alive today learn from the ancients? Does their experience tell us that cats are more than "animals," that perhaps they have a "culture" of their own? What does this knowledge tell us about the special—the unique and precious—relationship of our own cats today to ourselves?

As the Egyptians knew, the cat personified the revealing "otherness" of animals, thus ever expanding and enlightening our own human horizons. As my Burma search revealed, cats provide mystery in our lives and the capacity to imagine, to dream and to live on wholly other plains of existence, and yet in the end they somehow understand one another in ways we had never dreamed of. As the Siamese knew, the moon could indeed be caught and held fast in their cats' eyes, and that really meant that they were expressing the possible relationship between sentient beings and the light of the planets. And as the Japanese had discovered over the centuries, good cats do *surely* bring good luck!

There was a reason, too, that they would see things in animals that we, with that errant assurance and confidence of our secular times, barely recognized. For in brilliant ancient civilizations, in the so-called "pagan" religions like the Egyptians, there was abundant space for cat goddesses or sacred cows or even (ugh!) crocodile gods. Not understanding the world in which he lived, cautious early man safely worshiped everything that cried out in the night, shrieked in the forest, or glimmered like the moon. There were so many gods representing so many sides of the human soul and personality that there was plenty of space, too, for the animal qualities.

When the Judeo-Christian heritage came with its "One God," where could cats enter this single-minded world? Whether the frolicking gods of Mount Olympus or the stylized cat mother with her basket in the Egyptian Museum, all were equally banned! Now there was no more psychic and spiritual place for the relative virtues or vices. No longer could man relieve himself of some of his human pain by diluting his complexes in his sweet and transformational regard and love for a small creature who was alive like him, but different.

One must also ask: Is there perhaps also a *culture of cats?* In fact, there has been a world of discussion about this.

What we humans alive today, then, could and should learn from the ancients is that they can immensely deepen and broaden our emotional understanding of our cats. Just try to listen to them and to understand *their* perceptions!

"Animals have no culture," Konrad Lorenz, the great Viennese-born ethologist, animal behaviorist, and Nobel Prize–winner wrote, without the slightest hesitation, at the height of his work in the mid-twentieth century. But today, human researchers of high stature disagree with the venerable Lorenz.

Elizabeth Marshall Thomas, in her classic book, *The Tribe of Tiger,* answered Lorenz directly: "On the contrary, animals most certainly do have culture. We fail to realize this for no better reason than that our experience with populations of wild animals is so severely limited we are not often in a position to see much evidence of culture." She is thinking of culture not as theater, ballet, or art, but as a web of socially transmitted behaviors, and she writes that "culture in animals comes about in precisely the same way that it comes about in human beings, by each generation learning from the generation before." There is a growing school of thought across the country that reflects such ideas.

I have myself seen this reality acted out in dramatic form. Three times, I have been to the Galápagos Islands off Ecuador, the "enchanted isles" that Charles Darwin was drawn to when he circumnavigated the globe in the 1850s, studying natural species and developing his famous theory of the evolution of the species. (And, yes, that was the same time he wrote about discovering how the oriental cats lost their tails in Southeast Asia!) The first places I visited, the animals there had never known man, and for that reason, they did not fear him. It was a strange, lost world, but one of unique balance among God's creatures. The baby sea lions swam playfully with me in the shining seas, while their grandmothers rode the waves like dowager surfers. Ancient turtles, which disappeared elsewhere in the world seventy thousand years ago, moved so slowly that they seemed to be aching with historical exhaustion.

One day on the lava rocks of James Island, when we approached a group of furred sea lions on the rocks above a particularly beautiful grotto, the animals suddenly fled in terror. Had I done something wrong?

I asked our scientist/guide from the Darwin Station if there was an explanation for what had happened. "You may not believe this," he said slowly, "but this is the only island where the animals were hunted."

I then asked, aware of what he was really trying to tell me: "When would that have been?"

He looked directly at me as he answered, "Two hundred years ago."

Now, truly, I gasped. "You are trying to tell me that they have passed that knowledge down within them through the centuries . . ."

He nodded. "Yes," the scientist said, "I am."

I knew at that moment that there are stranger things in this world than we have allowed ourselves to imagine—but that we could imagine, if only we allowed ourselves to do so.

The longtime student and protector of cats, the late Roger Caras wrote about these questions once, with an appropriate, but rare, sense of wonderment: "We know that cats were objects of trade and were carried as symbols of status and exotics. Did the legends that so often parallel them, thousands of miles apart, travel with them? Did the magical aura of Egyptian, then Grecian and Roman gods and goddesses, travel as adjuncts to the cats themselves? We can't be sure, of course, but it would seem likely that two forces were at work."

And Nicholas J. Saunders goes still farther in his perceptive and original book *The Culture of the Cat:* "Today, the cult of the cat is more pervasive, and complex, than ever. Although magical images of huge cat-like monsters, sorcerers, demons and deities have been banished to the realm of fantasy and film, images of the big cats are still universally employed to convey authority, power, prestige and wealth. Countless households are the domain of a seemingly infinite variety of domesticated felines. Current ideas about cats as pets reveal much about the way we live, our mores and our ever-changing view of the natural world and our place within it, just as ancient attitudes revealed similar features of past societies.

"While modern attitudes would doubtless seem as strange and incomprehensible to our ancestors as their beliefs appear to us," he summed up, "the image of the feline has nevertheless retained its hold over the human imagination."

So, in effect, whether there is truly a culture of cats must be left up to every individual cat lover.

And, finally, *our* relationship with *our own cats?*

In olden times, the ancients looked at the animals' qualities and tried to emulate them and to learn from them. They transposed both their own qualities and questions upon them, watched to see what happened and then came out knowing far more about both the animal and the human kingdoms, infinitely deeper understandings of both their cats—and themselves. Today, instead, we egocentrically want cats to appear "human," and so instead we anthropomorphize, we impose our qualities upon them, and pretend that *they* are like *us*—and all because we so surely, casually, and worshipfully place ourselves, and not gods and goddesses, at the very center of the universe. Too often, we like to imagine that they are aspiring to be human beings, while they surely choose in their heart of hearts to think that we are honorary cats.

Even today they are, as they were in ancient times, the extension of our human souls. They represent man's spirit, in different form, yet in a form available to us. To truly understand this reality, think of the differences between humans and dogs—and humans and cats. Dogs have always represented man's physical being; cats, our spiritual being. Dogs work; cats *be.* Dogs search for attention; cats *demand it.* Dogs run or bark; cats *stretch and sleep.* Dogs are from Mars; *cats are from Venus.* We thought that by categorizing them in the breeds and in the cat shows, we could discipline their mystery, make them walk on a leash or dance on hind legs. Don't give it a thought. The mysteries are still there and always will be—we just call them by different names today. In the end, we complete ourselves in them and they in us.

Although I did not understand it when I began my search, I came to realize the degree to which, in the great anthropologist Joseph Campbell's understanding of the world, cats and our relationships to them were indeed part of the great subconscious of myth and legend that we all share together because we all partake in them. The cat is one of the archetypes of the collective conscious, one of the infinite images that are reflections of the myths we share, a revealing part of the "elementary ideas" at the base of human life that spread across and enrich and revivify virtually every culture.

And so, tonight, look carefully at your cat: if you do not see the moon in his eyes, if you do not sometimes feel him entering your soul and carrying it away, or if you do not in the next moment see her busily carrying her little basket to market or meticulously adjusting her earrings, you aren't really looking and you surely are not feeling or seeing as deeply as you could be.

It was the New Year's Eve after I had returned from Asia, and I was sitting quietly and thoughtfully in the comfortable brocaded armchair I usually work from. There was a sense of quiet in the air and, yes, peacefulness, too—for my quest was finally reaching its end, as I realized the extent to which my love for my own two cats had opened wholly new worlds, sentiments, and understandings to me.

Nikko seemed to think that his part was done, too. He was curled up on the ottoman next to me in one of those perfect little balls of fur. His pinched head was burrowed deep into his white chest and his front paws were turned in against themselves, resembling Japanese dancers with their wrists pressed together and their palms pressed outward in greeting. His eyes were so tightly closed that one had to wonder whether what other worlds he was now visiting. Yet there was also a new confidence in his walk. During the day when I was writing this book, he kept pawing and pawing and pawing at me for attention; finally, in desperation, I put my beautiful Belgian brocade pillow at the end of the desk and now he sleeps there all day while *I* work. At times I have had the distinct feeling that he now thinks of himself rather as my overseer, which might well be true.

Just the week before, I had received a welcome call from the Pentagon from Susan Wallace, the public information officer for Secretary of Defense Donald Rumsfeld. He had agreed to an interview. But before she hung up, Susan said, "Oh, I pulled up some of your columns and the cat column from Egypt was just great."

When I did the interview, Secretary Rumsfeld, by then the second most powerful man in the world, asked me what I was writing on. Since we were at war in Afghanistan, I demurred, fearing he would think me less serious than I wished. Three days later, I got a letter from him, saying in a devilish tone, "I wish you great success with your book on the *reigning cats*." How did he know? I can only guess that our intelligence agents were somehow onto Nikko, and so I double-locked the doors every night after that.

Then the strangest thing happened one night as I was finishing my quest. Little, modest, unassuming Nikko, who was always scared to death by the sound of the telephone or even the fax—went quite crazy. Unlike dogs, cats can suddenly revert, usually very briefly but noticeably, to the wild; I wouldn't say that Nikko totally reverted, but he did suddenly become a kind of crazy cat, doing things he had never done before. Perhaps he suddenly felt, for all his apparent modesty, that, since he now truly was a celebrity cat, he had to prove it. Out of nowhere, he suddenly decided he was going to play with the stone cat!

Nikko crouched down on the floor. (I put down the newspaper I was reading and I silently watched. What on earth could he be up to?) He took several very deep and melodramatic breaths and then he jumped . . . Not one of his usual halfhearted, really pitiful little attempts at jumping, but one huge jump. His short little legs seemed to disappear in the leap, which reminded me for all the world of the noble little cats of Inle Lake leaping till the end of time. My God, I thought, there he goes—and there, in fact, he went, up to the very top of my grandmother's hutch, where he immediately sidled up to the stone cat. It would have been pathetic, were it not so oddly charming, for Nikko now cuddled up to the stone cat, then rolled over next to it, eyeing it lovingly. Unlike Pasha, he did not try to go through the ceiling, but he did put his head next to the stone cat's and then, when he saw I was looking, leapt smartly down, clearly immensely proud of himself.

At this, he strolled away, head up and tail standing straight up, as though I had to be taught how woefully I had underestimated him. Before he left the room, he stumbled over a small stool displaced there, but he just picked himself up and bravely soldiered on.

And so at the end of my journey, I got out my map of the Cats of the World, their historic journeys and their many di*cat*sporas. Like some odd Marco Polo or poor-man's Charles Darwin, I had tried to lay out maps and family trees for

THE FAMILY OF CAT PHOTO ALBUM

1. **Abyssinian,** Dave Dybas, Highgait Paws, Clintondale, New York; 2. **Abyssinian,** Alana Hueston, Highgait Paws, Clintondale, New York; 3. **American Curl,** Keith Kimberlin, PROCURL HAREM, New York, New York

4. **American Curl,** G. Scheffer, PROCURL HAREM, New York, New York; 5. **American Shorthair,** Sharon A. Reuther, Fort Madison, Iowa; 6. **American Shorthair,** Linda Beard, Seaside, California; 7. **American Shorthair,** Linda Beatie, Paradox Photography, Petaluma, California

8. **American Wirehair,** Helmi Flick; 9. **Balinese,** Helmi Flick; 10. **Bengal,** Charlotte Norris, Suite Bengals, Augusta, Kansas; 11. **Birman,** Marilyn Rowley, Barmar Cattery, Beavercreek, Ohio

12. **Birman,** Linda Beatie, Paradox Photography, Petaluma, California; 13. **Bombay,** Helmi Flick; 14. **British Shorthair,** Helmi Flick

15. **British Shorthair,** Linda Beatie, Paradox Photography, Petaluma, California; 16. **Burmese,** Linda Beatie, Paradox Photography, Petaluma, California; 17. **Chartreux,** Helmi Flick; 18. **Cornish Rex,** Linda Usher, Cowboy Claws, Plano, Texas

19. **Cornish Rex,** Linda Usher, Cowboy Claws, Plano, Texas; 20. **Devon-Cornish Rex,** Linda Usher, Cowboy Claws, Plano, Texas; 21. **Egyptian Mau,** Jan Wydro, Matiki Cattery, Atlanta, Georgia

22. **Egyptian Mau,** Linda Beatie, Paradox Photography, Petaluma, California 23. **European Burmese,** Shelley Amundson, Mastrpeace Cattery, Shawnee Mission, Kansas; 24. **Exotic,** J. Faith Forrer, Faithful Felines, Neenah, Wisconsin; 25. **Havana Brown,** Linda Beatie, Paradox Photography, Petaluma, California

26. **Himalayan,** Linda Beatie, Paradox Photography, Petaluma, California; 27. **Himalayan,** Helmi Flick;
28. **Japanese Bobtail,** Linda Beatie, Paradox Photography, Petaluma, California; 29. **Japanese Bobtail,**
Carl Widmer, Marianne Clark's, Kurisumasu Cattery, Beavercreek, Oregon

30. **Javanese,** Helmi Flick; 31. **Korat,** Jim Brown, Li'l Minx Cattery, Calgary, Alberta, Canada; 32. **LaPerm,** Beth Fillman, Calico Rose Cattery, Bridge Hampton, New York

33. **Maine Coon,** Helmi Flick; 34. **Manx,** Helmi Flick; 35. **Mixed Breeds (left to right):** Domestic Shorthair "Tuxedo," Turkish Van, Tonkinese, Weems S. Hutto, Flower Mound, Texas; 36. **Mixed Breeds (left to right): Black British Shorthair, Maine Coon, Maine Coon, Blue British Shorthair,** Helmi Flick

37. **Munchkin,** Ken K. Taylor, Sandkats Cattery, Ledyard, Connecticut; 38. **Norwegian Forest,** Helmi Flick; 39. **Ocicat,** Helmi Flick; 40. **Oriental Shorthair,** Helmi Flick

41. **Persian,** Karen Claybin, EZ2LUV Cattery, Vancouver, Washington; 42. **Persian,** Linda Beatie, Paradox Photography, Petaluma, California; 43. **Pixie-Bob,** Linda Beatie, Paradox Photography, Petaluma, California

44. **RagaMuffin,** Kim Clark, Ultimate Rags, Fort Lauderdale, Florida; 45. **Ragdoll,** Helmi Flick; 46. **Tonkinese and Russian Blue,** Helmi Flick; 47. **Scottish Fold,** Ann M. Walkinshaw, Honolulu, Hawaii

48. **Selkirk Rex,** Barb Kimmet, Cuddly Fur Cattery, Spencerville, Ohio; 49. **Siamese,** Helmi Flick; 50. **Siamese,** Donna White, Sealed With A Kiss, Manhasset, New York; 51. **Siberian,** Korporate Kats Photographer, Kathy Wade's, Croshka Siberians, Winder, Georgia; 52. **Singapura,** Nicki Ruetz, Moontan Cattery, South Bend, Indiana

53. **Snowshoe,** Barbara Roth, SnowAngels
Cattery, San Marcos, California; 54. **Somali,**
Mary Ellen Zydell, Felidacity Cattery,
Havana, Florida; 55. **Sphynx,** Linda Beatie,
Paradox Photography, Petaluma, California

56. **Tonkinese,** Linda Beatie, Paradox Photography, Petaluma, California; 57. **Turkish Angora,** Barb Azan, Azima Turkish Angoras, New Ringgold, Pennsylvania; 58. **Turkish Van,** Donna R. Homann, Mattoon, Illinois; 59. **Turkish Van,** Jack Reark, Matabiru Cattery, South Miami, Florida

Pasha and Nikko. And I had tried to give to all cats everywhere—regardless of race, gender, creed, color, mixture of colors, spots, length of tail, temperament, spiritual or gender preference, or religious persuasion—a deeper understanding of themselves. For whether Egyptian Mau, Snowshoe, American Bobtail, Korat, British Shorthair, or Chicago alley cat, theirs was not some royal pedigree but a rich and true history.

And at the end of the trail, I had found, among my other discoveries, a truly amazing one: *all cats are royal!* After all, they all came from Egypt, every single one of them! Today all cats are related to one another, and all cats are interrelated to the breeds, every single one of them! They make up an acknowledged society: they have their own clubs, their own maps, their own family trees, their own genealogy, their own genetics, their own decor, and their own style of dress (although the earrings seem to have gone out of vogue). They have their own Vatican—Egypt. They have their own royal court—Siam. They have their own haunted house—Burma. And they have their own commercial trademark—Japan.

On my piano were pictures of Pasha next to pictures of Nikko. I did pause for a moment to wonder whether Pasha, were he still alive, would think of Nikko as rather an upstart? Or whether Nikko would think of Pasha as rather a pretentious old bore? (But I didn't dwell on this very long or go into it very deeply; good mothers never encourage jealousy and strife among their children.) For surely they were both part of my family, but they were also—now—part of their own family. No longer only pets, they were now relatives. Now I could not only *say* but actually *prove* that my two cats were related. So my instincts had been right from the very beginning . . .

Perhaps at first I had thought, with that accustomed propensity of humans to believe that they are the instigators of all things, that humans are the cats' inspiration and interpreters. Now I know that, in truth, the cats reveal us through what we choose to make of them. The cats lead us to interpret them so that they become the interpreters and symbolizers of us—and that is exactly what happened in the many societies that made them into royal and sacred creatures. We didn't give *them* meaning, they give *us* meaning.

And so, even though our beloved pets will die, as will we all, at least now they will not die some random, pitiful little creatures, without history, ballad, or manuscript. For if we choose to know them truly, they now will always live properly enshrined in stone and in sculpture, in genealogy and in legend, in map and in myth. And always, always, in our hearts.

PART TWO

THE FAMILY OF CAT

I believe that all cats are or can be beautiful and that they share in that sacred and royal spirit that they exemplify in themselves and inspire in us humans.

Often, nonpedigrees like my beautiful Pasha, who probably *was* an American Shorthair, just like the Chicago vets said he was, are far more beautiful and have more personality than the pedigreed cats. Besides, all cats are sacred and royal because they all originally came from Egypt and they partake of all of the beliefs and legends that accompany them around the world. Still, in the Family of Cat I have focused on the pedigreed cats because they are clearly defined and cats everywhere share some of their representational characteristics.

However, please do not think it was easy deciding which breeds to focus on, which breeds to just mention, and which groups and associations within the Cat Fancy to depend on. In fact, all of the groups have some discrepancies in the breeds they recognize, some are breeds-in-creation, and still others, breeds-in-waiting, and some will be your next most popular cat in America and England, and some, sadly, will wither by the wayside.

To name only a few of the major groups over the years, there have been the American Association of Cat Enthusiasts (AACE), the American Cat Association (ACA), the American Cat Fanciers' Association (ACFA), the Canadian Cat Association (CCA), the Cat Fanciers' Association (the CFA), the Cat Fanciers' Federation (CFF), Cat Fanciers, the International Cat Association (TICA), the

Traditional Cat Association, Inc. (TCA), the United Feline Organization (UFO), the Canadian Cat Association in Canada, the New Zealand Cat Fancy in New Zealand, the Governing Council of the Cat Fancy (GCCF) in the U.K., the Fédération International Féline (FIFe) in continental Europe, and other smaller ones. And, of course, there are special clubs for all of the special breeds.

But of all those worthy organizations, the Cat Fanciers' Association is the largest in America and is considered the most comprehensive. I have, therefore, profiled the forty-one they now recognize fully as breeds as well as some of the other most popular breeds. (Other organizations recognize at least twenty more.) At the end of this introduction, I will list many of the charming breeds-in-waiting. Forgive me if my numbers are not perfect, for the cat world changes every hour, if not every minute, and there are many breeders always rightly challenging the given numbers.

First, what *is* a breed? A recognized cat breed is defined by a breed standard, of the kind that Cat Fancy founder Harrison Weir first laid down in the late 1880s in Great Britain. This standard describes the cat and its physical characteristics, but it includes more than color, pattern, or hair length. A pedigreed cat will consistently produce kittens of the same physical conformation, coat quality, and temperament, while a cat of many "colors" will not. Years of selective breeding and the careful recording of all those generations of cats is the guarantee that each new litter of kittens will have specific qualities. The term "outcrossing" is used when there is breeding between two cats who have not had any ancestors in common for three generations.

Less than 1 to 3 percent of the cats across the world are pedigreed, that is, cats of a specific breed, and each cat everywhere is capable of being a wonderful pet, if well treated.

As I have already noted, cat breeding emerged in the middle of the nineteenth century in England when a middle class arose alongside the Industrial Revolution and new attitudes toward animals began to form. No longer just worker/dogs or mouser/cats, these animals could now become pets and so return to the royal status they had lost so much earlier. Today, too, there are other divisions even among the breeds: there are traditional cats—like the "apple-headed" Siamese up against the sleek new Siamese—and almost every short-haired breed now has its long-haired sisters and brothers. Others suddenly sprang up through a genetic accident—and were then bred.

Here are only a few of the cats I found waiting in line, perhaps to be taken in as full breeds and open to championship competition soon: the Highland Fold, the Munchkin, the Ruffle, the Snowshoe, the Chantilly, the Savannah, the York Chocolate, the Pixie-Bob, the Australian Mist, the Nebelung, the Sokoke, the Chausie, the Brazilian Shorthair, the California Spangled Cat, the Cherubim or Honeybear, and the Ojos Azules. Some of the new spotted cats, like the Savannah and the Bengal, are the result of matings to wild cats and are bringing in all sorts of new questions about "breeding" and the number of generations it takes for domestication. Good luck to all of them and to all cats everywhere.

I have deliberately named this section the Family of Cat for a precise reason. When I was in college at Northwestern University in the 1950s, the famous picture book *The Family of Man,* the book of photographs by Edward Steichen, was issued. It had wonderful photographs of human families across the globe and seemed to exemplify our idealism about human beings living peacefully together. It seemed to me that it was time for a Family of Cat to show the complexity and breadth of that animal family, as well.

THE BREEDS

- The Abyssinians and the Somalis
- The American Curls
- The American Wirehairs
- The Balinese and the Javanese
- The Birmans
- The Bombays
- The Burmese and the European Burmese
- The Chartreux
- The Colorpoint Shorthairs
- The Cornish Rex, Devon Rex, and Selkirk Rex
- The Egyptian Maus

- The Exotics
- The Havana Browns
- The Japanese Bobtails and the American Bobtails
- The Korats
- The LaPerms
- The Maine Coons
- The Manx
- The Norwegian Forest Cats
- The Ocicats
- The Oriental Shorthairs
- The Persians and the Himalayans
- The RagaMuffins and the Ragdolls
- The Russian Blues
- The Scottish Folds
- The Shorthairs
  - The Brits
  - The Yanks
- The Siamese
- The Siberians
- The Singapuras
- The Sphynx
- The Tonkinese
- The Turkish Angoras
- The Turkish Vans

THE ABYSSINIANS AND THE SOMALIS

If one breed most closely approximates the original first cat that strolled out of the darkness of Africa tens of thousands of years ago or stands as the standard bearer for the style, bearing, and physical presence of all the other cats descended from that breed, there is little question that the choice would be the Abyssinian or, as he is affectionately known across the world, the Aby. The sleek creature has Made in Egypt written all over him. The Egyptian Ur-cat, she is alternately the serious Bastet riding down the Nile or the mischievous prankster deftly opening doors with his paws. The Aby even chooses to pose on high places, as though invoking his ancient place on the walls of the temples and the tombs.

Oh, there are surely questions about whether this handsome fellow, with his dapperly ticked coat, sailboat ears, svelte body, racy whiskers, ruddy red-brown coat, and alert and almost illuminated eyes (which normally have a fine dark line encircled by a light-colored area to accentuate the gold or green eyes), is really the only or even the major descendant of the Egyptian god cats. Admirers of the Egyptian Mau cat, a beautiful creature as well but with a spotted coat that is much fuller, insist that their cat is actually the original Egyptian cat. The sweet and homey tabby, as well as a dramatic and wild-looking striped cat seemingly displaced from Africa, are both to be found in various places in the tombs.

As great a cat specialist as Harrison Weir wrote that he believed the Abyssinian was the result of intentional breeding in England from the old but supposedly more "common" tabby stock. Other specialists insist that the breed came out of the crossing of the various silver and brown tabbies. What is believed to be the first example of an Abyssinian—a taxidermy specimen dating from the 1830s apparently purchased from a supplier of small wildcat exhibits—is in the Leiden Zoological Museum in Holland and bears the name awarded it by the museum director of the time, *Patrie, domestica India* or "Born in India." Could the Abys' original home possibly have been India? No one can really know.

By far the most believable story about the popular Aby is that the first cat came from Abyssinia, commonly known today as Ethiopia, and was brought home, probably around 1868, by one of the British soldiers stationed there. The kitten was named Zula and she became the grandmama of all the Abys. In the January 27, 1872, *Harper's Weekly* one finds the first mention of an Abyssinian, when the third prize in the December 1871 Crystal Palace show—the first cat show!—was awarded to an Abyssinian cat. In Gordon Stables's early and influential book *Cats, Their Points, and Characteristics,* published in 1874, there is even a colored lithograph of a cat with ticked coat without the common tabby markings on its paws, face, and neck.

The other cats, while certainly beautiful and valuable in themselves, are almost surely pretenders to the throne. The Abyssinian is closest in appearance to the African wildcat *(Felis silvestris libyca)* that was the ancestor of all domestic cats. With their long, lithe bodies, deep-set eyes, their flying ears, their odd, serene demeanor, the Abys bear an eerie similarity to Bastet. At the same time, there is a touch of Africa in the Abys, just a hint of the wildcat transported into this civilized cat body. In fact, they look at you as though they know that you know that they know that you know from whom they are descended—and you quite rightly ought to! The Cat Fanciers' Association also designates the Abys as the most likely descendant of Bastet. The Abyssinian became a separate breed in England in 1882, with silver Abys among the early colors. They were imported to North America from England in the early 1900s and by the 1930s, they had formed the foundation of the American breeding program.

But how did the original god cats get to Abyssinia or modern-day Ethiopia? We can only conjecture that after the Persians kidnapped some of the Egyptian cats and took them to Persia, they became the Persian breed. After the Roman conquerers took hundreds, maybe thousands, of Egyptian cats to Europe, and after more spread across the Silk Road and the various trade routes to the Orient, somehow some of them ended up in Abyssinia on the east coast of Africa and there, in relative isolation, re-created themselves in the physiological and spiritual image of Egypt.

Whatever happened along the way, today the Aby is one of the most popular breeds in the world—almost always one of the Top Ten. Four colors are recognized. Besides the basic color, which is ruddy burnt-sienna with brown and red ticking, there are the blue (warm beige ticked with slate), the red (red ticked with chocolate brown), and the fawn (warm rose ticked with cocoa). All seem to be indiscriminately adored by their owners, who make up for their cats' relative quietness by bragging of their beauty ("A living work of art," says one owner), their intelligence, their activity, their love of water, their loyalty, their generosity of spirit (he always "wants to help," says one Aby mother), and many more wonderful qualities.

Then there are the Somalis, another CFA breed which is closely related to the Abys. Actually, the Somalis are simply long-haired Abyssinians, but they look so different that it is almost impossible to believe they are of exactly the same genealogical family (which happens often, as it does in your own family). When we say "long hair" in this case, we mean really long hair. The Somali is a gorgeous cat, usually of a wild reddish color, looking very much like a small fox with huge ears, a full ruff, and a bushy tail. Unlike your classic Aby—the perfect, coiffed, ready-for-any-civilized endeavor cat—this sister looks ready for action in the wild. That is her charm: she looks wild but is utterly gentle in nature, sweet-voiced, and totally companionable, despite the wild ruddy ruff, which in some Somalis looks like a huge beard.

The Somalis are always into everything, sometimes running sideways like a monkey. They have been known to turn faucets on and off, and they like water. Several times a day, they have bursts of energy, running around the house and leaping into the air. Somalis come in four colors, ruddy, red, blue, and fawn.

Oddly enough, this talented and colorful creature was a source of prejudice and resentment. (It has happened before in the Cat Fancy.) When the first long-haired Abyssinian, George, was born in 1969, he was brought by his fifth owner to a private Abyssinian breeder and shelterer in Gillette, New Jersey, Evelyn Mague. His parents had been pedigreed cats from fine Abyssinian lines, but Mague felt that her cat had been treated no better than a street tough because of his seemingly reckless '60s-style long hair. It almost became a civil rights case, for Mague was determined to get these cats accepted, but the traditional Aby breeders equally refused to allow their name to be used for a longhair. Finally, Mague cleverly chose the name "Somali" because the little land of Somalia was found at the eastern and southeastern borders of Ethiopia, which was once known as Abyssinia.

Today, there is no need to defend the Somali breed. It is an extremely popular breed. Many Aby breeders feel that because they are so close to the Abys genetically—only one gene that determines coat length differentiates them—they should not be a separate breed. But this is, always remember, the Cat Fancy, and one cannot always determine what moves its, well, fancy.

THE AMERICAN CURLS

When you try to encompass the extravagant spirit of this unique cat, think of the costumes at the Ziegfields Follies in New York in the high days of Broadway! Think of Catherine the Great's dressy balls at the glorious Catherine Palace outside of St. Petersburg in the eighteenth century! Or remember for just a moment the most dressed-to-kill movie starlet at the Academy Awards in Hollywood during the romantic age of the stars!

Then you'll have an idea of the irrepressible spirit, the vivid style, and the sheer outrageousness of this thoroughly and uniquely American breed. With its fantastic ears that curl back and give it the look of a cat that is always intently listening to you, its full and plush plumed tail, and its beautiful and expressive movie cat's face, the American Curl is not something you are going to find at a Quaker meeting in New England, at a Mies van der Rohe building in Chicago, or in a Finnish sauna in Helsinki.

This is a true cat of excess: *more is more.*

This unusual and very American breed, one of only a handful formed accidentally or deliberately in America in the twentieth century, was born one June day in 1981 when a stray long-haired black cat and her sister strolled into the family home of Joe and Grace Ruga in Lakewood, California, and soon became "the cats who came to dinner." Grace Ruga noted immediately, of course, that the kittens had "ears that curled back from their heads in a funny way" and that their coats were fine and silky. Although the sister disappeared only weeks later, the little black female was named Shulamith and was to become, beside the family's beloved pet, the Biblical "Eve" of the American Curl to which all bona fide pedigrees trace their origin.

When the family referred the genetic difference to the famous feline geneticist Roy Robinson of London, they discovered that the ear curling was "autosomal dominant," which means that any cat with even one copy of the gene will show the trait, caused by more cartilage along the inner lining of the ear than is present in most cats. (Thus, like the Curl's alternate version, or even feline nemesis, the front-folded ear of the Scottish Fold, the ear formation is a genetic mutation.)

Realizing that they could be on the brink of an entirely new breed, the Rugas, and soon others, fell in love with this very different, stunning, but not-at-all spartan-looking cat. In fact, within a mere six years of Shulamith's stroll, her descendants were competing in championship classes in the International Cat Association. This marked an unprecedented feat for a new breed. A quick rise to fame and an overnight star, indeed! And the names matched the theatrical promise: Curl Hand Luke or Apocurlypse Meow, or Lauren Baccurll.

Typical of the charm exercised by this cat is the story told by Caroline Scott, a major Curl breeder, who operates the Procurl Harem American Curls in New York City. It was 1986 and she was grieving the loss of her black-and-white domestic cat of nine years, Petal. Thinking a cat show in New York would cheer her up, she went to one but instead started to cry any time she saw a black-and-white cat. Then one of those "cat moments" occurred.

"Suddenly I had an eerie feeling that eyes were on me," she wrote afterward. "When I turned around, there was this handsome black-and-white cat rows and rows away staring at me. I walked over and his owner let me hold him. Immediately as if by magic, the grief lifted and I felt as if he was transferring the sadness out of me and into him. I know it sounds weird, but he mended my broken heart and I've since named Curls the 'spiritual healers of felines.'" A little later, she and her longtime partner, Michael Tucker, were actually able to get the cat, which was named Carbon Copy. He became the foundation male for their cattery and they now have an entire family, with many grand champions, blessed by him.

Sounds "weird"? Well, not really. Many cat lovers have had similar experiences, when they suddenly saw a cat who obviously looked at them as their special "human" and an understanding passed between them.

And the ears? Actually, when Curls are born, they have normal ears, but within three to five days they start to curl back into what breeders call a "rosebud position." As with the Scottish Fold, the Curls exist as a breed only because of their ears, which began as a mutation and ended up as a mark of beauty. The ears of the Curl can be most likened to those of the lynx, with the ears fanning outward with graceful long tufts of hair, giving them the sophisticated look of an exotically coiffed New York model. The Cat Fanciers' Association has as its ideal for the breed that the ears should curl in a minimum arc of 90 degrees, not to exceed 180 degrees.

But these cats are, as Caroline Scott puns it, far "more than meets the ear." They are snuggly, loving, personable; they give off trill-like cooing sounds; and like water, she insists they have an "inner light" and are the "Peter Pans of the feline world."

One thing, for sure: you are never going to mistake them for any other cat.

THE AMERICAN WIREHAIRS

Put your hand on its coat and be prepared to be pleasureably surprised! Instead of the usual sleek and shiny cat's coat, this coat is wiry to the touch—not even soft and wiry like the two Rex mutations, the Cornish Rex and the Devon Rex, but more like the coat of the wirehaired terrier. Sometimes when you pet it, the fur springs back at you when stroked, like a stubborn, spunky creature. The coat is crimped, coiled, and springy—and even its cat whiskers are curled! The American Wirehair's image strikes you at first a bit like that of the cocky, tough kid on the block but he turns out to be really only very cute and spunky. Wirehairs are a delight to their owners, an amusement to the observer, and a pleasant curiosity to scientists since they represent still another natural mutation.

The American Wirehair is purely American. It is one of only a handful of breeds created in the United States recognized by the American Cat Fanciers' Association. These include the long-haired American Bobtail, the swish-swish American Curl, the traditionalist American Shorthair, and that great old country cat, the Maine Coon. But the American Wirehair is perhaps the most unusual American breed of all because of its remarkable coat, every hair of which is "wired" or curled at birth. One could be forgiven for indulging the feeling that this is somehow an electrically charged and ready-to-go cat.

How did this happen? In 1966, in a barn littler in Vernon in upstate New York, the first Wirehair was discovered in a litter of five kittens. The two that survived were named Bootsie and Fluffy (no originality there!). What was original was the fact that one of them, a red-and-white male of undetermined lineage and light-years away from Egypt, had a very spare, very wiry coat, in which each of the longer hairs was bent into a hook at the end. The local "cat lady," Joan O'Shea, was called in to take a look and she soon decided to try to reproduce the "kinkies." Geneticists were then also called in to see this "curly-haired kitten." Its coat came from a mutant gene.

The first kittens were then bred, or outcrossed, with the American Shorthair and soon a new breed was born.

Owners who have these cute and somewhat humorous cats as pets adore them. They describe them as "sinewy, muscular, bright-eyed, and independent" and ruling the households with "iron paws." They are quiet, reserved, gentle, happy, and playful. People are enchanted by the crimped whiskers, which stick out at all angles and longer-coated kittens are sometimes born with veritable ringlets of curls. Today they are found in Canada, Japan, and Europe, where they are particularly popular in Germany. The Cat Fanciers' Association accepted wirehairs for registration in 1967 and the breed advanced to championship status in 1978. Their relationship to the Egyptian god cat is not clear, but we do know that today they are registered as a separate breed from their shorthair forebears. Could that perhaps show us once again that every new generation in America, even in the Family of Cat, is destined to have its own chance at the crown?

THE BALINESE AND THE JAVANESE

The first lesson to learn about the Balinese and their Javanese cousins, two of the most romantic-looking of all of the breeds, is that they are neither from Bali nor from Java.

Go to the isle of Bali or to the larger Javanese archipelago in Indonesia, and you will find none of these cats! Look at the stylized, quirky dancing of the Balinese dancers and you may see in your mind's eye the equally fine-boned and graceful Balinese cats or catch a fleeting glimpse of them luxuriating on the altars of the temples or wandering, deep in spiritual cat reveries, about the Balinese temples (or, more likely, given cat nature across the world, sleeping)! But those pictures will remain in your mind's eye.

One Indonesian scholar told me flatly that she had never heard of any cats in Bali at all! The embassy in Jakarta had never heard of any Balinese cats anywhere in the country. Finally, one specialist told me straight out, "There is no actual cat from Bali. In fact, there are no cats of any consequence or numbers in Bali. The supposed Balinese breed, whose relatives later also made up the Javanese breed, are both designer breeds," unlike, say, the Egyptian breeds, or the Siamese or the Asian bobtails, which we call natural breeds because they emerged naturally across history. Breeds like the Balinese and the Javanese were deliberately created through man-made intervention in the breeding of cats—through special breeding and interbreeding. Most of them are found in England and America.

No matter. Most cat breeds today are indeed mixtures of the few natural or "foundation" breeds and created breeds—and most of them came to birth, for better or worse, through the hand of man. That is why they are called designer breeds and this has nothing to do with either their beauty or their personality, for the Balinese and Javanese are both gorgeous cats, their bodies long and sinuous, their faces dark and sultry, their eyes rimmed with dark lines as if made up for the stage, their whiskers actually spotted, and their legs and tails often dramatically barred or ringed. They look very much like a Siamese, but not quite, like a bell that had chimed just a little off-key, and that is because they are both long-haired breeds of the sleek and svelte Siamese.

The Balinese began to see the light of history when, for many years, a few fuzzy little kittens would be born in Siamese litters. Even in earlier times, as cats began to be bred for their looks, the fuzzy ones did not meet the standards of the times and were simply given away or put down. Although unmistakably beautiful, they were considered to be "faulty" because they did not adhere to the foolish fashion of the moment. But soon, these "long-haired Siamese," as the fuzzies came to be known, began developing into an entrancing family of their own—they originated in American breeding circles—and they were almost surely first interbred in the West through the mating of Siamese and Persians. The Balinese are large and gorgeous cats, with graceful swaying tail plumes, with the same long svelte body of the Siamese, and with a wedge-shaped head and entrancing blue eyes. They are not as loud and boisterous as their Siamese forebearers (which is seen as a great advantage by many people who find the Siamese's little shrieks a trifle exhausting). The Balinese are, however, equally playful with their offspring and with all human company.

By the 1940s, breeders in New York and California began to work toward gaining recognition for them as their very own breed and in 1970 the Balinese were recognized for championship competition in America.

What is a Balinese like? Perhaps the best description comes from Sylvia Holland of Holland's Farm Cattery in Tarzana, California, who writes of her own beloved cats: "Picture an elegant, tall, slender Siamese, with a noble head, piercing blue eyes and a proud bearing. Clothe him in long, fine, silky hair, flowing back softly towards his tail, where it spreads out like a plume, Listen to his voice—not quite so loud and insistent as some Siamese we could mention, but unmistakably

Siamese in tune. Watch how he steps up graciously to make your acquaintance, tail on high, purring his loudest and ready for a romp. This is a Balinese."

And the name? It was a prominent breeder, Helen Smith of Merry Mews Cattery in New York, who proposed the name of Balinese. She admired the grace of the Balinese dancers and saw her cats as sharing directly in that grace and indeed dancing beautifully into the cat future.

As for the Javanese, which is now also a full second breed, they share all the same characteristics of the Balinese, except for color: the Balinese are the same colors as the Siamese, while the Javanese point colors are far more far-reaching in colors! The Javanese, too, are American-born and bred, their accession to becoming a full breed in 1986 being the result of a highly original campaign by their innovative breeders, which involved taking out full-page catalog ads to explain their love for their unique fuzzy Siamese!

What is the particular claim to royalty or to sacred status on the part of the Balinese and Javanese cats? Quite simply, like all of the many (many!) offspring of the Siamese, they partake directly of cat royalty through all the history of their royal forebears, the Siamese. All of the reasons why the Siamese became the favorite of the Siamese human royal family apply to them.

But, as with all the Southeast Asian cats, there remain outstanding mysteries. At least one ancient Chinese tapestry of many hundreds of years ago depicts long-haired cats that look almost exactly like today's Balinese and Javanese!

THE BIRMANS

This is a particularly exquisite breed, which has now become one of the most popular in the world. The strange and compelling thing about the Birman breed is first, its stunning and almost surreal beauty. The Birman is a fluffy, almost frothy, light-coated cat with the dark points of the Siamese and deep blue eyes that seem to be staring at you from another world; its body coat is described as a "golden mist," and its face is as sweet as the most adorable child's. It has a tender voice, too, not loud and boisterous like the Siamese. But if they do not scream like the Siamese, the Birmans do sometimes go off in what is known as "the Birman huff." They actually emit a huffing sound when they are, in fact, huffed. But it is the cat's pristinely pure white paws—its "white gloves"—that complete the enchanting ensemble. The

Birman is a little like the perfect lady who would be nothing without her hair done and her gloves on—but who is absolutely stunning when ready for show.

The Birman is accepted as a pure and separate breed almost everywhere now, having been registered by the Cat Fanciers' Association as early as 1967. The cat has been bred in many colors and is today to be found in no fewer than twenty variations, with the original Siamese seal or dun the most popular, and the blue, chocolate, lilac, red, cream, and tabby patterns following close behind.

But where did the Birman really come from? There are two theories. The purists and true believers, who will never give up on their cat legends, God bless them, insist to this day that they were brought from Burma, or perhaps Tibet and that they were the original "sacred cats of Burma"—who can be that picky or precise about something as "sacred" as this? The realists, who may in truth know little more than the purists and the true believers, say that the breed was the result of cats brought from Burma to France around 1919, or developed by breeding—matings between Siamese and long-haired black-and-white cats—in France at that time. Cats that appear very much in the same style as the Birmans have elsewhere also resulted from such matings. Like so many other breeds in Europe during World War II, they almost died out and there was at one time believed to be only one mating pair left in France. So the Birman was outcrossed to Persians, and possibly to other breeds as well, much like ancient royalty would search around for some "sturdy blood" to brace up some weakened royal families, or find a handsome courtier and—whoosh!—to the altar, all in the true name of genetics.

The full story of the great mystery of both the Birman and the Burmese cats—two of the most glorious and most beloved of cats today—has already been told in detail in the chapter on searching for the royal cat of Burma, so we will only review it briefly here to reflect on the historic beauty of the Birman.

It is the story of how, in a temple to Tsun Kyan-Kse, the sapphire-eyed goddess of olden days who was charge with the transmigration of souls, the noble pagan monk Mun-ha, was kneeling in prayer when some evil highwaymen attacked the temple, fatally wounding the monk. But he did not die before his good cat, Sinh, leapt on his chest and faced the goddess, the cat's fur taking on the golden hue of the goddess and his eyes suddenly glowing sapphire as the extremities of the tail, paws, face, and ears turned brown (as with the Siamese cat) but his paws remained white, a symbol of the purity of his act in defending his beloved master. Soon, he carried his master's lost soul to paradise.

Of course, the story is probably apochryphal—but who cares? The Birman, whether from Burma, Tibet, the Indian border, or from an apartment in France, is a perfectly beautiful creature, with a lovely soul to boot. And one can never think deeply enough that these stories and legends about the great cats, in themselves, symbolize for us the great sagas of human beings and make us wiser about ourselves.

Whatever the real background of these mysterious feline ladies and gentlemen, they are at the very top of just about everyone's list of the "most beautiful cats." And somewhere along the way—sometime, somehow—one has to be convinced that they did have a relationship to the mysterious land called Burma, where the kings were known as "Arbiters of Existence," and "Lords of the Earth and Ocean," and "Lords of the Sunset." What more romantic a cat could you possibly hope for?

Oh, there is one other thing: during my time in Burma, when I traveled around the country, I never saw any cats at all. Most people did not even know that there were Burmese, much less Birman, cats in the world. It's a shame, but one has to face the truth.

But there is still one more mystery. One is hard-pressed to describe any real relationship between the Birmans, who are big and fluffy with plumed tails and white paws and have the point coloring of the Siamese, and the Burmese, who are small and pert and cute as buttons and nearly all of one color. To make it even more confusing, the Burmese, as well, are often described as the "Sacred Temple Cat of Burma." I give up, at least on this particularly popular legend of the Family of Cat.

THE BOMBAYS

The Bombay slinks and strides into the room like a small black panther surveying the jungle. One black paw forward, then another, slowly, thoughtfully, and methodically, black head held poised and at the ready for anything the "jungle" has to send. The cat's black-as-midnight coat shines in the sun and his three-in-the-morning black tail waves ever so slightly in the winds of the romantic mood that the Bombay evokes.

But panthers are huge, ferocious, deceptive creatures, always on the look-out for trouble. Panthers prowl the mountains and jungles of Southwest Asia; they do not serve as company and amusement for the living rooms of Chicago, Los Angeles, and Boston. And this . . . why, this is a trim, small cat, sweet and loving, a domesticated feline. Suddenly the cat sees a string ball and begins to chase it around the house like a child at play, and our confusion grows: Who are you really, Mr. Bombay?

In fact, this striking little carbon copy of the big black leopard or panther, with its black-to-the-roots patent leather coat and its hypnotic deep copper eyes, was created in the 1950s through the deliberate mating of a black American Shorthair male with a Grand Champion Sable Burmese female. Then, through patient breeding, the Bombay, which has come out with a remarkable combination of the practical common sense of its father and the slinky sable mysterious femininity of its mother, emerged as a distinctly different breed. Yet the cat is said to combine incongruously the easygoing temperament and robust nature of the American Shorthair and the social, inquisitive lap-loving manner of the Burmese.

Typical of the Bombay breeders who fought to have their cat recognized—and typical, indeed, of all cat breeders—was Nikki Shuttleworth Horner of Louisville, Kentucky, who was highly successful in breeding black kittens with black kittens, working through the Burmese–black American Shorthair cross. Realizing that the purist and finicky Burmese breeders would never accept the idea of a "black Burmese" for showing in cat shows, she hit upon the Bombay name to evoke the magic of the black leopard of India and the city of Bombay.

About this cat, there does swirl plenty of the deception, conspiracy, and intrigue that also surrounds Bombay in India! At times, the cat has been said to be merely a "black Burmese," the charge hinting at the mysterious matings behind those closed doors of the convent-like catteries. Those complaints outraged the "purist" Burmese breeders, who accept the rich, deep brown Burmese color of sable as the *only* acceptable color of their breed: there are stories of "falsified pedigrees" (Good grief!) and everywhere endless trickery and subterfuge in the courts of the Cat!

Many of the court squabbles over mating resemble those bitter disagreements of European royalty across the centuries. But whatever the court intrigue flowing around this beautiful cat, after the first mating in the fifties, the Bombay achieved Cat Fanciers' Association championship status in 1976. Today, it is prized as the perfect answer to those people who say, "I'd love to own a panther" or to the famous comment that owning a house cat is the equivalent of "caressing a tiger." Sometimes the Bombay is called a "mini-panther" or a "parlor panther."

But the Bombay is also an intelligent, affectionate companion who enjoys playing "fetch" and is highly inventive. It has been said that, "If you want a dog, a cat, or a monkey, you want a Bombay."

THE BURMESE AND THE EUROPEAN BURMESE

Perhaps no feline in the Family of Cat is so universally and uncritically loved by its owners and by so many others! They like to call them "little love bugs," the "dog cat" (oh my!), "Velcro cats" (because they cling to you), and sometimes the "Teddy Bears of the Ring."

What seems to really create this adoring public for the Burmese is the fact that this is still another of those Ur-cats or basis cats around which so many other cat families and cat qualities revolve—like the American Shorthairs, the Siamese, the Japanese Bobtails, the Turkish Angoras, the Persians, and the various big cats of the north. Burmese are little square cats, enormously clear statements of their Creator and as no-nonsensical as they come. They are bold little pusses, usually of clear, strong colors and they make adorable—and adoring—pets.

There is a word or term in the Cat Fancy—"cornerstone" cats, which is used to describe the few individual cats who set their stamp on an entire breed because they have such outstanding qualities that the breeders try to copy them in new generations—but in general, the term applies to single, special cats, and, after, to mutations that made them special. The Burmese is a kind of "cornerstone" breed because it has helped in siring so many other breeds, but also because its little body, form, and spirit make up the essence of natural and unexaggerated "cat."

Not that their human choruses are exactly "unexaggerated"! The Cat Fanciers' Association profile of the Burmese, for instance, reads: "Burmese carry surprising weight for their size and have often been described as 'bricks wrapped in silk.' Their coats are very short, satinlike in texture and generally require little grooming other than daily petting . . . Burmese have large, expressive eyes that are great pools of innocence and seductive appeal, irresistible in effect. These eyes are their most persuasive weapon in an arsenal of endearing traits that mask an awesome power to hypnotize their owners into life-time love affairs through which they effortlessly rule their families."

See what I mean?

Now, I know you are going to ask me, "But where did they come from?" Well, as related earlier, the first American Burmese was developed in San Francisco by the naval psychiatrist Dr. Joseph Thompson, who received a little cat from Burma in the 1930s via a traveling sailor. He began a controlled breeding program for his new breed, directed by serious professional geneticists. The cat, Wong Mau, was mated with a Siamese male, their offspring were carefully bred to one another, and the Burmese breed was born in America, christened "Burmese" for the supposed country of origin.

As with all the breeds whose founders originated in foreign countries, the true story is steeped in such mystery, in such legend, and in such contradiction that one can only stand back and wonder.

The entire story of "The Sacred Cat of Burma," which involves the Burmese breed as well as the very different Birman breed in ways not truly known to man, has been related in chapter 4—the Burma chapter—of this book, so the interested reader can see it there, in addition to the fact that there are virtually no cats of the Burmese style in the totalitarian Burmese state today—or at least none that I could find. The history of Ayudha, the capital of Siamese royalty, which was taken by the Burmese kings in 1767, when it is believed that Siamese-style cats (not only today's Siamese, but the Siamese "coppers" and probably Korats) were taken back to Burma to mix with whatever local cats were there, has also been gone into in some depth.

We know that Burmese cats are of very similar genetic makeup to the Siamese, although their wondrous and largely solid colorings (from blue to lilac to red) are quite different from the Siamese. And the wondrous "cat treatises" in the Bangkok regime, written and drawn with such care and love by the Siamese monks between the fourteenth and sixteenth centuries, in fact show all of these cats, at play, at work catching mice, and in thoughtful contemplation of their worlds.

Suffice it to say here that all of these Southeast Asian cats did mix and meld, beginning with "natural" breeds, which developed more or less in historic isolation and then formed new breeds. The Burmese were also instrumental in the formation of many other breeds. There is the pert little Burmilla, a mix of Chinchilla and Burmese, the Bombay, a mixture of a Burmese and a black American Shorthair, the Tiffany, which is really a long-haired Burmese created out of a mix of Burmese and Persian, and finally the Tonkinese, bred from the crossing of Burmese and Siamese and said to combine the best qualities of each. There is also a European Burmese, which came from the same original matriarch, Wong Mau, but whose male ancestors came from the United Kingdom.

The only thing we really do know about the Burmese cats' wondrous history is that this fine little feline developed in Southeast Asia, along with the other fine families of cat from Burma and Siam and the Malay Peninsula, and that there is probably no more generally beloved cat in the entire Family of Cat.

THE CHARTREUX

There is a lovely tale told about the blue or gray Chartreux cat that is about as romantic as any of the great Family of Cat stories that are so steeped in legend.

Storytellers would have us believe that the robust, deep-chested, gray Chartreux—known for their "smiling" faces and upturned lips—were the favorite cats of the Carthusian monks of France. The monks originally were able to get the cats from the Christian knights returning from the Crusades, some said. They spun tales of how, on cold, wintry days when snow lay on the grounds of the La Grande Chartreuse monastery near Grenoble, founded in 1084, the beautiful cats even shared a little of the monks' famous, vividly light green Chartreuse liqueur!

Actually, the Carthusians were originally known for their excellent steel work, and somewhere along the way they began fermenting their delicious, but dangerous liqueur—that much is true. But all of the legends surrounding their link with the Chartreux, or with any cats at all, turn out to be just that, legends. In fact, the Carthusian archives mention no cats at all, a fact that surely does not make these special little cats any less special at all!

What is known is that this Family of Cat has long been considered a national treasure in France and that references to the blue-gray felines are to be discovered across French literature, the earliest recorded use of the name having been found in the 1723 edition of the *Universal Dictionary of Commerce*. In fact, gray or blue-gray cats were common in France as early as the sixteenth century, and gray cats always had a special place in the cat shows; in Harrison Weir's first cat show in 1871, when separate or distinct breeds were as yet unknown or at least ill-defined, the categories for judging were all simply by color—and the blue or gray cats were considered to have a special magic.

When we move beyond legend, it seems that the first real Chartreux breeders on record were two sisters, surname of Leger, who lived on the small island of Belle-lle-en-Mer off the northwest coast of France and who originally bred Persians and Siamese. They discovered a large colony of blue-gray cats on the island, origins unknown, and began breeding them, showing them first at a cat show in Paris in 1931. Probably because of the wooliness of their fur, according to the Cat Fanciers' Association, these cats were given the same name as a well-known Spanish wool of the early eighteenth century, just as the Angora cats in Turkey had the same name as the Angora sheep and goats. Once breeding started with the Chartreux in the early 1950s, the breeders attempted to strengthen the breed by mating it to blue Persians and British Shorthairs. The Chartreux came to the United States in 1970 and remains a rare creature—there are probably only about a thousand of them in the entire world!

They are especially known for those fine, woolly coats, which hide a dense undercoat. Their eyes are particularly lovely, being rounded with the outer corners curving slightly upward and eye color ranging from gold to copper. They are smart, even precocious. Yet their most striking feature is to be found in their sweetly upturned mouths—they are, indeed, the "smiling cats" of the family.

THE COLORPOINT SHORTHAIRS

These exquisite creatures, which are arguably the most exotic example of the creativity of the wondrous world of "designer cats," are today structurally indistinguishable from the Siamese. There is good reason for that: they were bred almost entirely from the Siamese family of cat, with only a small input of shorthair and occasionally Abyssinian to give them the sturdier blood and all the different colors that make them so unique.

In fact, the percentage of non-Siamese blood in Colorpoints today is very tiny, with only the colors of their "points"—the color in the Siamese breed that flows out to the tail, legs, head, and ears from the usually basically dun color of the Siamese coat—distinguishing them from the classic Siamese. They were the creation of breeders who just got bored with the four limiting colors of the traditional Siamese—seal point, chocolate point, blue point, and lilac point—and wanted to create cats with the Siamese body but with a veritable rainbow of "point" colors. (And, yes, boy, *were* those Siamese breeders persnickety about those colors!).

One cannot deny the sheer gorgeousness of these cats. They are a little like beautiful stage actresses with a shadowy past, like a sunset gone a little wild, or like Jack Frost having moved his artistic hand from trees to felines.

But why then are they listed as "Shorthairs?" Therein lies still another strange story of the Cat Fancy, with all its pride, prejudice, and promise.

Since the Colorpoint Shorthairs originated generally as a hybrid of the Siamese and the American Shorthair, the beautiful creature soon got lost in the mazes and the myriad multiple and inevitable quarrels of the Cat Fancy. The traditional Siamese breeders did *not* want these multicolored Siamese stealing their show—they were purists and there was only *one* type of Siamese. Objectors talked in grand terms, like the association's attempting to "legislate morality," and some Colorpoint breeders insisted upon believing, despite all the evidence, that their cats resulted from a spontaneous mutation.

So it was that, in 1963, the Cat Fanciers' Association denied these cats the right to be shown as Siamese. Instead, in one of those many weird compromises that characterize the cloistered world of the Cat Fancy, they were accepted as a separate breed to be known as the Colorpoint Shorthair. Thus today (or at least at this moment), both the Cat Fanciers' Association and the Canadian Cat Association treat them as a separate breed under the umbrella name of shorthair, even though they bear virtually no resemblance to either the British Shorthairs or the American Shorthairs. The lengths to which godlike breeders will go to design new creatures!

They share directly in all of the Siamese royal cat history, for instance, but they also have their own strange modern history, which brings us into the worlds of science and of genetics. Indeed, the breed was started by experimental geneticists and breeders, and this kind of breeding was referred to by British cat fanciers and judges as early as 1893. Around it all, there raged one great, operatic quarrel, with the true believers of the Siamese breed talking more like Marxist theologians about "deviations" from the "pure breeds" and onlookers wondering if some "Cheka" of the cat world was about to be called in to "resolve" the "differences."

The outcome is that today fully sixteen different "point colors" are now bred. You can find a "red point," an elegant cat with clear white coat, deep red points, and coral-pink paw pads; a "cream point," a cat with a clear white coat, apricot points, and coral paw pads or even a "lilac lynx point," a cat with a white body, gray-pinkish points, frosty gray ears with pinkish tone, and nose leather and paw pads of lavender pink. And they breed not only separate colors, but tabby and other designs on the points of the cats so that now you might see a purely Siamese-looking cat with a ringed tail and a tabby head and legs. All as beautiful as sin itself!

Many of the Colorpoints also have extraordinary, intense deep blue eyes, described as sometimes having an "electric" quality. Although the practice may seem a little precious to owners of more ordinary cats, Colorpoint breeders recommend polishing or "finishing" the cat by smoothing the coat with a chamois cloth.

The odd thing is that, despite all of this funniness, the Colorpoints are not only gorgeous and svelte cosmopolitans, but very pleasant cats. They are intelligent, sweet, and devoted. And if the entire process seems a little strange to some outside the Cat Fancy, they should remember that cat shows, cat breeding, and cat designing began as a means to make the public respect, love, and honor cats. This beautiful cat is one of the outcomes of those attempts and has surely helped in every way and everywhere to raise the level of respect, if not awe, for these once helpless and despised little creatures.

THE CORNISH REX, DEVON REX, AND SELKIRK REX

It was a hot July day of the post–World War summer of 1950 when an unusual discovery was made in the town of Bodmin Moor in Cornwall, England. In her barn, along with her white cat Serena's newest litter, Nina Ennismore discovered a highly unusual kitten. There, among the other kittens, was a tiny cream-colored male, normal except that he was covered with row after row of tiny curls. At first, Nina Ennismore thought she had come upon a miniature lamb—later, these cats would be called the Marcel cats after the tiny-waved hairdo so popular in America in the 1940s and 1950s. And as the cat grew, he became odder and odder: far from his British Shorthair roots, this kitten had, in addition to its charming curls, very long legs, a fine-boned body, and perfectly enormous "bat ears," along with a tail that whipped around at an unusual speed. At first, he looked oddly Egyptian, then his coat seemed like cut-velvet, or perhaps karakul lamb or silk: it was the softest thing people had ever seen.

Mrs. Ennismore liked this odd, curly cat, decided to keep him as a pet, and responsibly took him to the vet to be neutered. It was only when the veterinarian told her that this unusual birth in Cornwall marked something unique, and even important, that she realized something that special had happened—she took the cat back home and named him Kallibunker.

The prominent British geneticist A. C. Jude told Mrs. Ennismore that her pet marked the arrival of a genuine mutation, and so they bred him back to his mother; soon two more curly kittens were produced and the Cornish Rex breed was born. Since Mrs. Ennismore had already bred Rex rabbits of the same coat type (rather like the Angora cats and the Angora sheep and goats in Turkey), she decided to continue with the Rex name. By 1956, *Life* magazine published an article and pictures of the by-then renowned Kallibunker, and cat devotees across the world noted with pleasure the advent of a new breed!

I saw my first Cornish Rex at a very emotional time—when my dear and accomplished friend Dr. Barbara Stein, of Chicago, lay dying. We had been friends since the early 1960s; she was then struggling against all the odds as one of the first women veterinary students. By the late 1990s, this charming, gracious, and brilliant woman was a huge success, having started the Chicago Cat Clinic on the Northwest Side, and having become an important international cat specialist. Once, on a lecture tour to Japan, she had the pleasure of speaking to the emperor, a great cat lover, about their common love of the little creatures.

But this day, as my beloved friend lay in bed, soon to die of still-mysterious maladies, her two Cornish Rexes, one mostly black and the other a combination of browns, played all around her, jumping on the bed, loving her, and playing in my lap. They were such small creatures, and so *curly,* and so cute, that I could hardly resist them.

None of the pictures of the members of the Rex family do them justice: they are really adorable little pixies, and their whippet tails and bright, alert little faces hint at more than the sense of humor that delights so many with this breed. They are so loving that they can often scarcely get them loose from their owners—or any other human who happens to wander by or offer a warm and willing lap. They are extremely active and even fun-loving.

Barbara died soon after that bedside chat, but the young cats were taken by her niece to love and to raise to old age and I envied her the sweet little pussies.

The Rex breeds in general mark another one of those spontaneous mutations, like the Japanese Bobtail, for instance; and well before Kallibunker there had already been a German Rex in East Germany, but it had not been bred. The more important next Rex mutation also occurred in England, this time in Devon, when another kitten, soon to be named Kirlee, was discovered in 1960. Cat Gene 1 was the name given to the Cornish Rex; Cat Gene 2, to the Devon Rex; but when they tried to mate the two cat families, only straight-coated kittens came out. It was soon decided that the two mutations were actually two entirely different breeds of cat, though both bore the Rex name and both had curly coats and looked quite similar. They were recognized as different breeds in England in 1967—in America, in 1979. They began appearing at cat shows in Europe in the 1950s and in the States soon afterward.

Both breeds are extremely popular, because of their looks, their affectionate qualities, and their pixieish playfulness. They often play catch and even pick up objects with their paws and toss them around. They are truly part of today's generation of cats, modern and filled with fun, with thankfully no memory of and aeons away from the torments of the medieval cats of Europe or the poor cats of the streets of London in the nineteenth century, much less the jungle cats of history.

Some uninformed observers may not exactly be able to tell the two breeds apart, but in fact, they boast quite different characteristics. The Cornish Rex has large ears, but of a normal type—the Devon Rex has a small, devilish, triangular-shaped face with huge, pointed ears. Both have curly whiskers, of course, as is only right and correct, to match their curly coats. The Cornish

Rexes are much larger, resembling a street cat that had been to the coiffeur, while the Devon Rexes were "much smaller in build with large, round eyes and ears that appeared to be quite out of proportion to the size of their bodies"; at times these cats seem to be some kind of gremlin! Both breeds are noted for their distinct senses of humor, bordering on a seemingly instinctive naughtiness, but the Devon Rex is the very quintessence of impishness, enchanting its devotees with the devilish look that never seems to leave its little face.

Finally, there is a third Rex, the Selkirk Rex, one of the newest natural breeds, a curly cat that was found in a shelter in Montana. The original Selkirk was bred to a black Persian and she produced three curly kittens out of six. The Selkirk Rex is a larger, more heavily boned cat than the other two Rexes and is sometimes compared to the British Shorthair. Its coat is full and loosely curled and there is also a long-haired version of the Selkirk. They are described as patient, loving, and tolerant, curly whiskered, and another credit to the charming and original House of Rex, which has offered so much playfulness and fun to the great Family of Cat!

THE EGYPTIAN MAUS

When cat lovers think about the cat family living today that is closest to the royal and sacred quintessential cats of ancient Egypt, they think first of today's Abyssinian breed. But there is also at least one other cat who many believe to be at least as worthy and accurate a descendant of the Egyptian god cats, and that is the Egyptian Mau, whose name can mean in Egyptian either merely "cat" or the "light" of the moon that the ancient cats were believed to hold in their eyes while the earth darkened. While there are other spotted designer cats, specially bred to look wild, this breed has the distinction of being the only domesticated natural breed of spotted cat. They are strikingly different, with their silvery-gray fur, their bold jungle spots, and their gooseberry-green eyes lined with cat "mascara" lines. The scarab beetle pattern on their heads and their banded legs and tail complete the picture; cat books warn owners that they are so beautiful, they should not let them run wild, or they are likely to be kidnapped!

Are the Maus descendants of the ancient Egyptian cats? Well, first, their shape and form are remarkably close to that of the Abyssinians; but far more revealing is the fact that, as I myself saw in Egypt, on the tombs and in the museums, there are in many artworks spotted cats, sometimes called "hunting cats," in addition to the svelte Aby-style goddess, Bastet. In the ancient capital of Thebes, for instance, there is a wall painting dating from about 1400 B.C. showing a spotted cat that looks much like today's Mau—it is demonstrating its training in hunting ducks for the Egyptian hunter.

But, while the Egyptian Mau cat is surely the type and style of cat seen in the tombs, most probably the relic of an ancient past, there is little or no evidence that it is directly related physiologically to those original cats of the Abyssinian type. Probably it is true that the Mau was introduced to the United States from Europe, from Egypt, via Rome, in the early 1950s. Many cat analysts still insist that the breed does not come directly from Egypt at all but that it was bred in the West for its coat pattern to resemble the spotted cats of ancient Egypt.

The most divine story of all about the Egyptian Mau, or indeed any cat, has to do with an exiled Russian princess, Nathalie Troubetskoy, born in Poland in 1897 and educated at the art theater and the medical school in Moscow. She served throughout World War I on Russian battlefronts and lived in England for twenty years. While in Rome, she was given a spotted silver female kitten from one of the Middle Eastern embassies. She was a beautiful kitten, and the princess named her Baby. Veterinarians and professors having told her that the kitten was of Egyptian stock, she set off for the United States in December 1956 with Baby and two other Egyptian Maus, a group of travelers which then gave birth to the new breed in America. The princess was unable to book her trip on the *Andrea Dorea,* which sank in the Atlantic off the coast of North America. Had she and the cats been on that sailing, there most probably would not have been any Egyptian Mau breed in America.

What we do know is that today Maus come in five colors, silver, bronze, smoke, black, and blue, and they are recognized as one of the most popular—and elegant—of the championship breeds.

Part of the Mau's enchantment is that it seems to have a perpetually "worried" look on its tiny face—but, in fact, it does not seem to be worried at all about where it stands in the pantheon of sacred cats.

As to whether or not the Egyptian Mau actually came from Egypt, the answer is that such a question is totally irrelevant, for the essence of the sacred cat of Egypt was that its spirit would always be found in all cats; it would inspire both cats and humans; and it would enrich and ennoble both animals and mankind.

THE EXOTICS

And then some cat lovers dreamed a new dream:

A Persian cat with short hair!

You could combine the wonderful, loving and sweet personality of the Persian—that saucy pug nose that made the small cat's little face and bright eyes look a bit like an exclamation mark staring at you out of a bundle of fur—with the practicality of the short-haired cats whose hair does not need to be so constantly washed and brushed, or its long and abundant fur, untangled. Once again, the breeding dreamers got to work—and what came out was a perfectly charming little cat with a lush/plush coat and a breed often called the "lazy man's Persian." Having an Exotic around the house might be compared to being married to a Marilyn Monroe who was a great cook or being in love with a Gary Cooper who just loved to do the laundry.

For many years, some breeders in North America already had been systematically mating American Shorthairs with Persians, but it was really only in the mid-1960s that some actually made the decision to create a whole new breed of cats with mixed Persian and shorthair ancestry. They were wildly successful in achieving their goal: to create the fullness of the Persian coat while at the same time shortening its overall length, and to gain a cat with delightful companionability, which has virtually matched that of its Persian ancestors.

The nose of the Exotic was shorter than the shorthair's, not quite so pronouncedly pushed-in as the Persian's. There has also occasionally been some Burmese input, and even some Russian Blue, both introduced to supply the short-haired gene.

But no one should think that these Exotics were simply a commercial enterprise, a practical endeavor, or even a genetic experiment—no, these breeders were definitely into the cat world's "vision thing." Breeders spoke with deep conviction of the "spirit" and of the "vision" of a beautiful short-haired silver Persian, and then began to breed their good old American shorthairs to silver Persians to try to get the lovely silver coat and the vivid green eye color on a short-haired cat. At first, they were going to be called Sterlings, but that proposed name was for some reason dropped. And—why are we not surprised?—for a long time in the early years, the Exotics met perfervid resistance from Persian breeders, just as, for instance, the Colorpoint Shorthairs had met fervent resistance from Siamese breeders, because the breeders would simply not countenance mixing their lines with other breeds. Slowly, some outcrosses were found and this new breed was started! By 1990, the breed some liked to call the "plush-coated Persian" was well on its way.

And, once again, as with so many breeds, there were long periods of waiting, once kittens were born, to see exactly how they *did* come out. In a piece for the Cat Fanciers' Association on the breed, writer Barbara Sims shows the air of expectation that accompanies the emotions of the ever-zealous cat lover and breeder: "Once your breeding is done and the kittens arrive, then comes the wait to see which are longhairs and which are shorthairs . . . While the kittens are still wet, the longhair coat may have a wavy appearance. After the kittens are dry, rub the hair backwards on the back of the cat. The shorthair kittens will have a more bristly feel to the coat. Hold the kitten up to the light and look at the hair on the top of its head. The shorthair kittens will have a halo-like appearance with guard hair sticking slightly above the other hair. Then you wait three weeks. They'll get fuzzy. Don't get discouraged, just watch their tails. The longhair kittens will have tails that resemble little Christmas trees. The hair on the tails of the shorthairs will stay short." You are home free! Whew!

Such a dear little cat—but perhaps not such a *lazy* man's cat, after all!

THE HAVANA BROWNS

Ahhh, Old Havana! Sloppy Joe's Bar, Rum and Cokes, Tropicana at midnight! Ernest Hemingway, in his white sharkskin suit and with his handsome swagger, and George Raft, sinister in his casino gangster hats, roving about the sensuous old Spanish city at midnight! Perhaps Graham Greene is there, too, writing, *Our Man in Havana.*

And then—and then—right into their path and out of the Spanish baroque elegance of Old Havana, there strolls a gorgeous, sensual cat—all-black with the sheen of the moon on a gleaming coat—and the cat crosses the paths of the men. Startled, they pause. They are stunned by the threat of the gorgeous creature, which looks as though it had been modeled out of mahogany, but also by the promise of such beauty.

There *is* such a cat, and it is the Havana Brown; it is just as beautiful and it looks just as slightly sinister as cat lovers think. The only problem is that the Havana Brown never had anything to do with the city of Havana, Cuba. The breed is the outcome of many years of reverence for the dark brown cat, which started many centuries ago in Siam and Burma with the sleek little Burmese brown cats, which then finally made their way to Europe and to America, and its name comes not from the city but from the rich color and perfume of the tobacco of the Cuban Tobacco Company!

Actually, deep brown–colored cats have been revered for centuries, particularly as a branch of the royal cats of Siam, a country in which the ancient poets ordained the all-brown cats as "protecting their owners from evil." Such dark cats, known as "coppers" in Siam and "Burmese" in Burma, probably came along with the lighter and more exotic Siamese to England in the nineteenth century and immediately became popular. The Havana Browns would later become confused with the brown Burmese and, in Britain, similar cats were known by the name of Chestnut Brown Foreign (which, however, is really a different kind of cat that belongs in the Oriental Shorthair group).

But then, enter once again the pride and prejudice of the Cat Fancy! These beauteous brown cats had been winning prizes—one won a first prize at a British show in 1888 and forty years later one won a special prize at a Siamese Cat Club show for having the "best chocolate body." The cat club purists had to strike back! The Siamese Cat Club of Britain in the 1920s announced with the typical haughteur of the purist cat breeders that it, regretfully, was "unable to encourage the breeding of any but blue-eyed Siamese!" The brown, black, mahogany, and chocolate cats, with their dark eyes, were out in the dark once again and, in fact, brown cats were not seen in competitions in England again until 1954 when photos of two chestnut-colored kittens appeared in the new edition of Harrison Weir's book *Our Cats and All About Them*.

Finally, in the mid-1950s, the first chestnut-colored cats arrived in the United States from England and were given the name Havana Brown, by which they are known today. They are beloved for their glistening, rich, mahogany brown coat, their powerful muscles, their long head and pert muzzle, and their chartreuse eyes—even their whiskers are deep brown! They use their paws a lot, offering them in friendship, and today the Havana Browns are considered a uniquely North American breed, with a fine temperament and intelligence. This is a cat who talks constantly to its kittens.

Pity the poor city of Havana—it doesn't know what it has missed.

THE JAPANESE BOBTAILS AND THE AMERICAN BOBTAILS

The little Japanese Bobtail cat most definitely does not strike you at first like one of the Cinderellas, Scarlett O'Haras, or Madonnas of the Family of Cat. Unlike the glamorous, sultry, psychologically "complex" Siamese, or the pure, virginal, otherworldly Turkish Angora, or the American Curl, with its jaunty in-your-face ears and its gloriously operatic plumed tail, the historic bobtail is a generally unassuming little cat. It is snappy and suave in its appearance as though always wearing a tuxedo and top hat, but is also so happy just to be with you at home and loved by you at every possible moment that this cat can scarcely believe the great good fortune the bobtail symbolizes for others!

If you are seeking a gorgeous, plumed tail on your cat, do not look to the modest bobtail—he has at best a small bunny tail, sometimes called mischievously a "shaving brush tail," that quivers like jelly when he is excited or alarmed, sending ripples down the soft, fine fur of his back. If for some undefinable reason you are looking for a large, ponderous, and arrogant cat who will keep you in your place and hide under the bed when guests come, only to be drawn out with penitentially offered tidbits and promises, the bobtail is surely not for you! For not only is the bobtail a perfectly adorable—and adoring—cat, rather like a pert, pleasing little jockey out every day to run the best race of his life, but oddly enough, this "modest" little cat has also one of the very most romantic and wondrous histories of any of the felines in the great Family of Cat!

The bobtails can surely be considered one of the founder cat families, a natural breed that developed by itself in certain of the protected peninsular recesses of Southeast Asia, somehow wandered to the Korean Peninsula and then to China, and finally found its natural historic home in Japan. Seen as an inspiration by Japanese artists for hundreds of years, the bobtails grace and lend enchantment to much of the greatest artwork of medieval Edo Japan (in nearly every painting, there seems to be a bobtail, dancing, rolling about, daring the children, or leaping through the air in some comical manner). They were pampered in the Edo palaces by prince and princess alike, by shogun and warrior and poet and painter, as precious and furry handmaidens and manservants of royalty.

To be honest about it, it is surely odd to find such a rich, deep, and complicated history for such a sweet, modest, fun-loving little cat.

First of all, the bobtail is very tiny compared to even most cats of moderate weight (most bobtails weigh in at only six to nine pounds, whereas big cats can go up to twenty pounds or more). It is a long and lean little puss, with a pinched face, elongated eyes, and high-set ears positioned slightly forward to create such an unusually alert expression that, to everyone's initial surprise, the bobtails look distinctly Japanese! (But then, so too do the Japanese dogs, like the Akita and the Japanese Chin.) For the bobtail, of course, the tail is of great importance: it must be clearly visible and less than three inches long (unlike the other totally "tailless" cat, the faraway Manx from the Isle of Man off Britain). Some tails are rigid, while others can be wriggled. Bobtails are also smart cats: their kittens are active earlier, walk sooner, and get into trouble at a younger age than other cats, according to the Cat Fanciers' Association. They are good travelers and like to suddenly spring out of nowhere. The most highly prized bobtail is called the Mi-Ke or the Japanese-style calico.

But it is not a surprise to find that, since these cats are related to the Buddhist religion, which stresses less the worship of gods than good and kind behavior, that the bobtails are not really considered royal or sacred but rather, in keeping with the religion they represent, seen as the good fortune or good luck cat of Asia! This innate characteristic is most beautifully contained within the representational cat figure of the Maneki Neko, a cute, fat, and rather self-satisfied–looking bobtail. Dressed in the appropriate apron and jewelry, its fat little paw raised in greeting, the Maneki Neko has traditionally stood outside the shops to welcome buyers into the stores.

As has been related earlier in this book, there are several temples in Tokyo and other Japanese cities where cat figures guard the Buddhist altars, but there is one temple in particular in Tokyo, the Gotokuji temple, where there live hundreds and hundreds of Maneki Neko statues, on the altar, in the temple, even in the cemetery. There, many bobtails are buried, a practice that assists the cat on its journey to Nirvana, freeing the human soul that was contained within the animal form on earth so that it may attain its eternal perfection. (But one should add that Japanese history is also rife with stories of "monster cats" since, as in Egypt and elsewhere, the cat can be both the good cat—and a very, very bad one.)

I, of course, have a bobtail, my beloved little cat Nikko, and I can surely attest to the good luck he has brought me every day. Whether he's going to carry me to Nirvana, I'm afraid I really can't say.

What we know about the bobtails' historic hegira across Southeast Asia is that they almost certainly developed in the Malay Peninsula, around today's modern-day city-state of Singapore, sometime deep in the mists of history. There are historians who say they, or at least some cats, had already come to China as early as 200 B.C. But they began to be "seen" in history about the sixth century A.D. in Korea where, under the rule of the Emperor Idi-Jo, A.D. 986–1011, they were sent to travel on ships to protect religious parchments and silk garments. It is believed that Buddhist priests coming from China during the Heian period, A.D. 794–1185, brought the cats to the Heians' Kyoto court, where they became such a rage that, in the Heian classic, the *Tale of Ginji,* a cat plays the unwitting role of Cupid. By the Edo period, particularly between A.D. 1600 and A.D. 1868, bobtails had become a crucial and loving part of every cultural level of Japan: from some of its most gorgeous paintings (Hiroshige's *Cat Washing,* and Kuniyoshi's *A Woman Sewing and Her Cat,* for example) to ukiyoe prints to haiku to novels. For the tailless cat had so come into its own that, as Katherine M. Ball points out in her *Decorative Motives of Oriental Art,* "as this short-tailed variety became the familiar type, the long-tailed animal began to be regarded with superstition, since cat demons were believed to be thus identified."

Then, suddenly, as so often in truly great families, tragedy struck—and again through the foolishness and falsity of the Family of Man, never the Family of Cat! At one point in the seventeenth century, the little bobtails were thrown out on the streets to catch mice. From that moment on, the once-pampered bobtails, the adored subjects of great artworks and the beloved pets of the palace, were street cats, scavenging for food and begging for mercy. So it went until World War II, when Americans in Japan deliberately brought the little bobtails home to America to breed them. In America, they soon became a respected breed and are now a favorite among many cat owners. In today's Thailand the Siamese are largely forgotten or dismissed, and the favorite cats in Japan today are Persians and Siamese. (A cat is surely not without honor except in its own country.)

Once in America, the Japanese Bobtail also gave birth eventually to another full breed with the legendary bobtail name. This is the American Bobtail, which some, when they first glimpse it, compare to the bobcat because it is a long-haired Bobtail with a seemingly untamed manner. In fact, the American Bobtail has thick and beautiful fur and a tail just a bit longer than its Japanese forebears. May find utterly charming the rare combination of the wildcat's feral stare balanced against a domestic temperament.

At the same time, it is said that these American Bobtails are so patient and well-adapted that long-haul truck drivers have purchased them as cabin companions and that psychotherapists use them in their treatment programs because they are sensitive to people in distress. Actually, the American Bobtail breed, while it has been in the creation for some thirty years, was accepted for registration by the Cat Fanciers' Association only in 2002, making it one of the most recently recognized breeds in the world. What religion they are here in America, no one can really quite figure out.

Still, what will go down in history for the original Japanese Bobtails is their special relationship to Japanese Buddhism and to the Japanese spirit. As Barbara Nixon has written in *The Cats of China and Japan:* "In Japan, the cat enjoys a more revered position. Japanese people believe in a sense of brotherhood between men and all living things. Sometimes this is inspired by religious faith, sometimes by superstitition. Often it manifests itself as homage to unseen powers, as in the Japanese veneration of animals after their death. This special devotion, Buddhist in origin, is to remind followers of their duty to pray, work and be selfless. To attain ultimate Buddhist perfection, Nirvana, one's life must be lived beyond self and senses, suffering and existence."

Jana Martin wrote in her book, *Zen Cats,* with exquisite photos by photographer Yoshiyuki Yaginuma, in which she analyzes sensitively the place of the bobtails in Zen Buddhism, with its abstract manner of looking at the world: "Serene, living in the moment. Existing in harmony with its surroundings— which, in Zen terminology, are qualities of the enlightened. If so, the cat is the embodiment of Zen. But it's an unwitting embodiment, a natural one . . . To coin the term more casually, it's a Zen kind of embodiment. You don't really have to explain it. As a Zen expression goes, it is."

We might turn here for just a moment to former President Bill Clinton's inspiration and interpretation, when he said so famously that, indeed, everything ultimately depends upon what "is, is."

THE KORATS

Most cat observers would have to agree that the Korat cat of ancient Siam and of today's bustling Thailand started life under a cloud, probably a monsoon cloud. From its very beginning deep in the history of Southeast Asia and the Malay Peninsula, the Korat had to deal endlessly with the abundant charms of *that other cat* of Siam, the "gorgeous . . . aesthetic . . . wondrous" Siamese cat!

From the very beginning, even though we know from the famous Thai cat manuscripts in Bangkok that the Korat is at least as old as the Siamese, the burly, chesty, saucy Korat was the village cat of Siam, used by the villagers of the northern Korat Peninsula to beg rain from the gods and crops from the field, while the long, lithe, languid Siamese was the royal cat of Siam, used to represent the palace and the bedchamber and to please the tastes of the royal foreign visitor for things of the exotic Orient.

Yet—wonder of wonders—the little gray-blue Korat, that gentle and modest creature, with its bold, single-colored body and its eyes, which become a luminous green color as it matures, has become at least as popular a cat as its favored Siamese cousin. Indeed, today, Korat lovers, perhaps reflecting the love of the defense of the under*cat*, wax insatiably poetic in praise of their breed. "The eyes shine like dewdrops on the lotus leaf," wrote one Korat lover. The cat's body seems to have a "silver halo" that is like "delphinium dust," another writer wrote rapturously. It is "silver-tipped blue, rain-cloud gray, like sea foam on a beautiful morning." And, as some disdainfully add, unlike its royal Siamese cousin, its eyes are not crossed.

What so enchanted so many about the Korats was, first, their unique color. In sharpest contrast to the Siamese, the Korats are of solid, shimmering silver, right down to their roots. Their faces are heart-shaped and seem to have been formed by the hairs around the face. They are heavy little bundles, far heavier than they look, and their owners clearly adore them. They are very sensitive to noise and it is said by breeders that, if one wants to show a Korat, one has to accustom him or her to noise by keeping a radio on in the "nursery."

What we know about the history of the Korat, or the *Si-Sawat* as it is called in Thai, is that it was one of the seventeen "good cats" described in the *Cat-Book Poems* or *Cat Treatises* or *Tamra Maew,* the oldest breed standard for cats. These pages of drawings, writings, and poetry were painstakingly put together by Thai Buddhist monks between A.D. 1350 and A.D. 1767. They were cosseted over the centuries and during invasions and today are housed lovingly in the National Library of Thailand in Bangkok. On page after page, one finds the various cats of Thailand, leaping, thinking, playing with mice, dancing, dreaming, representing man's love for books. Many are spotted, some are clearly the forerunners of the Siamese breed with its elongated body and the colors that dramatically run out to the ends of their tails, paws, nose, and ears, and others are clearly the square and bold original Korats. The six "bad cats," representing the bad graces of mankind, are there, too.

Historically, one finds genetic ties among many of the cats of Southeast Asia. Across the centuries, the Korats were surely taken to Burma and other neighboring countries during invasions. Some of the breeds are so similar that it has been suggested that the Korat might actually be a Blue Burmese, but Burmese cat breeders would have none of it, insisting that their cats must always be sable or brown. Yet the Korats have an unmistakable similarity to the Burmese breed; reddish-brown cats in Thailand are called coppers even today in the country, and except for their color they look almost exactly like the silver Korats. Some of the different cats from Siam do have kinks in their tails, as do, of course, all Japanese Bobtails.

The Korats were first shown in 1896 in the London cat show and, as the new breed moved across the world from success to success, they appeared to be a village maiden who had enchanted the cosmopolitans and often sped right by the often-spoiled cosmopoli*cats.*

In the ancient Thai *Cat-Book Poems,* there is a lovely poem about the Korats that reads:

> The hairs are smooth
> With tips like clouds and roots like silver;
> The eyes shine like dewdrops
> On a lotus leaf.

Korats were first imported into the United States in 1959 by the Cedar Glen cattery in Oregon, and in 1966, they were accepted into championship status. It is considered one of the "natural breeds" and, indeed, Korat clubs insist that the cat not be outcrossed or mated to other breeds and that all Korats should have ancestry tracing back to the original cats of Thailand.

As to their status within the Family of Cat, the Korats are not considered royal or sacred, as are the Siamese (despite, one is pained to mention once again, their bawdy bedroom behavior); the Korats represent the joys—and needs—of the villagers. Thus, the Korats became representationally more like the Japanese Bobtails than like their much closer-related, but snooty, Siamese cousins. Like the bobtails in Japan, the Korats became the good luck cats of Siam, bringing good fortune to the people.

Interestingly enough, in the end, the Korats had the final say. As the country modernized and democratized, it has been the Korats, and not the special-taste Siamese or the mysterious brown coppers that became the "national cat" of Siam.

THE LAPERMS

Relatively little is known about the LaPerm breed, except that it is one of the "curly cats," a little like the Rex family in appearance. It is a beautiful, loving, curly creature with a sweet face and even a full and curly tail. Its coat can be a simple wavy coat of the marcel type or it can range from curls that form little tight ringlets to long corkscrew curls. It often has a full and curly ruff.

What we do know about LaPerm, one of the very newest and most recent of the American breeds, is that it emerged out of hardy "barn-cat" stock only in 1982 on an Oregon farm located near the ancient hunting and fishing grounds of the Wishram Indians. When the lady of the farm noticed that one kitten of six was born completely bald, and looked nothing like her mother or her siblings, she became curious. Then, when in eight weeks the kitten began to grow very soft, very curly hair, she named it Curly, and in a short time it had a full coat of curly hair.

In the next ten years, bald kittens continued to come in the breeds at the farm—and finally the owner realized she had something highly special and unusual. Soon she was controlling the breedings, and this new breed almost immediately evinced great interest. Today the LaPerm, so named because of the curly "permanent" style of the coat, comes in all recognized colors and coat patterns, and each kitten goes through the same process as the first, adorable Curly—from baldness to beautiful curly heads and bodies of curly fur.

Amazingly, there is little in the cat books about this interesting new breed—hopefully, soon there will be.

THE MAINE COONS

If there is one other indigenous American breed that could rival the sovereignty of the American Shorthair, which has lent such a confident and practical air to American catdom and given its good, solid genes to enrich so many other cat families, it is the Maine Coon. This is the famous "gentle giant" from one of the founding colonies of the United States, a natural breed that sometimes weighs in at forty pounds and has feet so big they are comically referred to as snowshoe feet. The huge and beautiful creature can easily walk on the snow through the long and snowy winter months. Sort of a trusted Great Dane of cats, without the liquor!

New Englanders are convinced that this—their own Maine Coon cat—is simply the biggest, smartest, sweetest, most innovative and lovable cat to be found anywhere, and they were giving cat shows starring only this pet as early as the mid-nineteenth century, when there were no cat shows even in England or America.

Now, all that may well be right, but the fact is that the Maine Coon, like so many breeds of cat, is deceptive. It looks so homey, so natural, so cozy-by-the-fireside that one can scarcely believe it has a very romantic and cosmopolitan—at times, even quirky or eccentric—history.

Take the story about the Pilgrims in 1640 bringing Angora and Persian cats to the country, cats which then mated with native cats, probably by that time only shorthairs, creating the Maine Coon breed! Or the favorite story, even in some places today, that the Maine Coons came out of the mating of a domestic cat and the raccoon! Or the very possibly true legend that the cats were named after an English sea captain named Coon, who was most fond of cats, sailed around the New England coast with a horde of them, in particular longhairs like Persians and Angoras that were popular in England in the nineteenth century, and duly took his foreign cats ashore, where they mated with the "native" Yanks! ("One of Coon's cats," a New Englander supposedly commented when long-haired kittens began appearing locally.) There is also evidence, which seems obvious to the eye, that the Maine Coons are related to the Norwegian Forest Cat of Norway, another big, furry, and beautiful cat from the northern regions. Or, the most superromantic story of all, that when the French Revolution occurred in the 1780s, Marie Antoinette's beloved cats were sent to America for safekeeping and ended up in Maine, becoming the ancestors of today's Maine Coons!

Well, let's step back and unweave some of the legends. The Angoras and Persians of that time certainly could have mated with the American Shorthairs already here—that's a real possibility. So is the Captain Coon story, although there doesn't seem to be a whole lot of confirmation of its veracity. The tie with Norway makes perfectly good sense. As for the raccoon story— No!

It doesn't mean anything if the Maine Coon sometimes speaks with a trill or chirp similar to the cry of a young raccoon, if it has a brush tail similar to the raccoon's, and if it has rings around that tail. It is genetically not possible for domestic cats to breed with raccoons, or even bobcats, for that matter. The faces on some of the bigger Maine Coons look more like a lion than any other cats I have seen—but does not mean they are lions.

As to the Marie Antoinette story, one can surely not dismiss it too quickly, not only because it is too delicious but also because there is some historic veracity. It seems that one Captain Samuel Clouch, probably an Englishman, was involved in a plot to smuggle the French queen out of France and bring her safely and victoriously to Wiscasset, Maine. The plan did not work, but he was able to load his ship, the *Sally*, with many of the tragic queen's personal belongs, which included six of her favorite pet cats, before the queen was seized and executed. He probably did set sail and supposedly took her beloved cats to Maine. It's a nice story and—who knows?—it might even be true.

What we do know is that these gigantic cats dominated the only cat shows in America before the 1890s. The Coons came from all over the territory to complete for the treasured title of Maine State Champion Coon Cat in places like Skowhegan Fair in Maine. But they were soon set aside, once again due to the fancy tastes of the new cat breeders. After the 1890s, when larger and more inclusive cat shows began in America, the Maine Coons were forced to live in the shadow of the more flamboyant Persians and Siamese from cat breeders in Britain.

Today not only do they have a valued place at the cat shows as well, but they are now a breed sent to England and Europe—a belated return visit to thank Marie Antoinette, perhaps.

THE MANX

Pick one of three answers to this question: "What would you think if you heard of a group called "Stumpy, Stubby, Rumpy, and Cymric?"

They are:

1. a vaudeville combo that played the Borscht Belt in the 1950s.
2. a new law firm in a TV sitcom that makes fun of attorneys.
3. a television ad for diet foods.

Actually, none of the above! Stumpy, stubby, rumpy, and cymric (and occasionally a Longie, with a full tail) are the names given to the types, sizes, and configurations of the tails of the chubby, pert little Manx cats, which are to be found today on the remote and historic Isle of Man. One of the British islands in the Irish Sea off the northwest coast of England, it is administered by special agreement with the British Home office. With its wildly rocky coastline and a "landmass" (if you can call it that) that stretches barely thirty by ten miles wide, the island was Norse or Viking from A.D. 800 to about A.D. 1266, when Norway thoughtlessly sold it to Scotland. But it has a special history: it is home to the Manx cat, which takes its name from the island.

All right, then, pick one of the next three answers to this question: "How on earth did a little cat with no effective tail at all get to the north of Europe and become its own charming breed, where, unlike Southeast Asia, there had not been any tailless cats?"

1.   A cruise ship from Singapore came up the Suez Canal and across the Mediterannean and, when the tourists stopped off for a bit of lunch at the island's local inn, several of the famous Singaporean tailless cats hopped off—curious of course, as are all cats—missed the call to return and lived there ever after.

2.   The Spanish Armada stopped there on the abortive voyage to conquer Britain in 1588 and several cats aboard the ships swam to shore.

3.   A local cat got its tail caught in a door, the tail had to be amputated, and, against all the laws of genetics, the results of this accident were passed down to the next generations.

This time, the answer is almost surely Number 2. It was 1588 and Catholic Spain, as so many nations before her, was filled with a hubristic glory about ruling the world. Her coffers were filled to overflowing with the looted gold of the New World—she saw nothing wrong with seizing and stealing the solid gold flowers that stood as tall as man in the gardens of the Peruvian Inca in Cuzco, melting down such irreplacable treasures and carting the soulless boullion back to Spain—and so she determined to attack the other power of the age, Great Britain. How grandly the great armada of Spain, with its 130 ships, eight thousand sailors, and nineteen thousand infantrymen (and apparently a good many ship's cats!) sailed up through the English Channel to assert the right of Spain's ownership of Europe from the motherland to the Spanish Netherlands!

But when the final story was told, the Armada was roundly defeated by the more modern and spartan British, who had learned to employ smaller, faster, and low-lying ships against the clumsy and hulking armada, with the only results of the battle being the grand defeat of acquisitive Spain and the founding of the Manx breed from the ship's cats that got ashore! On that isolated island, genetic changes could easily become permanent. The Vikings got in there somewhere, as well, probably carrying some of the evolved heavy-coated and long-tailed cats from the northland to mix with the Spanish kitties and give them the strength and health of mixing types of cats.

Yet—and herein lies a charming tale, not tail!—there are old beliefs on the isle which say that the Manx is actually the result of a crossing between the domestic cat and the rabbit! In fact, the Manx cat does rather hop when it runs and, with its distinctly raised hindquarters and bunny tail, but that is no more true than the Maine Coon and the raccoon story.

For those people used to long-tailed cats—or perhaps very long-tailed or very grandly plumed cats—it may be a little difficult getting used to the tailless cats, but I insist that that is true only in the beginning. I happen to have one myself, a Japanese Bobtail, which is a totally different strain of cat from the Manx, and there is something so sweet, so lovable, and so, well, dear about them that, when you get used to them, you begin to look at cats with tails as being a little weird.

One of the early great admirers of the Manx cats was the famous English romantic painter Joseph Turner, who lived from 1775 to 1851 and was considered by many to be the greatest nineteenth-century landscape artist. He painted in Yorkshire, in the Lake District, in Wales and Scotland, and, ever and always, at the sea. Many things about his life were secretive, but we do know, from the book about him, *Turner's Golden Visions,* by C. Lewis Hyde, that at least in 1810, when the artist was thirty-five, he claimed he had seven cats that came from the Isle of Man, almost surely all of them Manx cats.

But in fact, the Manx is an old cat on the island. Even if one were to disregard the Spanish Armada story, which I do rather believe, we know that Dr. D. W. Kerruish, a Manx breeder, in his book *The Manx Cat,* insists that the breed was known on the Isle of Man for at least two hundred to three hundred years. They were recognized by the Cat Fanciers' Association as a breed by at least the late 1920s, although with "details unknown." Another Manx owner insists, with the pride typical of apparently all the breed owners, that "Manx are the feline sports cars of the car world with their acceleration and quick turns." They are also loyal and easy to bond with, but once they bond, they tend to be a one-person, or at least one-family, cat.

Perhaps the highest moment in the evolution of the Manx cat came in 1970.

The island had passed back and forth between different nations; in 1840, as the British Empire was reaching its heights, the island decided to accept British money instead of its local currency. But in 1970, the island again issued its very own coin—on one side is the picture of Queen Elizabeth II and on the other side . . . is the Manx cat!

Ah, but what *about* those odd names for the tails? Some Manx, of course, are still born with a full tail, and they are considered extremely useful for creating robust new cats without the genetic defects that run in some of the Manx—but most are tailless to some degree or other. Some have a small rise or knob at the base of the spine—these are the "rumpy riser." The ones who are completely tailless with only a hollow or a kind of dimple where the tail would normally be are the "rumpies." Then come the "stumpys," which have a visible tail stump that's described by the cat books as "usually movable but often curved or kinked." Fully tailed cats are "longies" and the long-haired Manx are the Cymric.

Oh, I almost forgot something: the Gaelic-type language of the island is also called Manx. Do you suppose some of the cats ask one another when they chance to meet at a foreign cat show: "Do you speak Manx?"

The Norwegian Forest Cats

These big, furry, perfectly gorgeous cats of Norway—the Norsk Skoghatt, in Norwegian—have an old and revered history and their relationship with their land is, in many ways, similar to that of the Maine Coons' to New England. Most probably, there is a solid historic relationship between the two cat breeds, since both have adapted in similar ways over the centuries to the cold, snowy northlands of the world and since the trade routes, from the time of the Vikings until today, were long traveled across the North Atlantic. There is also speculation that they are related to the Manx cats of the nearby British Isle of Man.

The Norwegians, in fact, would like to believe that their gorgeous and sturdy big cat—who were some years ago already designated as the "official cat of Norway" by the late King Olaf—has been around for some four thousand years (unlikely, since most cats came even to southern Europe from Egypt only about the time of the Roman Empire, but like all things in *cat*dom, possible). In fact, their origins are unknown. It is said in Norway that one day they just "came out of the forest," although we may note that we have had evidence before of sudden and unexpected appearances of cats far away from what is believed to be their origins—the appearance of a Van cat drawing in eastern Turkey at the time when cats were reigning in Egypt is only one curious instance of that.

But we do know that these lovely cats are to be found all through Norse mythology and that they take active part in the Norwegian fairy tales that were gathered and written down between 1837 and 1852. Nor can we forget the story of Freyja, the Norse cat goddess, who went riding through the sky in a chariot pulled by young virgin cat goddesses through generations of Norwegian legends and who looked suspiciously like the Egyptian cat goddess, Bastet.

The fact is that there most definitely is a magical quality to the Norwegian Forest Cat. It has developed its wondrous heavy coat in a Darwinian fashion over the centuries in order to protect it from the bitter cold of the north. It is an unusual double coat with water-resistant guard hairs over a downy, warm undercoat. But then in the spring—these cats actually molt! Their hair naturally loosens and, by rubbing themselves against tree trunks and brambles (or, of course, being brushed), they rid themselves of the unwanted hair. "They unzip their winter overcoats and step out of them," one breeder is quoted as saying of this amazing annual event, rather like women taking their spring wardrobes out in April. They "take off their winter underwear," said another. So in a sense, you get two cats for one: a big bundle of fur in the winter and a pleasantly normal cat in the summer, before the fur starts to grow again in the fall in order to protect the creature from the snows.

Another amazing part of the breed is the strikingly beautiful faces of these forest cats. Now, I think that almost all cats have beautiful faces, even the poorest little wretch on the streets of the Middle East or Asia. But the Norwegian Forest Cat's faces are truly transformational. They stare at you out of exquisitely ethereal and sensitive faces, the face often flat-haired, the eyes brilliantly and magically engaged with you, while a great, rich ruff surrounds the entire face.

As with so many cat breeds, there was a time when the existence of these great members of the Family of Cat was threatened. As with other cats of Europe, after

World War II the forest cat was in danger of becoming extinct. Not only had the war taken its toll, but no one had stopped them from interbreeding with other free-ranging domestic cats. Then a good Norwegian, Carl-Fredrik Nordane, took over as president of the Norwegian Cat Association and organized a breed club to oversee the preservation of this breed through planned breeding programs. By 1977, the forest cat was being accepted in Europe for championship competition, and upon Nordane's return to Oslo from Paris at that time, music, flags, and parades greeted him. Two years later, this lovely creature arrived in the United States and is now a popular and beautiful contender at American cat shows.

Do the Maine Coons and the Norwegian Forest Cats ever get together at those shows and talk about a common history? And perhaps include the Manx cats and the American Shorthairs? Given the intelligence of these creatures, one can only imagine that they do.

THE OCICATS AND THE BENGALS

This first stunning cat, another of the "manufactured breeds" of cat, was developed and has become very popular for one major reason: the lure of the jungle cat, the fascination of sleeping with the leopard, or, as Victor Hugo said in his favorite aphorism, "God has made the cat to give man the pleasure of caressing the tiger," or the "kick" of seeing a small leopard that opens doors and fetches! One would only have to add to that, "and to relive the glory days of old Egypt."

However, it was not God, at least in this case, that got things moving to develop the Ocicat; it was a Berkeley, Michigan, breeder, Virginia Daly, who in the sixties got the idea of trying to create an Abyssinian-pointed Siamese, that is, a Siamese with dark-ticked Aby tail, paws, legs, ears, and face. She had already done a number of experimental breedings. Now, through the interbreeding of Abyssinian Siamese and American Shorthairs, along the way she produced a large, ivory cat with bright golden spots and copper eyes, which they named Tonga. Her daughter immediately named this breed-in-the-making an Ocicat because of its coat's resemblance to the spotted coat of the ocelot.

At just about that time, a geneticist wrote an article in the *Journal of Cat Genetics* suggesting that someone ought to try to re-create the long-extinct Egyptian spotted fishing cat in an attempt to save some of the vanishing wild species for humankind, and Virginia Daly was on her way. When I toured the agricultural museum in Cairo while doing research on the Egyptian cats, the director specifically pointed out old spotted Egyptian cats in various paintings and impressed me with the knowledge that these spotted cats, as well as the sleek cat goddess type, were found deep in Egyptian lore.

There are other spotted domestic cats. The Egyptian Mau is the only natural spotted cat, and another is the designer Bengal. But the Ocicat is larger than either of those; weighing in between twelve and fifteen pounds, it is a large, muscular cat. Once the word was out on the "jungle cat," their popularity surged. Two Ocicats were registered with the Cat Fanciers' Association in 1970; in the years between 1986 and 1989, annual Ocicat registrations jumped 292 percent.

Ah, but somehow fate has played a curious trick on the Ocicat owners who take such pride in their "wild cats"! These charming creatures are not wild at all, but sweet, intelligent, and loving home cats. That's the way life goes.

As for the Bengal, the second striped "manufactured cat," it is of a totally different genesis, but the inspiration was the same as with the Ocicat—to create a domestic cat that looked for all the world like a wild spotted cat of history. The Bengal was created by crossbreeding the Asian Leopard cat, a rare Asian semiwild cat that was being used at the University of California, Davis, to research feline leukemia virus, with (again) domestic cats like the all-purpose American Shorthairs, a feral organ domestic cat from a zoo in New Delhi, India, and a brown-spotted tabby domestic shorthair from a shelter in Los Angeles. Other designer spotted cats also keep coming to the fore—the new and beautiful Savannah is one of those. Talk about multiculturalism in cats—here it is!

More "lap leopards" of the cat family!

But the crossing of these wild or semiwild cats with domesticated cats to come up with a dramatic spotted wild-looking cat is becoming a highly controversial practice in the cat world. One reason the Cat Fancy does not recognize most of them is because of the uncertain domestication involved.

THE ORIENTAL SHORTHAIRS

The meticulous writer comes to a question when addressing these perfectly gorgeous—even ethereal cats—who so exemplify in their long, lithe bodies, their regal carriage, and their expressive faces every principle and standard behind the sacred and royal cats.

Where should *they* be placed in the great Family of Cat? Physiologically and genetically, they are intimates of the Siamese family—the Oriental Shorthair Standard differs only in minor points from that of the Siamese and, in fact, the only real difference between the two breeds lies in its color and pattern and in the fact that the Oriental Shorthair allows green eye color. They even have the loud and insistently boisterous voices of the Siamese (to some people's dismay). Yet, Oriental Shorthairs *are* listed by most of the major cat institutions as a breed of their own, because they are, after all, the result of the mating of the Siamese and a veritable parade of Shorthair cats, with their partners giving them their extraordinary rainbow of colors and patterns.

So, yes, I made a decision: With some of the cats in these profiles, I blended one or two together even if they were recognized as separate breeds, particularly if the only difference was that one was a short-haired cat and the other, a long-haired cat. But with the Oriental Shorthairs, there seemed to me to be enough difference to address them separately. And those are, in fact, the kinds of decisions that the judges and adepts of the Cat Fancy have always had to make. If trying to herd cats is difficult, just try putting them in *cat*egories.

It is believed that the first Oriental Shorthair was born in 1950, on a winter night, when another of those British cat fanciers of apparently unclear royal background herself, one Baroness von Ullman, decided to create a new variety of cat, which was a brown shorthair with green eyes and a Siamese body. Four years later, two lovely kittens appeared in the issue of the British journal *Our Cats*, named Bronze Leaf and Bronze Wing. The mother was Our Miss Smith, a seal-point Siamese, and the father, a brown hybrid named Elmtower Bronze Idol.

This was the result of another of those longtime dreams within the Cat Fancy, this time of creating cats of Siamese-body type, but without the special colors of the Siamese that occur on the "points" or the feet, tail and face, and ears area; these new cats were to be of one block color, or of tabby or other patterned coloring, or Angora. Soon, as with the Balinese and the Javanese, there was also a long-haired sister. And the experiment was wonderfully successful. By 1977, the Oriental Shorthairs were competing well in championship classes everywhere.

As a matter of fact, these are perhaps the most elegant cats of all. You see one of them, all in black, or in a soft lilac-mauve, or perhaps with a tabby coloration, and you see the most spiritual-looking of cats. Their faces are dominated by a very long nose, tiny lips, and large ears, and when they crouch down it is as if a ballerina is taking a long and beautiful bow. But then they fool you: these elegant creatures are also playful, filled with spirit, and utterly loyal.

With the Oriental Shorthair as a friend, therefore, you can savor the feeling of having a beautiful princess or dancer in your lap or snoozing next to you at night: another transformational experience in the sacred and royal experiences of humans with cat.

THE PERSIANS AND THE HIMALAYANS

The Persian is most definitely a cat with a past.

History says that they were originally found in the cold, high plateaus of ancient Persia or today's Iran—and even perhaps as far away as Tibet and Afghanistan—and that they made their way westward with the caravans of silk and jewels, bounding along on camelback. Surely the cats got to Persia from Egypt, possibly after the evil (to cats!) King Cambyses defeated the Egyptians near the Suez in the fourth century B.C. through the ploy of placing the beloved and sacred Egyptian cats in the arms of his fighters.

But the picture is clouded by the fact that, within Persia, there are hieroglyphic references to such unusually formed cats as early as 1684 B.C., at the same time that the Egyptians were at the height of their domestication of the cat. Could they have somehow come much earlier?

Then there is the "Angora" connection. It is generally assumed in Turkey by cat geneticists whom I talked to—and by the Persian Cat Fancy itself—that the Persian and the Angora were originally closely related, if only because the areas of eastern Turkey and Persia are so close and the cats are so furrily alike. But the Angora, and the other Turkish cat, the Turkish Van, have a more prosaic, normal if you will, body formation; whereas the Persian is known for its gorgeous coat, yes, but even more so for its charmingly, sometimes snippily, pushed-in nose and the big eyes popping out just above it. In the early years of the twentieth century, geneticists noticed a feature of the Persian cat skull that was special, a marked shortening of the facial region that compacted the teeth, causing an overshot lower jaw and a widening of the facial region. This skull, interestingly enough, bears a striking resemblance to that of the Pekingese dog, which was bred for hundreds of years in China. Nevertheless, they are one of your basic, cornerstone families of cat, and have long stood for the standards for beauty and form for the entire Family of Cat.

It is believed that cats from the blended lines from Persia, Afghanistan, Burma, China, and Russia were brought to Europe at least three hundred years ago, but exactly how no one knows. They seem to have mixed in the Caucasus, the present home of Georgia, Azerbaijan, and Armenia, then moved northward, and, as they did so, formed different modern breeds. By 1871, at the first cat show, which took place at the Crystal Palace in London, there were 160 entries, among them many Persians, which were immediately highly praised.

It was suddenly the modern era, when the poor cats of the world and of the streets of Europe were suddenly being transmogrified into admired and cosseted creatures, but there were as yet no breeds and so the cats were shown according to color ("blue" or gray was big) or according to length of hair. The Angoras were the first long-haired cats in England and were always referred to as the "French cats." The Persians came in, too, under the "long-haired" title. Then, in 1920, the artist, critic, and cat lover Karl Van Vechten published his classic on feline history, *The Tiger in the House,* dedicated to his beloved Persian, Feathers, thus instantaneously furthering the appreciation of this unusual breed. Today, Persians are almost always the number-one most popular breed in America.

Why do people love the Persians so much? Well, they have those long, flowing coats, almost like a beautiful woman with a long cape, and their open faces are sometimes described as "pansylike." The word "sweet" only begins to describe their personalities, for they are serene and loving. Because they have short legs, they play but are not given to jumping and climbing, which is a comfort to some of the owners of the long-legged breeds, like my own first cat, Pasha, whom one could often find flying through the air.

However, because of their coats, Persians must be kept indoors and they must be combed daily. Occasional baths are highly recommended. This is not a low-upkeep cat. Says the Cat Fanciers' Association: "Owners should be prepared to spend time each day grooming. A routine should be established to include a daily cleaning of the face to remove stains and a complete run-through with a metal comb to eliminate tangles." Baths are necessary once a week, and some breeders bathe them with bluing rinses that reflect light, giving the wonderful coat an even more sparkling appearance; some black and red Persians are groomed with Bay Rum as a finishing spray (which would also make them smell good at night, particularly if they sleep with you).

On the other hand, what many people fear—that the pushed-in nose of the Persian will cause breathing or pulmonary problems—does not seem to be true. There was also informed speculation that both Angoras and Persians might have been descended not from the Egyptian *Felis silvestris* but from a wild cat whose remains were found in Central Asia by naturalist Simon Pallas, sometimes called Pallas's Cat or *Felis manul* or the Manul cat. This was a small, long-haired wildcat native to deserts and rocky mountain regions from Tibet to Siberia and perhaps related to the Tatars or Mongols, who also did surprisingly keep and appreciate cats. But that link, while interesting, does not seem to hold true, either.

Like the Siamese, the shorthairs, and the Burmese, the Persians have often been mated (outcrossed) in attempts to create new breeds. There is, for instance, a somewhat controversial breed, the Peke-faced Persian, found generally only in America, which has been bred so that the nose is so short as to be almost flat on the face.

Better known—in fact, very well known and loved—is the Himalayan, which is a breed of its own today in many organizations, but one that is so close to its Persian roots that I decided to include it with the Persians. Breeders wanted a Persian-style cat with Siamese coloration and patterns—and that is what they got. Himalayans are a most sought-after breed today and, by all accounts, lovely companions; they come in a rainbow of colors from shaded and smoke, black, cream, bicolor, calico, and even (of course, the good old) tabby pattern. In fact, there are over 343,000 Himalayans registered in America since 1957.

Thus, the Persian Family of Cat goes down in history among the most accomplished and admired. Dramatic, theatrical, and different, but also loving, sweet, and incongruously homey, they are a "special taste" but one that has enchanted tens of thousands of admirers.

THE RAGAMUFFINS AND THE RAGDOLLS

Here are two mystery cats with similar names! Two created breeds, big cats, charming cats, beautiful cats! Do they belong together? Who knows, because, although both are recognized breeds by major associations, astonishingly little is known about them from books or searches.

The RagaMuffins come in all coat colors and patterns and are very large cats, with females weighing between ten and fifteen pounds and males, fifteen and twenty pounds. They are gorgeous, with large expressive eyes, sweet personalities, and calm, yet playful, natures.

Where did they come from? The Cat Fanciers' Association says in its breed description only that "The exact development and early history of the Raga-Muffin breed is clouded. The full story will likely stay a mystery forever." Yet, they are increasingly recognized as a major breed or at least one moving up fast. It's more than a little like having a cousin in the family that no one quite knows.

The Ragdoll got its name from the fact that it likes to just flop in your arms when handled. We know that the first Ragdoll kittens were born in California to a white Persian queen with Siamese markings named Josephine—the father's identity is open to speculation but Josephine's owner in Riverside, California, thinks that he was a Birman. After a road accident in which the cat suffered a broken pelvis, she gave birth to an entire litter of kittens who flopped in your arms when handled. Specialists say the accident could not have created this reaction, but the fact is that no one really knows.

What we do know is that the breed began in the sixties and we can speculate that that is the reason why this is one of the most laid-back of all breeds. It is loving, undemanding, gentle, and (very) relaxed. They are light-colored with darker Siamese-type points on the face, legs, tail, and ears. The Ragdolls are beautiful creatures, but, while it is sort of curious that an entire breed should be created only on the basis of the cat flopping in your arms, odder things have surely happened in the Cat Fancy.

Won't someone do the great Family of Cat a favor and tell the stories of these lovely cats?

THE RUSSIAN BLUES

Of all the mystery cats of the Family of Cat—and there are many whose origins and history remain shrouded in mists of the past—none is more mysterious than the Russian Blue.

First, it is supposedly from Russia, and we find almost no cats at all with any Russian historic links. Second, it is supposedly from Archangel, which is a historic port of Russia, having been founded as a fortified monastery for the Archangel Michael in 1584. Think about it: little Archangel sits right alongside the White Sea, just south of the Arctic Circle and roughly six hundred miles northeast of St. Petersburg. It is snowed-in and iced-in most of the year, dark around the clock in winter, and sunny around the clock during the too-brief summers.

How did this beautiful little blue cat, with its exquisite blue-gray coat, its pert face, and its smart, alert eyes, get there—and from there, at least so they say, to London and finally to America, to be shown proudly at cat shows everywhere? Was it really, as is also said, the pet of Tzar Nicholas II? Frankly, nobody knows! But what we do know is that, in keeping with the mysteries of Russia and with the conspiracies and Byzantine nature of its courts, the Russian Blue has, over the years, gone by a number of different and probably deliberately deceptive names, among them, the Spanish Blue, the Archangel Cat, the Maltese, and the Foreign Blue. (Everything but "007"!)

It is said that, in keeping again with the habits of its country of origin, the cat has never revealed which name it itself preferred.

Russian Blue owners love their cats because they are especially gentle and affectionate; but they also love their double coat, so short, dense, and plush, so almost blue as if each hair were dipped in silver, so silky and upstanding that it is often compared to the Russian beaver. Like Russian humans, these cats do not like change, but they do show inordinate loyalty to their human family and are excellent parents. Playful, they love to sit atop door frames and hide in small places. Russian Blue owners enjoy telling stories about how their cats can turn doorknobs when your poor old cat can't!

Historians stress that the origin of the Russian Blue is still not documented, yet they also say that its "determinable origins" have been in England and the Scandinavian countries of Sweden, Finland, and Denmark, in addition to the northern reaches of Mother Russia. It is believed that sailors from the Archangel Isles carried the first cats to England and to northern Europe in the 1860s and one rumor has a Russian Blue as a favored pet of Queen Victoria. They were first shown at the Crystal Palace in England in 1875 as the Archangel Cat, and, since no one could figure out exactly what they were, they were set up to compete in a category of all-blue cats. Not until 1912 was the cat given a class of its own.

Russian Blues almost surely existed in North America as early as 1900, but they were then called Maltese and it was only in 1947 that they were actually bred in America and only in 1964 that they achieved their first grand championship in the Cat Fanciers' Association. There are still small numbers of the cats in North America and their dedicated breeders nevertheless keep the numbers small, because the Blues seem to need an inordinate amount of attention and individualized care.

Meanwhile, history holds its tongue. How on earth did this sensitive, beautiful, plush little cat get from Egypt to the Arctic Circle? Like most Russians throughout history, the Russian Blues are not telling.

THE SCOTTISH FOLDS

Many observers describe the Scottish Folds, one of the most charming and easily distinguishable members of the Family of Cat, as looking both sweet and sad. They look rather like puppies, some say, with their ears that fold forward. Or they look like a pixie, an owl, a teddy bear. But I think they look just a little charmingly dizzy, with their big dark eyes and their ears pulled down over their foreheads like some poor guy who's had a pint too many in Scotland. Adorably drunk!

The first Scottish Fold in modern times was discovered in 1961 at the McRae farm at Coupar Angus in the Rayside Region of Scotland, when a shepherd spotted the first known cat of the breed, to be named Susie, a white barn cat, both of whose parents were straight-eared farm cats. Susie's uniquely curved ears were due to a spontaneous mutation, and soon others near the farm began breeding these cute, distinctive little cats with the intent, childlike expression, making them into a very popular breed, particularly in America.

But as with so many of the cat breeds, every once in a while in the scarce literature on them, a beam of light comes shining out of the past, bringing us back to ancient days. The 1975 *Guide to the Cats of the World* states that, even in ancient China, "The idea of a drop-eared Chinese breed was a persistent one," and avers that at least one British sailor returned home with a "drop-eared cat." But the first known reference to such cats appeared as early as 1796 in the *Universal Magazine of Knowledge,* in which fold-eared cats were mentioned as wild cats in China.

There is no record of Scottish Folds having any connection to royalty, except, one might at least say, in the best-selling books of Peter Gathiers, whose beloved Scottish Fold, Norton, stars in his *The Cat Who Went to Paris* and *Cat Abroad.*

Some in the Cat Fancy believe that the Scottish Folds should actually be a member of the shorthair families and not a breed of their own, because they were mated to so many Shorthairs. But the Folds did become a breed of their own, both in Britain and in America, although in the 1970s the British Cat Fancy decided to stop registering the Folds, banning them from all shows because of fears they would be prone to ear mites and deafness. There is no proof of this if the cat is well cared for. Only about 50 percent of the Folds have litters with the drop ears, so in essence, your true Scottish Fold can have both drop ears and regular ears. But along with the American Curl, whose ears go equally enchantingly the other way, the Scottish Folds are the only other breed to exist only because of the ears! Looking at them, you could be forgiven for feeling that you were always at a party.

THE SHORTHAIRS

The Brits

"My first love will always be for the short-haired domestic cat."

Those were the unforgettable words of Harrison Weir, in his famous book, *Our Cats and All About Them.* With those words alone, the Shorthair had found its place in the great history of the Family of Cat! In fact, those words were something like getting a foreign policy strategy award from Henry Kissinger or a dancing certificate from Fred Astaire. Weir, a British gentleman and a Victorian who started the first cat show in England in 1871, was the noble founder of the Cat Fancy.

Once this practical, down-to-earth, cozy, homey, elegant cat of Europe and

America received that precious accolade, it was clear that the supposedly "ordinary" and "everyday" shorthair was neither ordinary nor everyday.

For the homey shorthair, or the "Domestic" as the cats were once called, has just as romantic and historic a story as any of even those superromantic families like the Siamese, the Burmese, or the Persians. The shorthairs only seem unprepossessing, whereas, in fact, their histories are rich and storied and their inner confidence is of the very essence of "cat."

First of all, the British Shorthair comes to us with a good two thousand years of history on its strong and furry back. It traces its ancestry back to the early domestic cats of Rome, the city that was the Egyptian cats' first port of call after having been catnapped from a declining Egypt. Roman troops carried the first British Shorthairs to Britain, where they are found in paintings and engravings for several hundreds of years. The breed is a favorite of animal trainers and the picky producers in Hollywood, for its intelligent and easygoing nature. Always very special in the breed was the short-haired cat of the tabby coloring, which is the oldest recorded type of shorthair.

But the Shorthairs, both British and American, fell upon hard times for many centuries. In their early years in England, they were called mongrel or street cats. In World War II especially, they suffered terribly, the early attempts at breeding all but destroyed. Today, instead, they win inordinately large numbers of Best in Show and Grand Champion in the cat shows of both countries and they also almost approach the fecundity of the Siamese in taking part in the breeding and the creation of sturdy, but also gorgeous, new breeds, thus belying the picture they often give of an asexual and homey domesticity!

At that first cat show in 1871 in the Crystal Palace in London, Best in Show was awarded to a fourteen-year-old female "blue" or gray tabby British Shorthair, owned by (who else?) Harrison Weir. The blue shorthair has always been considered a very special cat, a cat with a certain magic, and was often confused in later years with the Chartreux until the Chartreux was made a separate breed at the insistence of its own jealous breeders.

When you look at the sturdy and square shorthairs at first, they seem sometimes to be a bit like an uncle from the "Old Country" or a guy who is a just a little "square," particularly when compared to "designer cats" like the American

Curl, the Sphynx, or the Birman. That is only to be expected since they are the direct descendants of the working cats of Europe. Before Harrison Weir and the cat shows gave all cats a new and respectable lease on life, the British Shorthairs and their continental brothers, the European Shorthairs, had been rather looked down upon, with their massive round heads, broad furry chests, cobby bodies, dense fur, full cheeks, picture-book colorings, and the look on their faces of perpetual perplexity bordering on indignation.

But once they were bred in the late 1800s, they became Britain's all-time favorite; registered British Shorthairs were carried to America about 1900, thus giving rise to the formation of the American Shorthairs. They were found in all the colors of the rainbow: black, white, and blue in solid colors; brown, red, and silver in tabbies; spotted tabbies; narrow-striped tabbies; smoke; black-and-whites; white-and-blacks; tabby and white; tortoiseshell; and tortoiseshell and white. One of the great favorites remains the glamour-puss cat that developed later, the shiny and elegant Silver Tabby Shorthair.

With all this history behind them, perhaps it is not surprising that the British Shorthairs stand today like the patriarch and matriarch figures of so many other fine breeds, overseeing the great family that they have helped to father and mother. They seem today like the steadiest and most reliable of cats. Like my Nikko, they are not fast, not great leapers—"When gracelessness is observed," the Cat Fanciers' Association profile says, "the British Shorthair is duly embarrassed, quickly recovering with a 'Cheshire cat smile'"—and that is surely because, in their heart of hearts and of all the cats in the world, they know who they are, that they are the very essence of "cat."

The Yanks

The American Shorthair came early to America. The very first cats to arrive on the New World shores came with the first shiploads of colonists—records show that there were even several cats aboard the *Mayflower!*—because cats were carried as working mousers and good companions. Yet, without question, those first American Shorthairs were certainly a scruffy bunch compared to today's neat and naturally regal (but also, oddly enough, comical) shorthairs. They were, of course, of the same original blood as the British and the European ones, and thus of the same Egypt-by-way-of-Rome voyaging. After 1900, this New World cat would be widely and deliberately mixed with the British Shorthairs, which had been so successfully bred in England in the 1880s and 1890s.

After the American Revolution, these stalwart and sturdy fellows made their way around America, serving as loyal friends of the pioneers, all the while doubtless looking on with envy as the first cat shows were held in New England almost exclusively for Maine Coons—until the cat shows began in America at the turn of the nineteenth century and American cats began to come into their pedigreed own. Once that early Cat Fancy took root, it truly took off. As early as 1896, at the Second Annual Cat Show in Madison Square Garden, an American breeder was offered $2,500 for a particularly beautiful brown tabby American Shorthair, a huge amount of money for that time! It was after that that friends of the cat began acquiring the best examples of the breed and mating them selectively to preserve the American Shorthair's wonderful disposition and strong physical features.

The first red tabby British Shorthair was sent to an American cat lover only around 1900, so the two Anglo Shorthairs developed separately until then. It was a pedigreed red tabby, a male inexplicably named Belle, and he/Belle was the first short-haired cat to be registered as a pedigreed animal by the Cat Fanciers' Association. Others followed, like a male silver tabby named Pretty Correct, to take their place next to newly registered American cats, the first having the hearty all-American name of Buster Brown. The new American breed was already recognized as one of its first five registered breeds as early as 1906; they were also called Domestic Shorthairs until 1966 when they were officially named American Shorthairs.

How, then, are the British Shorthairs and the American Shorthairs different?

Both cats are intelligent, affectionate, and homey. They don't leap or scream around, like the Siamese. They are quiet, having developed out of the harshness of the northern winters and defined by the hardiness that comes out of early survival. But the Cat Fanciers' Association says that the American Shorthair is less square in shape than the cat's British cousin and that the feline has an oblong rather than a round head, plus larger ears and longer legs.

The American breed is not supposed to have a soft fluffy coat, for instance—these are supposed naturally to be tough, good-tempered, and easy-to-care for cats; they are often described as being the antithesis of those fashionable, theatrically difficult fancy cats, exemplified by the Siamese, with their displays of temperament and excitable natures. No, your American Shorthair is your quintessential Good Citizen cat, but no dope, either: in America, every year these cats win about a hundred Grand Champion and Grand Premier and Distinguished Merit Cat titles and for a long time they were ranked ninth in popularity among Americans.

If you need a real star American Shorthair, just think of Morris the Cat, who won over the nation in the 1960s with his delightful catfood ad starring his beautiful big furry body and his cat/persnickety "Why-are-you-bothering-me?" expression.

There are fancier cats in catdom and there are more dramatic presentations; there are longer tails, odder ears, stranger kinked tails, crimped whiskers, curly fur, and smiling lips. But somehow, at least in the West, both the British and the American Shorthairs are the cats upon which all the others build; they are the baseline, the family album. If the Abys are the Egyptian-style royalty of the cat's royal court, if the Siamese are the courtesans and sexpots of the cat's boudoir and if the Japanese Bobtails are your classic merchandising good fortune cat, then the American Shorthairs are your hardworking cat who has made good, your All-American cat straight from Hollywood—right out of central *cat*sing.

THE SIAMESE

Alone in the low alluvial monsoon planes of Southeast Asia where the great muddy rivers of China meander their way into the South China Sea, there developed over many centuries a small, enclosed familial enclave of cats that was destined to stun the world with its sheer strangeness and beauty. These creatures would become one of the true "royal" families of cat and they would even also give rise to an entire "royal family of cat," one part of the genealogy emerging onto the world scene more gorgeous than the other.

When the outside world discovered them, in the nineteenth century, the Europeans gasped at their stage presence and at their exotic bearing, for these were no ordinary cats. They were not even the ordinary bold colors of most other cats. Instead, somewhere along the line down the centuries that they were developing on that landmass, so remote from their Egyptian homeland, there occurred a mutation of the gene that governs the color of the coat. The dark colors of the fur of the Siamese cats passed to the extremities of these cats: to the edges of the ears, of the tail, of the paws (the famous "points"), while the bodies remained a pale cream or fawn color, making these cats not only breathtakingly different, but sometimes even somewhat frightening.

We have already related in detail how, in those remote plains, this breed developed naturally with an extraordinarily sophisticated world built around themselves. Not only were they beautiful but they had their own history books, meticulously and lovingly written and sketched by the Buddhist monks in the fourteenth and fifteenth centuries—these were the *Cat-Book Poems* or *Cat Treatises* of the *Tamra Maew,* written in old folded books and with exact drawings of today's Siamese cats, with all their special coloring. Then some of the Siamese were carried as bounty to Burma by Burmese invaders during the sacking of the Siamese capital of Ayudha in 1767; finally in later centuries, they became the royal symbols of the Siamese monarchy, which presented these exquisite "royal" cats to distinguished and royal personages as special gifts of the monarchs. The king of Siam had given a pair of Siamese to Consul-General Owen Gould in 1884, and after the cats made the long and onerous trip to Great Britain, they were exhibited at the Crystal Palace cat show in 1895.

In those days, no one was too careful about calling the Siamese royal, because many of them were billed as "imported from the royal palace, Bangkok." In truth, not only the dozens of princes but also high officials in Siam called their homes "palaces," so one could never be too sure.

These cats seemed "different" in virtually every possible way. They also had a "special" voice—it was, in fact, more like a yowl—which, in truth, could grate on many people's nerves. They were squinty-eyed. Their tails were usually kinked, but mostly only inside the furry tail. They had different patterns and habits: they gestated five more days than most cats, for instance, and the Siamese males were unusually attentive to their kittens—admirers of the breed pointed out that, unlike other breeds, the fathers did not eat their kittens, surely an admirable trait but also not one that should be overly praised. And from the very beginning, the Siamese seemed to provide a repertoire of starlets for theater, screen, and stage.

How such a rarefied, aristocratic, and almost eerie creature developed on the monsoon plains of Southeast Asia, an area known for its huge and often savage animals, among them the gibbon tiger, the leopard, the wild pig, the python, the king cobra, and the crocodile would be an amazing story, if ever we could learn it.

Somehow the Siamese, themselves unwittingly to be sure, always came to extend beyond themselves and to represent far more than themselves; for as it happened, they had entered into that moment of history when, following the publication of Charles Darwin's work on *The Origin of Species by Means of Natural Selection,* European societies were gaining new understanding of the process of evolution; at the same time, the Industrial Revolution, large-scale urbanization, and the increased leisure of people working in the manufacturing industries were causing widespread interest in the "improvement" of domestic animals. Prospering families, moreover, came to want "special" cats, to feed the new middle-class need for badges of superiority.

It was into this era that there stepped the Siamese cat, a new-style feline that one cat book describes as "extra-affectionate, extra-noisy, extra-demonstrative, extra-angry, extra-active, extra-sexy, extra-fertile, in fact extra in every way!" Thus, the Siamese spread from Bangkok to Britain, and from there to America, to South Africa, to New Zealand and to Australia, where they were madly popular.

But it must be pointed out that the original Siamese were not at all the long-headed, sylphlike, elongated Siamese of today, bred down to the fashion-magazine model figure of finely chiseled face and slim haunches. Before man put his intrusive hand in to breed the Siamese to society's image of the most special cat in the world, the original "traditional" Siamese were far healthier-looking than the "modern" Siamese of today. In fact, the original Siamese had very attractively homey round heads, and later came to be called the "apple-headed Siamese." There was also something about the Siamese that seemed to make humans want to define them ever more exactly on their own terms and soon cat fight after cat fight was erupting in the Cat Fancy over the popular Siamese.

By the mid-twentieth century, the apple-heads were out and the Siamese Cat Club of Britain issued a definitive and snippy statement that it would encourage only the breeding of blue-eyed Siamese. From that moment, the beautiful yellow or green eyes were excluded from the Siamese showings. This could have seemed tragic, except that what it did was to encourage the beginning of the history of an entire separate breed of cats, the gorgeous and ethereal Oriental Shorthairs. In addition to the ruling on eye color, the Cat Fancy decreed that the original genteely kinked tail of the Siamese was no longer acceptable, and step by step, the entire breed standard was rewritten to reflect changing tastes, which, of course, the breeders had themselves created.

For a time, such fights marked a sad period for the traditional Siamese cats and their admirers across the world, and by 1986, there were no apple-head Siamese being shown anywhere. Even worse, the new breeders were trying to rewrite history by actually refusing to believe that the apple-heads had even been the original Siamese! But eventually adepts of the apple-head lobby, enraged at being sideswiped and forced either to take their cats out of the show ring or to breed them to fashionable thinness, regained their confidence and struck back. They formed their own Traditional Siamese Association and dedicated themselves to bringing back the apple-heads. In addition, they later opened up their shows to include other traditional breeds whose original—and natural—qualities were being bred out of them. These include the Burmese, Persians, Balinese, Bengals, and Himalayans. Not only do they now hold their own shows, but they have influenced the entire Cat Fancy to criticize the practice, largely in America, of breeding to extremes.

Meanwhile, particularly after the breed was brought to America in the twentieth century, the Siamese were becoming the stars of stage and screen, appearing in the 1950s and 1960s in such films as *Bell, Book and Candle,* Disney's *That Darn Cat,* and *Lady and the Tramp.* Perhaps this theatrical bent of the breed went along with the indisputable fact that the Siamese were also highly sexually explicit. In their highjinks, they managed to father and mother (perhaps in part because they were not eating their kittens) an entire new family of families of cats, including the Tonkinese, Himalayas, Havana Browns, Singapura, Javanese, Oriental Shorthairs, Balinese, Tabby Oriental Shorthairs, and even a wavy-coated rex cat. Some cat students say that the Siamese are surely also related to the Burmese, the Birman, the Ragdoll, and even the Ocicat; the Burmese are sometimes called chocolate Siamese and come from exactly the same area of Southeast Asia.

In one of those many great mysteries of the sagas of the Family of Cat, the famous naturalist Simon Pallas, in 1793 even discovered an old engraving on a journey into southern Russia showing cats with exact Siamese markings! The markings were of a much darker coloring and Pallas described the cats as having light chestnut-brown body color with the same black extremities as the Siamese from Southeast Asia. How such a cat got to southern Russia, a good thousand miles away, is a mystery as great as the mystery of the Russian Blue cat from Archangel!

Eventually, ironically, the slim-modeled "modern" Siamese began to lose out. They began to look a little like some faded aristo*cats*, like the faded White Russian princesses in flats in Shanghai in 1948 with no home to return to. Although the Siamese do remain almost always on the list of the ten most popular cats, they no longer have the popularity that they enjoyed, particularly in America, in the middle of the twentieth century. In Thailand (modern Siam), you scarcely find a traditional or a bred Siamese at all, and Thais widely believe them to be "foreign cats" and "too difficult . . . too high-strung . . . too foreign."

Still, historically they remain one of the greatest of the Family of Cat, with their romantic, complex, and compelling history and with the veritable "worlds" that were built around their small and dramatic figures. And by the early years of the twenty-first century, the historic fascination with the Siamese was to be revealed in all its charm and elegance still once again, as on American television, a charming and fluffy Siamese cartoon cat named Sagwa, the Chinese Siamese Cat, was enchanting audiences young and old with his charming adventures into Chinese history!

THE SIBERIANS

If you move with the cats of the northern hemisphere—in those regions of ice and snow, where the long winters create cats with lush, rich, long coats to protect them—you can move eastward from New England in America to Norway and then to Russia and, perhaps not so amazingly, find much the same type and style of cat. In fact, there is a tremendous likeness in the figures and in the personas of the Maine Coon, the Norwegian Forest Cat and, now, the Siberians of the taigas of Siberia and northern Russia.

But not surprisingly, there is much more mystery about the Siberians, just simply because, unlike the other two cats, they came from that closed, isolated, neurotically ingrown world of the Russian steppes and snows. Siberians will insist that the cat has been around for at least a thousand years—and then they say no more. The Siberian cats were first mentioned in Harrison Weir's great book, *Our Cats and All About Them,* and they took part in his first 1871 cat show, but before that—who knows? Cats were always unappreciated in Russia, a country historically so poor that it could hardly appreciate animals when people appreciated themselves so little.

Today, Siberians are being imported into the United States and, in 1987, as life began to get better and freer in Russia, even Russian cat clubs began registering the breed. After the fall of communism in 1991, the world opened to Russia; the cats really came into their own, in part because for some reason they seem to be hypoallergenic—humans are not allergic to them, and that has been a major factor in their new popularity, so much so that they are now becoming great favorites at cat shows as the "strong, silent Siberian."

In truth, they are a beautiful, sturdy breed with triple layers of fur in the winter. They have lovely expressions, are playful and loyal, rather like a very dependable and loyal big man who knows exactly who he is. It is also often described a being "doglike," because of its loyalty and playfulness, and can be found playing catch and fetching toys or forest objects like branches and leaves for its people. And while it does bear a striking resemblance to the Maine Coon and to the Norwegian Forest Cat, in truth the three are quite different. The Siberian is round-bodied and triple-coated; the Maine Coon is rectangular-bodied and less furry, and the Norwegian Forest Cat is double-coated.

But the Siberian is now here to stay and even to travel around the world, thanks mainly to the end of the Cold War and to welcome changes in the geopolitics of the world.

THE SINGAPURAS

Poor little creatures, these cats started out as the famous drain cats of the rich city-state of Singapore, one of the most prosperous places on earth. While everything gleamed and glittered outside in the sunlight due to the polished autocratic hand of Lee Kuan Yew, until the 1980s nobody cared about the miserable little brown-ticked cats, with their little pinched faces and their big pop-eyes, in the Loyang district of the city. They quite literally inhabited the drains, rather like Dickensian orphans in old London before the Industrial Revolution and the Victorian age, hiding away from a world and from a population that cared little about them.

Then something happened that turned out to be so amazing that one can only look at it as a Cinderella story or a morals story, or both, as these poor little creatures were rescued by an American couple, made into a breed of their own in the Western world, and finally into the "national cat of Singapore," and even (isn't tourism wonderful?) a "living national monument." In 1991, the Singapore Tourist and Promotion Board actually placed statues of the Singapuras, by then rescued and redeemed, along the river as models for modern Singapore!

The tale of their historic rescue is filled with pathos, but also with stories of intrigue in the international cat world, of alleged conspiracies to defraud immigration and customs' authorities, and of Americans smuggling cats across borders! We will take no position on the total veracity of any of the various versions of the story here, (as, indeed, with all the cat legends!) but only relate them here, with love and affection.

According to the stories, the Americans were a couple named Hal and Tommy Meadow. He was a geophysicist from New Orleans and he was sent to Singapore on business. One story has him finding four, brown-ticked cats in the Loyang district, paying a crewman on a ship bound to the States to transport the animals to his fiancée, Tommy. Since there were no import or export papers on the animals—they were, after all, drain cats, and what exactly would they be worth?—no one knows exactly what happened. But then the various stories have the couple returning to Singapore in 1974, and taking three of the grandcats, named Ross, Tickle, and Pusse, of the original Singapuras back to the homeland.

It seems, from the many stories told about them, that the couple then brought the three back to America, pretending they were cats they had just found. They were going to start a new breed based on this unique, naturally occurring Singapore drain cat. All of this was reported in the United States, but later all hell broke loose. The Singapore tourist board was about to launch a big promotion based on these tiny cats—had they been taken in? Had this "original, naturally occurring" Singapore street cat actually been bred in the basements of the United States? As we have already seen, anything is possible in the Cat Fancy, but in truth, who really cares?

The Cat Fanciers' Association did not, and one leading member declared nobly at a board meeting in October 1990 that the gene pool that created the Singapura (the same gene pool that created my cat, Nikko, incidentally) had always been in Southeast Asia, coming from the Burmese or Siamese copper gene pool that has been there at least until the good monks of Siam put it down in their treatises in 1350. "Whether they mated on the streets of Singapore or whether they mated in Michigan," the woman said, "it doesn't really matter." What a wise woman!

What matters, it seems to me, is that here we have an example—of conspiracy, yes, probably, but of conspiracy to save some poor little rascals from a terrible fate—to bring them to the avid attention of the world, and to give them finally their place in the sun of the Family of Cat. So now there are statues to the little cats in Singapore and they are drain cats no more. They were accepted in the United States for registration in 1982 and for championship competition in 1988. Most of all, they are beloved by their owners, known for their tiny bodies, for their reddish-ticked coats, but most of all for the deceptively sweet look on their faces—a look that is both angelic and devilish.

They seem like very small, cute little friends, and that, in fact is what they are—and if anyone can really blame someone else for smuggling them out, then those are very foolish people, indeed.

THE SPHYNX

There is little question that this cat, the "hairless" Sphynx, is the strangest member of the Family of Cat. It is a bright, alert, natural breed of cat produced not by man but by Mother Nature, and most of the cats have a perfectly charming personality, being loyal and devoted and full of fun. "They are loving, patient, tolerant and social, getting along well with children, dogs and other animals," writes Bev Caldwell in the magazine *Cat Fancy* in the Spring 2004 issue. The article has picture after picture of them, with their pink, gray, and wrinkled skin, with their beautiful, almost entrancing eyes, white whiskers, long pink or dark gray whippet tails, and paws so thick that they sometimes appear to be air cushions. They are described, she says, as "part kitten, part child, part monkey and part puppy," as she quotes a devoted Sphynx owner telling how they "run to the door to greet visitors, climb into any unsuspecting person's arms, wrap two paws around the person's neck and start to smooch and purr."

But the fact is that the Sphynx is hairless—well, almost hairless. In truth, it has a very soft kind of peach fuzz all over it, which has been likened by cat observers to suede, to a hot water bottle, or to a heated chamois. In fact, there are two distinct feelings to the touch, the article says, the "true chamois feeling" and a "sticky rubbery feel," both very "soft and supple to touch." That may sound strange to cat lovers who can only conceive of a cat as a creature whose abundant furry coat is a great part of the enchantment, but it is not at all strange to the Sphynx lovers, who are an utterly dedicated bunch and will hear nothing against their breed, thank you!

The breed started in 1966 as a spontaneous mutation when a domestic cat in Canada gave birth to a hairless kitten in Toronto. There have been other hairless cats found worldwide, and the cat can be bred to normal coats and then back to hairless. The dramatic breed found its descriptive name in 1975 when a Cat Fanciers' judge, David Mare, said, "When I first saw these magnificent creatures, I thought of a famous Egyptian cat statue in the Louvre, which bears some small resemblance to the breed." Out came the bonding of the cat to the Egyptian Sphinx (Egypt, yet again!) which though not really a cat does have a catlike dramatic face. These cats have a normal body temperature but, like humans, will get cold if let outside in the cold weather. They are not hypoallergenic, they have dander and a protein in their saliva that makes many people allergic, and they do have health problems. They must be bathed every seven to ten days and in general taken care of more than the furry cats, but to their devotees, these little E.T.s with the bright eyes and the smashing personalities are more than worth it.

THE TONKINESE

Upon hearing the name of this lovely, silvery creature, cat lovers who are sensitive to history will immediately think back at an unfortunate historic incident. It was 1964, and Lyndon Johnson's administration wanted the American public to believe that North Vietnamese torpedo boats had fired upon two U.S. destroyers in the Gulf of Tonkin between Vietnam and China and the Red River Delta. Still unresolved is the question of whether the American government used the alleged situation to upgrade the Vietnamese conflict to a full-scale war.

We should immediately discard that unhappy incident when we think of this gorgeous gray animal with its brilliant aqua-colored eyes. This is an exquisite cat to whom the word "mink" is constantly applied. The "Tonks" come in natural mink, blue mink, platinum mink, champagne mink, and honey mink colors. (You get the idea!) Some say that the word describes the luscious feel of the Tonkinese coat, but other specialists say that it only refers to the original Tonkinese pattern of a medium brown/gray that shades to a lighter hue on its underparts and to a Siamese-like dark brown at its extremities or points. Of course, the Siamese comparison is apt, for the Tonkinese is the result of a crossing a sealpoint Siamese and a sable Burmese by Canadian cat fancier Margaret Conroy, who wanted a cat intermediate in type with a temperament falling between those of the two star breeds and without the extreme stylization of the Siamese.

In fact, this is one breed to originate in Canada, and it was accepted for championship competition by the Canadian Cat Association in 1965 after Margaret Conroy began her breeding. For a while, New York pet shop owner Milan Greer was breeding similar cats that he called the "Golden Siamese," but he eventually gave up his project. Still, the Tonkinese grew steadily in popularity, being not only gorgeous but also outgoing, friendly, and affectionate, almost like a beautiful silver copy of its two parentages. It is now a full breed of the Cat Fanciers' Association and is also recognized Europe and Australia.

This little cat, like so many others (Javanese, Balinese, Havana Browns, Somalis, Bombays) was named by its breeders to associate it with the "Old Countries" of its dual parentages in Siam and Burma. They chose a romantic name from the region—that of the bay where ancient Vietnamese kingdoms and imperial China faced each other down.

THE TURKISH ANGORAS

The pleasant and scholarly middle-aged professor's voice grew sweet with memory as she reminisced about the first Turkish Angora cat that she thought she might have known. She was only a child then, filled with a child's capacity for wonder, and her voice betrayed the emotions still there after so many years.

"I remember a cat when I was young and it wandered in the corridors of our building at home in Ankara," she was saying softly, as she sat in her office in the Veterinary Faculty of Ankara University. "It was white in color and it had two different eye colors." She paused. "It was a very strange cat," she went on. "Sometimes, we would feed it because it didn't seem to have a home. Yes, it *was* a very strange cat. Later in my life—maybe after ten or twelve years when I first read about the Ankara cat, I thought, 'Maybe that cat really was a pure white Ankara Cat.'"

Maybe it was and maybe it wasn't—cats do have that mystical quality of drifting in and out of human lives and imaginations, rather like spirits in the night or mirages in the desert—but Professor Oznur Poyraz now probably knows as much as can be known about the beautiful and mysterious Ankara or Angora cat of Turkey.

First of all, she explained to me that spring day of 2002 in the Turkish capital, Turkey has two national cats—the first is the Angora cat, also called the Ankara cat, with its classically all-white mystical look and either staring blue or mixed color eyes; the second is the far heavier and less delicate, but equally interesting, Turkish Van cat.

The Angora, which has been found for two and a half centuries around the central highland Turkish capital, changed names along with the city when the capital changed in 1930 from Angora to Ankara—to avoid confusion, I shall refer to it hereafter as the Angora cat, by which it is today generally known. The Turkish Van cat is a related, but different, breed with a long, full, furry white coat but one with beige and brown colors on its head and tail and a most strange propensity for swimming!

Both have been closely related for at least 250 years to the Persian cats found along the border in neighboring Persian provinces. Indeed, at one time, Angoras were actually called "Persian." The Angoras, the Vans, and the Persians seem to have stopped for a while in the Caucasus (the present home of Georgia, Azerbaijan, and Armenia). There, they mixed and mingled and then separated to go their own way and become breeds in and of themselves. Amazingly, this faraway area is also believed to be the origin of other breeds who moved far and wide, for example, the Norwegian Forest Cat and the Maine Coon.

The Angora's ears are extremely high-set, vertical, and erect, which gives the cat the sweet look of always paying vivid attention to your every word. But in fact, at least 40 percent of them are deaf and about 70 percent have different eye colors because of a special genetic makeup called the pleiotropic trait. The cat has long hair on its neck and strangely carries its tail nearly parallel to its back, which surely cannot be a comfortable way to go through life; and while everyone thinks of this breed as always and only pure white, in fact there are other colors of the Angora cat, including a gorgeous, but quite properly scary, pitch-black one. There are also Angora goats and sheep around the city of Ankara, from which the precious Angora and mohair wool comes.

The Cat Fanciers' Association describes the Turkish Angora as "elegant, ethereal, regal, statuesque, strong, and opinionated." Turks like to use the Turkish word *yaman* in referring to the cat—"strong, smart, and capable."

The Angora also share preternaturally in the stories of other royal cats. In the sixteenth century in Turkey, as with the Siamese rulers in the eighteenth century, the Ottoman Empire's Turkish sultans would present their beautiful white cats, with their hair as fine and soft as ermine, as special gifts to European monarchs. Thus, the cat came to symbolize, if not a religion, at least an empire. In another example of cross-cultural cat stories—and the meaning given them in different societies—the Angoras play a role in Turkey similar to the bobtails in Japan: they, too, stand proudly as mascots in some merchants' shops, welcoming people in.

The Angoras also pass into Turkish legend in the story of the wishcats. It seems that someone having a strong wish should put one of these cats on his lap and whisper his wish into the kitty's ear. After the due presentation of tidbits, the kitty is supposed to make the human's wish come true. But—ahhh!—this can only happen if the cat truly is a wishcat, and no one knows for sure which cats are wishcats because no one dares tell whether his wish came true or not. Cat politics is complicated indeed.

After they were brought to England in the 1870s, when long-haired cats were becoming popular, and then to America, the Turkish Angoras were recognized in 1973 by the leading cat registries.

The story of the Turkish Angora cat has a happy ending. By the beginning and mid-twentieth century, the breed had become extremely rare in Turkey and had nearly died out in the rest of the world. The Turkish government suddenly awakened, declared the Angora the "National Cat of Turkey," and put the breed under national wildlife protection, even going so far as to forbid their export. In a series of acts that should stand as an example of animal husbandry, Turkey put out a nationwide appeal to private households and others to bring in every Turkish Angora they could find. The animals were thus collected by the state-owned zoos in Ankara and Istanbul, where they are today protected, bred, cosseted, appreciated, and preserved. Unlike the stories of many princes and princesses in the world, the Turkish Angoras today live happily ever after.

THE TURKISH VANS

There is nothing more unexpectedly breathtaking in all catdom—no, not even the wonderful hoop-leaping cats of Burma!—than watching a Turkish Van go for its afternoon swim.

First, this lovely cat pauses on the side of Lake Van, a beautiful high lake in eastern Turkey near the Armenian and Persian borders, its paws gripping the earth, its head extended, almost like a bird about to take flight or a racer getting ready to run his race. As intent and initially uncertain as any racer in the opening line, the cat pauses for a moment and then off it goes! It dives straight into the cool lake, its head momentarily under the water. Then it is up and swimming energetically across the lake, its head perched bravely atop the waves, its little ears down and its whiskers barely touching the water. It doesn't seem to mind, as do other cats, that its fur is all wet or that (perhaps they didn't know?) cats are not supposed to swim! Turkish Vans just love to swim—they are the only small cats in the world who do swim—and legend would have us believe that when Noah's Ark arrived at Mount Ararat in eastern Turkey some five thousand years ago, two cats, white and brown it is said, being cats were of their own minds and simply leapt into the waters and swam ashore. Once the floodwaters receded, the doughty chaps set out for Lake Van, which was about seventy-five miles to the south of Ararat and there they are today!

The biological part of the story is that the Van has a unique "water-repelling coat," totally unlike the coats of most cats, which is water-resistant and allows the cats to go for a dip and emerge at the end of the day almost dry. Remember, most domestic cats hate getting wet, perhaps in part because of all the grooming that must then go into looking their best, which is an onerous task when one considers how small their little tongues are for such heavy work. Finally, one must also factor in the terrible heat in this part of Turkey in the summer; perhaps the Vans originally just fell in and then found that they liked it.

"Why *do* they swim?" I asked Professor Oznur Poyraz of the Veterinary Faculty of Ankara University. "I don't know," she said, which is about as accurate an answer as anyone will get.

Although the Turkish Vans, with their ample white coats and their red or brown markings, are a separate breed from the Turkish Angora of Central Turkey and the Persians from neighboring Iran, historians are certain that all were related originally and then, like all families, spread out and formed their own households.

But there is one very strange and striking historical twist. There are native ornaments in the Lake Van region dating as far back as 5000 B.C. depicting cats that look remarkably like the Turkish Vans. This would make them one of the very oldest existing cat breeds and, remember, 5000 B.C. was in the earliest years of Egyptian cat lore, the cat becoming a full-blown god in Egypt only by 2000 B.C.! The Vans again emerge into focus historically when soldiers of the Christian Crusades to the Middle East returned to Europe between A.D. 1095 and A.D. 1272 and carried the Vans with them. In all this traveling and mutation, they came to be known by a rich dictionary of names: "Eastern Cat . . . Turkish Cat . . . Ringtail Cat . . . Russian Longhair . . ." They didn't seem to mind what they were called so long as no one tried to interfere with their afternoon swims.

This illustrates, too, how the godlike qualities of the cat in ancient times were transmogrified into the spiritual and the religious in modern times. The Vans also have a special symbolic status under Islam. Many of them have a color patch between their shoulder blades called the Mark of Allah. This is so close to the M on the Egyptian-born tabby's head, which is supposed to be the "thumbprint of God" of the Virgin Mary, that one can only wonder anew at the awesome similarity that man has invested in these strikingly similar spiritual stories of cats all across cultures, and indeed across the entire world.

The Cat Fanciers' Association accepted the breed for registration in 1988. Meanwhile, like their relatives, the Turkish Angoras, the Van cat story is one with a happy ending. In the 1990s, the Vans were rounded up from the streets by the Turkish College of Agriculture in connection with the Ankara Zoo, the longtime breeder of the Angora. They are today cared for and preserved as a national treasure.

appendix

HISTORY and GENEALOGY OF THE ROYAL and SACRED CATS

50 million years ago

There was a split between the catlike creatures and the dog- and bearlike creatures, stemming from a prehistoric ancestor called the miacis. Even today, most people do not realize that cats have the same genetic origins as the dog, the raccoon, the bear, and even the pig. The cat evolved out of one branch of this family; the other animals, from the other. But the cat was domesticated thousands of years after the dog, leaving even today's beloved pet house cat with a certain aura of wildness attractive to many people.

40 to 25 million years ago

The cat itself began to evolve as its own particular animal. Some 12 million years ago, the South American wildcats evolved and the first true cats, the Tuscany lion, the lynx, and the great cheetah were found in northern Europe, to disappear later with the advent of civilization. Between 8 and 10 million years ago, the relatives of today's domestic cat came onto the scene; and from 4 to 6 million years ago, the big cats moved into history. Finally, the small African wildcat, scientifically known as *Felis silvestris libyca*, the father of all the domestic cats, came out of Africa. Amazingly, it was a small tabby cat that looked very much like today's beloved and peaceable domestic tabby cat, except that it walked on tiptoes and had "stabbing" teeth more commonly found in dogs. All cats today carry the tabby gene inherited from their wild ancestors, the word tabby indicating a particular coat found in many breeds. Eventually, cats evolved naturally on every continent except Australia and Antarctica, but it was not until several thousands of years before Christ that they began to be adopted as royal and sacred creatures.

8000 to 7000 B.C.

Fossilized remains of a cat were found on the island of Cyprus. Scientists believe that this shows that those early felines came by boat, alongside humans who also carried with them from the African continent grain and mice. This find was important because it marked the first scientifically registerable association of cats and humans. Recent dramatic archaeological finds in Cyprus even indicate that a tamed cat's bones found in an ancient burial place the domesticated cat there as early as 9500 B.C. These findings occurred in 2004.

6700 B.C.

In a prehistoric site in present-day Jericho on the West Bank, pottery has been found showing what was apparently a wildcat, thus suggesting that Egyptian cats had been carried there not only in Roman times but far earlier.

6000 to 1700 B.C.

As trade routes developed and trading ships sailed the seas, probably beginning in 6000 B.C., the cat evolved from a semiwild to a domesticated creature, all beginning in Egypt. An ivory statuette of a resting cat was found, dating from about 2700 B.C., in ancient Lachish, the site of which lies now in Israel. From this era, the British Museum has further identified a terra-cotta head said to be a cat from a Minoan site on the eastern shore of Crete, apparently proving how the cat had already moved from its "home office" in Egypt.

EGYPT

4000 B.C. onward

The ancient Egyptians enthusiastically began the domestication of the cat because the inventive Egyptians had built silos to preserve their grains and these silos attracted rats. But rat-catching cats soon so endeared themselves to the Egyptians that they were made sacred within the Egyptian pharaonic religion and were worshiped across Egypt (with, of course, their knowing all the time that this was exactly what they deserved!). The cat was worshiped for its agility, virility, and strength and, while other animals were also considered sacred in Egypt, only the cat was worshiped in every region of the reign.

3500 to 2500 B.C.

The cat actually became part of the theology of the pharaonic religion of ancient Egypt. In the sacred *Book of the Dead,* the Egyptian pharaohs equated the cat with the sun god Ra, who could take the form of a cat at will and who was often referred to as the Great Tomcat, thus giving the animal divine masculine status in addition to its female goddess Bastet. The cat was also seen as standing guard (although that seems unlike the cat!) at the great battles of the people, thus illustrating the degree to which the animal was growing in royal and sacred presence.

Although there are no physical remains of cats from the prehistoric period in Egypt itself, the first finding of a carved figure of a cat appeared in Egypt on the famous tomb of Ti in Saqqara during this period of the Old Kingdom or about 2563 B.C.—and the cat moreover appeared as an honored figure, wearing a collar. This figure is the first representation of a royal cat that we have in history.

2000 B.C.

Over this entire millennium, the Egyptian cat was domesticated and was worshiped as a god across Egypt. The first actual cat name in recorded history, Bouhaki, was carved on Hana's tomb in the Necropolis of Thebes. The cat goddess Bastet soon had her own temple, the beautiful temple of Tell Basta on the Bubastis branch of the Nile in the northern Nile River Valley, where tens of thousands of Egyptians came to worship and where Bastet was particularly honored in the highly sexualized spring festivals. The ruins remain to this day but the actual details of the faces of the cat deities in the stone have long been weathered away by sand and time.

1500 B.C.
By this time, during the New Kingdom, the domestic cat was welcomed everywhere in Egypt and often was treated with such sophisticated humor that many analysts see the representations as the "first cartoons and caricatures" in history. One famous carving in the tombs had a spotted cat herding geese; another, a cat waiter serving a tableful of mice. It became a crime punishable by death to kill a cat and mourning for family cats was enforced by the state.

1400 B.C.
Pictoral representations of cats appeared everywhere, including a particularly beautiful picture of a cat in a papyrus swamp near the tomb of Nebamun. But while most observers today think of the quintessential Egyptian cat as the sleek Bastet, there were also spotted cats, hunting cats, tabby-patterned cats, and other types of cats on the walls of the tombs.

950 B.C.
The cat had become one of the most popular goddesses in Egypt, with even Queen Cleopatra modeling her style, her costume, her eye makeup, and her bearing after the goddess Bastet.

900 B.C.
Cat carvings appeared on the tombs in Beni Hassen in central Egypt, from which in later centuries hundreds of cat mummies were taken by the British colonialists back to London and to the British Museum. Many were later believed to have been offerings to the gods, since their necks had been broken.

525 B.C.
By this century, the cat had become for the Egyptians a figure of geopolitics and diplomacy. Sometimes they were held captive by the enemies of Egypt to gain

privilege, with complicated negotiations ensuing for their freedom. The Persians laid siege to Pelusium near present-day Port Said, and it is said that the Persian monarch Cambyses, father of Cyrus the Great, cleverly ordered his troops to capture and carry Egyptian cats instead of shields before them into battle; this way, the Egyptians would not attack them. Supposedly, the Persians carried the cats—and the day. After that, Egyptian cats were carried back to Persia by the victorious legions, most probably becoming the ancestors of today's popular Persian cats. How exactly the Persians captured and supposedly held all those cats, cats being what they are, without being clawed or mauled, is nowhere explained.

450 B.C.

By this era, the great literary figures of the Greek, Roman, and Mediterranean world were deeply involved in descriptive analysis of the importance of the cat. The Greek historian Herodotus visited the cat goddess's temple at Bubastis and described it in great length as the most beautiful of all of the temples of Egypt. He called the attention of the world to the fact that all wild animals had been made sacred in Egypt. In his *History,* he also tells how the Egyptian cats strangely sought out fires and seemed to be driven to run hypnotically into them.

425 B.C.

The Greek playwright Aristophanes in his *The Acharnians* used the word "cat" for one of the first times in literature, thus showing the spread of the cat across the culture of the Mediterranean.

350 B.C.

The Egyptian cat cult began its decline and, as foreign occupiers took over Egypt for long periods of time, cats were carried across the Mediterranean to Europe and down the trade routes by traders and travelers.

60 to 57 B.C.

The Greek historian Diodorus Siculus visited Egypt and wrote *Bibliotheca historica* in which he tells how dangerous and unacceptable it was to kill a cat in Egypt, because of the perfervidity with which they were still worshiped.

Birth of Christ: B.C. *to* A.D.

The world of the ancient cat changed forever. Now, in a syncretism of pagan religion and Christianity, the cat was still worshiped, but in confusing ways. Sometimes it was a "Virgin" deity, comparable to the Virgin Mary, and the cult of Bastet remained present even in pre-Roman and Greek cities, in pre-Roman Pompeii and Rome as well. But the coming of the Christian era, with its faith in the One God of Judeo-Christianity, precluded the worship of any other gods, much less animals. The cat entered into a long period of decline and persecution.

200 B.C. *to* A.D. *1400*

Cats spread from Egypt throughout Europe and Asia, across the Roman Empire, down the Silk Road and other trade routes and through the religions of Christianity and Buddhism, to almost every corner of the globe. They became a crucial part of the religious, spiritual, and social syntax of cultures as different as those of Egypt, ancient Siam, Burma, Japan, ancient Persia, Turkey, and even parts of Europe.

A.D. *390*

The Egyptian cat cult was banned by decree of the imperial Roman emperor and, for the cats, a "Dark Ages" fell like a curtain all across Europe.

A.D. *600*

Despite the di*cat*spora after the fall of the Egyptian empire, cats continued to be the source of a syncretism between the old religions and the new. In part because of the Prophet Muhammad's love for cats and in part because of little creatures' own meticulous habits, cats were sanctified for Muslims and were considered the essence of cleanliness and purity within Islam, while dogs even then were regarded as dirty and impure. Later, the Prophet carried cats to Mecca, thus giving cats an eternal religious blessing within Islam. This allowed cats to bridge the gap from being sacred in ancient Egypt to still being appreciated and respected in later centuries and in later devolved cultures.

China

500 B.C.
In China, it is said that Confucius was also one of those many spiritual leaders who owned a beloved cat; but Confucianism, being more a set of moral guidelines for right living than exactly a religion, never worshiped cats or enshrined them in any way.

400 B.C.
Buddhism arose out of India and then spread across Southeast Asia. Cats played an important role later in the history of Buddhist countries as a good fortune cat, but when legend tells us also that the cat was the only animal to fall asleep at the Buddha's funeral (and why are we not surprised?), for a time the animal was looked down upon in the religion. Cats were already domestic animals in China, and some historians argue that they were portrayed in some forms of Chinese artwork as early as 2000 B.C.

206 B.C. to A.D. 220
Cats were known in China during this, the Han era, with its great expansion of Chinese culture, apparently having come down the trade routes from Egypt to various parts of Southwest and Southeast Asia, but they would never gain the love and respect from the Chinese that they would receive from other Asian societies, like the Siamese and the Japanese, and were never exactly royal or sacred, although certainly aristocratic. (Some authors also argue that, as early as 4000 B.C., Sanskrit writings indicate that cats are known to have existed in the Harppa Indus Valley in what is today India—this would surely be the earliest reference to cats in Asia.) Some also insist that the cats of China closely resembled the Pekingese dog.

A.D. 600 to A.D. 700
Chinese cats and most probably tailless or short-tailed cats from Southeast Asia, in particular the Malay Peninsula, were systematically taken to Japan, where they became first, excellent ratters, but later beloved pets of the royal court with a royal and good fortune aura all of their own.

A.D. 1162 to A.D. 1227

Genghis Khan kept cats in his kingdom and capital city in Mongolia. They had heavy coats and were probably related to the Manul wildcats found later in Central Asia.

SIAM AND BURMA

Somewhere in the deep recesses of history

The legend grew in the Cat Fancy that, long before Buddhism spread across South Asia and after the Buddha's life in the fifth century B.C., there existed a Lao-Tsun temple in what is now northwest Burma (or somewhere) where Royal Burmese cats, and probably Birman cats as well, were protecting the high priest, supposedly known as Mun-ha. Attacked one night by highwaymen, the high priest lay dying when his pet cat, Sinh, climbed on him, faced the sapphire-eyed and golden-haired Goddess Tsun Kyan-Kse, and appealed for the transmutation of the priest's soul. The priest's soul entered Sinh's body and the body of the little cat began to transform itself as he died, later carrying the man's soul to paradise.

Unfortunately, there is no proof of this story, but it is inordinately important in the sagas told by the sometimes impressionable students and followers of the great stories of the cat. It is repeated everywhere as verification of the sacred qualities of the cat and is offered in many cat books as proof that the Birman's beautiful paws magically became white, as they are today, at the moment that the cat touched the dying priest's body. Who are we to contest such beliefs?

A.D. 1350 to A.D. 1767

By this era, the Siamese or Thai tribes that came out of China in the tenth century had settled in the great monsoon valley of today's Thailand and Burma. The new Siamese royalty and Buddhist monks obviously adored the cat, for the hundreds of pages of the *Tamra Maew* or the *Cat-Book Poems* or *Cat Treatises,* were painstakingly created in those centuries by Siamese monks in the royal Siamese city of Ayudha, the ruins of which lie north of today's Bangkok.

But conflicts between the Siamese and neighboring Burmese royalties continued. Finally Ayudha was destroyed in 1767 by invading Burmese armies and many Siamese-type cats were taken by the victors to Burma, where they would gradually mate and become the Burmese and Birman cats. The *Cat-Book Poems* or *Cat Treatises* are today lovingly housed in the National Library of Thailand in Bangkok and they show clearly the manner in which the various cats of neighboring Siam and Burma were historically intertwined. In today's breed terms, these include the Siamese, the Korat, and the copper in Siam and the Burmese and the Birman in Burma. (Only the copper is not a recognized breed today, but rather a local name for any brown cat.)

1873 to 1910

Chulalongkorn or Rama V became the progressive and beloved king of Siam. He is said to have had a beloved white cat, probably one of the all-white, otherworldly diamond-eyes cats. He also took joy in giving the traditional Siamese cats, which are the "royal cats of Siam" as special gifts to royal and respected visitors, making them one of the highest representations of the royalty and of the kingdom.

1884

The king of Siam gave a pair of Siamese cats to British Consul General Owen Gould, and the Siamese was thus introduced to London, where the cats soon came to be a smashing success.

About 1900

Buddhist missionaries from India founded the Nga Phe Kyaung monastery at Inle Lake, Burma, but it was not until almost a century later that the "hoop-leaping cats" would become a favorite of tourists from all over the world who traveled to the remote spot to see the cats leap hypnotically for hours through hoops held by the loving monks.

1930s

A kitten named Wong Mau was brought from Burma, probably by a sailor, to an American doctor in San Francisco. It is believed that Wong Mau laid the basis for the entire highly popular Burmese breed in the United States. In these same years, the Siamese breed had been carried from England to America and become a wildly popular breed in America, starring in many popular movies, in the modern-day "royalty" of Hollywood. The sleek and sexy Siamese also became the "father" of an unusual number of multiple beauties of other breeds when they were mated to Persians, shorthairs, and other sturdy cats.

1944
British forces in Burma adopted the symbol of the Burmese cats as mascots and put their pictures on the sides of their army vehicles to keep spirits up during the Pacific campaign.

1986
The original Siamese cats, known as "apple-heads" because of their round heads and robust bodies, were out in the cat shows, and the highly bred (and also highly temperamental and yappy), slim, long-headed Siamese were "in." Today, the highly bred Siamese are barely known in modern-day Thailand and are iron-ically thought of as foreign cats, but the old apple-heads are enjoying a comeback.

JAPAN

A.D. 500
Asian cats, many of them tailless or with small bunny tails, were carried by sea from China to Korea and Japan, giving birth to the founder breed of the Japan-ese Bobtail, the American Bobtail and even a rare Kurile Islands Bobtail of today.

A.D. 794 to A.D. 1185
Cats were sent traveling on ships to protect religious parchments and silk gar-ments and, in those same years of the high culture of the Japanese Heian period, Buddhist priests coming from China brought the cats to the Heians' Kyoto court, where they were a huge success with the aesthetically minded Japanese at the historic moment of their blooming new culture.

A.D. *1000*

Japanese Bobtails were becoming known and feted throughout Japanese art. In later centuries, such artists as Utamaro Kitagawa, Utagawa Kuniyoshi, and Ando Hiroshige would include the beautiful little cats, with their tiny tails, in painting after exquisite painting, where the little bobtails were dancing, nursing, loving children, or directing the Japanese on their daily ways.

1457

In the Battle of Ekodagahara, Lord Dakon Ota was saved by a small cat who led him away from the forest to safety on the land of what is today the Jiseiin temple in Tokyo. The lord soon also built the original Edo Castle, which eventually became the official residence of the Tokugawa or Edo rulers and was later expanded to become the imperial palace of the Emperor.

1603 to 1867

During this progressive and prosperous Edo or Tokugawa period, the little bobtailed cats of Japan become popular symbols of joy and vitality and are, if not sacred, closely related to Buddhism and to the shogun society. At one point, they were considered to be on the fifth rank of royalty. But generally, they were the good fortune cats and became so beloved that long-tailed cats came to be thought of as cat demons. In one sad period during this time, however, because of the proliferation of mice in Japan, the formerly spoiled little bobtails were suddenly loosed on the streets, giving rise to their "time of troubles."

1636

The Buddhist-Shinto shrine at Nikko in the mountains of Japan was blessed by a beautiful painted *Sleeping Kitten* or *Sleeping Cat*. After this, the bobtails became unofficially and informally known as the "national cat of Japan" and the nation's good fortune or good luck cat, a Buddhist/Shinto version of the royalty and sacredness accorded them in other cultures.

1945 to 1946

Japanese bobtail cats were brought from Japan to America by Americans and GIs involved in World War II. They soon became a favorite in America but, like the Siamese cats in Thailand, in Japan today the bobtails are little known.

TURKISH AND PERSIAN CATS

5000 B.C.

Native ornaments were discovered around Lake Van that depicted cats that looked much like today's Turkish Vans. This indicated to anthropologists that cats must have migrated here very early from Egypt, an amazing discovery that is bested only by the discoveries of cat fossils in Cyprus in 2004 that pet cats had been there for 9500 years.

525 B.C.

The Persian breed most probably stems from the era of the battle of the Persians against the Egyptians near Pelusium not far from present-day Port Said, when the Persian King Cambyses apparently defeated the Egyptians by the ploy of carrying sacred Egyptian cats into battle and thus forcing the Egyptians to stop fighting (or so it is said). Cats were carried back to Persia, where they devolved into heavy-coated Persians in the colder, higher plateaus and atmospheres. The Persians are also believed descended in part from the wild cats of Iran and Afghanistan.

A.D. 1095 to A.D. 1272

The European Crusaders carried Van cats from the area around Lake Van in eastern Turkey back with them to Europe, thus bringing still another biological strain into the European cat family.

1793

The famous naturalist Simon Pallas in Southern Russia discovered an old engraving showing cats with exact Siamese markings. This cat was the semiwild Manul cat.

Eighteenth to Nineteenth Centuries

The beautiful and delicate white Turkish Angora cats had developed around the Turkish capital city of Angora, whose name was changed to Ankara in the 1930s, and the Turkish sultans made special gifts of them to European monarchs and to other high-level visitors, just as had the Siamese kings to foreign visitors. Thus, the Angoras had a certain royal presence in Turkey and it was believed superstitiously that the great Turkish reformer, Ataturk, would come back to life in the "person" of a Turkish Angora.

1990s

Turkish naturalists and scientists from the Ankara Zoo and the Turkish College of Agriculture rounded up both the Turkish Angora cats and the Turkish Vans to breed and protect them, thus offering a wonderful and unique example of respect for animals and for their preservation for the entire world.

ENGLAND

Tenth Century A.D.

By now, domestic cats had arrived in England, having made the onerous trip for several centuries, first across the Mediterranean from Egypt, to Rome, and then northward to the farthest margins of Europe. In Scandinavia, the Egyptian god cat had been adapted to a spirit of a cat goddess called Freyja, who represented sex, motherhood, and destruction and whose pictures show her driving a sled pulled by other cats. In fact, northern Europe had maintained contact with Egypt through various trade routes since a thousand years before Christ. After arriving in England, it was not long before cats were transported to the New World with the first ships carrying colonists.

1400

Cats began crossing the seas. By the fifteenth and sixteenth centuries, cat colonization was common in European countries and, by 1850, cats could be found anywhere there were people.

1566 to 1684

In medieval times, the cat was more and more seen as a "witch's familiar" and was often put on trial and burned with witches. Cats now faced the polar opposite of the golden days of worship in old Egypt. This was soon to change as Europe modernized and, after the Industrial Revolution, the rising middle class began to look upon cats not as mousers but as beautiful accoutrements to the modern lifestyle and even as status symbols in an open, upward-striving society.

1598

A cat show, little-known yet still a cat show, was held at St. Gile's Fair in England, thus showing very early on how cats were beginning to be appreciated in certain areas, despite their persecution in medieval Europe.

1600s to 1700s

In 1607, the English naturalist Edward Toprell wrote the groundbreaking *The History of Four-Footed Beasts,* with some of the best and most sensitive descriptions of the cat ever before seen. In that same late medieval Europe, the famous Sir Isaac Newton invented the cat door, or cat flap, allowing cats to go in and out of the house at will; such inventions, besides of course being pleasing to the cat, showed the extent to which they were beginning to be redomesticated in late medieval Europe and established as house pets.

Mid-1800s

The idea of the selective breeding of cats and the production of pedigrees began to develop in England, leading up to the prizing of the cats in a modern society in ways seen before only in ancient aristocratic Egypt. The dog had already been bred for several centuries and dog shows were common.

1868

Naturalist Charles Darwin published his important book, *The Variation of Animals and Plants Under Domestication,* one of the first books outlining the development of cats and other animals and giving a great boost to the caring and breeding of felines.

That same year, it is believed that a British soldier who had been serving in Ethiopia providentially brought an Abyssinian kitten, which was then named Zula, to England. This kitten probably laid the basis for the beloved Aby breed, which is considered even today to be the breed of cat that is closest to the original Egyptian cats.

1871

The first cat show, at the Crystal Palace in London, was held with more than nineteen thousand people visiting the show in one day! The Siamese cats, never before seen in the West, garnered worldwide acclaim. But the top prize was given to a fluffy and equally exotic Persian. The show was so popular that a second cat show was held that same year.

1887

The first National Cat Club was formed in England.

1889

Harrison Weir, the founder of the cat shows or the Cat Fancy, published his classic book *Our Cats and All About Them,* giving the general reading public for the first time a general and even worshipful look at every aspect of the modern cat's life and how to love and care for him and her.

1898

The Cat Club, rival to the National Cat Club, was formed in England, and there soon began the tensions, jealousies, and envies that would from then on become so endemic in the entire human part of the Cat Fancy (although, frankly, the cats seemed loath to take any part in these fights).

1910

Various clubs were amalgamated, forming the Governing Council of the Cat Fancy, which would be the more-or-less senior governing group of the cat shows and world. This laid the basis for the development of other cat clubs and shows and, by the way, for the peevish jealousies about breeds and superiority that inevitably followed. "Cat fights" abound even today. Different cat clubs have different standards and recognize different breeds: that is why, although the number of breeds is generally recognized as being the forty-one recognized by the Cat Fanciers' Association (and sometimes up to seventy, according to smaller cat organizations), many people judge it to be higher—and who can dare quarrel with such dedication, especially since the major breeds today were only relatively recently recognized? Who would endanger his or her very life by challenging such passons?

1963

F. E. Zeuner published his important *A History of Domesticated Animals*, which among other things delved into the origins of the names used for the cat.

AMERICA

1500s and 1600s

It is believed that the first cats came to America with the *Mayflower* and other early colonial ships. The cats brought from England were also, of course, the same descendants of the Egyptian god cats, and the influence of Egypt could soon be seen to have devolved to the colonies, as Bastet and her stringed musical instrument, the sistrum, found themselves transmogrified in Americana to, "Hey, diddle diddle! The cat and the fiddle, the cow jumped over the moon!" right on the frontiers of America! The first cat shows and competitions were held in New England.

1749

The importation of cats into America was officially approved and encouraged.

1887

The National Cat Club was formed.

1895

The first American cat show was held in Madison Square Garden in New York. Largely modeled after the London show, it had 125 exhibitors and 176 cats and was a huge success despite temperatures that soared to 96 degrees. A brown tabby Maine Coon cat named Cosey won first prize at this show, which only seemed sort of "right," because Maine Coon fanciers in New England had for some years first promoted exhibitions of their cats in New England.

1896

A second Madison Square Garden cat show, with 130 entries, was held and this one laid the basis for the first registry in the United States under the American Cat Club.

1899

Two cat clubs were founded in Chicago, the Chicago Cat Club and the Beresford Club.

1904

The American Cat Association, generally referred to as the oldest registry in the United States, was formed.

1906

From this date on, many cat organizations formed, split up, reformed along new lines, and fought with one another over everything from breed standards to fur color to length of tail. Over the years, the American Cat Fanciers' Association came to be the major group in the Cat Fancy, but many other groups also had their own, differing standards for the breeds, which has led to the confusion over numbers of breeds and their popularity and importance. They are listed in the introduction to the Family of Cat—and please don't blame me for any discrepancies!

1919

Felix the Cat became the first animated cat film star, starring in a three-minute short named *Feline Follies,* but it would be in the 1930s that cats would come into their own in Hollywood, with the sleek, sexy, and exotic Siamese leading the Hollywood cat parade.

1945

The choice of pedigreed cats was still generally limited to only six: Abyssinians, Burmese, Manx, Persian, Siamese, and Domestic Shorthair.

1947

The first commercial cat-box litter was invented by Edward Lowe and this development led to an explosive increase in cat ownership and to the popularity of the beloved house cat. The descendants of the Egyptian god cats, the Siamese and Burmese royal cats, the Japanese good fortune cats, and all the others now stepped into still another golden age, much like that of pharaonic Egypt when cats were petted and cosseted—and the breeds became the new cat royalty!

1985

Cats for the first time outnumbered dogs as humans' most numerous animal companions, according to the Pet Food Institute, with 56 million house cats across America. By the year 2000, cats would outnumber dogs in American households by 10 million animals.

1989

The famous Moscow State Circus Clown Yuri Kuklachev founded his *Teatr Koshek* or Cat Theater in Moscow, in which cats break all the rules—and all records—for performing. This includes leaping through hoops, riding wheels across the stage, walking on horizontal poles, dancing between his legs, and wheeling chihuahuas in a baby buggy. The theater was still booming in 2004 and Kuklachev insisted that he discovered the performers according to their talents—and then practiced with them several times a day for about a year before they, his cats, were composed enough to go on stage. The cats, his son told me, had to *want* to perform and so the trainers used love and treats.

1996

The Cat Fanciers' Association by then named thirty-six breeds, the most popular ones being in this order: Persians, Maine Coons, Siamese, Abys, Exotics, Scottish Folds, Oriental Shorthairs, American Shorthairs, Birmans, Burmese,